W9-BKO-538

Randolph Bourne

LEGEND AND REALITY

By A. B. Jackson

Randolph Bourne

LEGEND AND REALITY

John Adam Moreau

Public Affairs Press, Washington, D. C.

419 New Jersey Avenue, S.E., Washington 3, D.C.

Printed in the United States of America
Library of Congress Catalog Card No. 66-17651

FOREWORD

This is the story of an unjustly obscure, physically damned man who had an extraordinary influence on the conscience of America. His words and ideas have much meaning for our time, for the problems of his day are surprisingly similar to those of our own. In virtually all the areas he commented on—youth, war, education, society, arts and letters, the melting pot, and human nature—there remains a meaningful, pertinent legacy.

In a time when the United States is deeply committed in Vietnam, the writings of Randolph Silliman Bourne (1886-1918) about war and the nature of the state are vital and challenging. Since much of American youth is restless and angry, or satisfied and indifferent, the ideas of this man who became the champion of youth seem almost directly applicable to the 1960's. One of the nation's most insightful commentators on education, Bourne said much that still applies to the need for reforms in this area. And as Peace Corps activities expand at home and abroad it is well to consider his early proposals for such endeavors.

This man, who was the symbol and the leader of the artistic and intellectual rebellion which occurred in the second and third decades of the century, spoke unforgettably about the potentialities of American culture. That is largely why much that he said is still read and extensively quoted. There is no thorough book on American literary history and criticism or on intellectual and cultural history which does not discuss his ideas.

Of late there has been a rediscovery of Bourne which demonstrates that his ideas remain both exciting and relevant. With astonishing frequency writers in many different fields continue to remind us of this unusual man. Aside from the essays which are still written about him and the large number of his writings which continue to be included in anthologies, three collections of his work have been published in the last ten years, two of them since 1964.

As is evident in these pages, Bourne's vision of America profoundly influenced contemporaries as well as many who came after him. Like such persons as Herbert Croly, Walter Lippmann, and Van Wyck Brooks, he shared the conviction that the nation was approaching maturity in culture and intellectual life. He and they foresaw much that we enjoy and are perplexed about today.

This is a biography of a man who tried to mend the world's broken heart. To know Bourne one must know of his sense of isolation because of his physical affliction, of his genius for friendships, of his constant longing for deeper relationships, and of his fear that he never would know adult love. What also must be taken into account is that toward the end of his life he learned that he could be accepted and loved without reserve, romantically, and by a talented, sensitive, and beautiful woman.

We cannot know whether being a hunchback with a disfigured face prevented Bourne (pronounced Boorn) from being as great as he might have been if he were unmarred. Nor can we say with assurance that deformity prevented his becoming a towering figure in American life. It is, of course, possible that misfortune helped carry him to the luminous position he held and still holds. Had he not been blemished, he may never have escaped the mediocrity which as a young man he came to detest so bitterly. Nevertheless, we do know that Bourne was an inspirer of men and that his articulate protests, sophisticated hopefulness, and pungent observations played a major role in the transition from the Victorian Age to 20th century America. When he died in 1918 there was deep and widespread anguish. Floyd Dell spoke for many when he wrote in the January 4, 1919, *New Republic*:

"Those who are not in some sense of the younger generation will hardly realize the poignancy there is for us in the news of the death of [Bourne, who] . . . belonged to us, and stood for us, in a way which he perhaps did not fully know, but which we now very keenly feel. . . . In literature, in art, in politics, in all departments of life, there has been an alienation of the traditional activities and the traditional activities have seemed unformed, fantastic or half-hearted —even insincere. Randolph Bourne was part of this revolt, its blood pulsed in him, he breathed its air. . . . So it was that his achievement seemed to us the promise of our specific contribution to American life. He was by virtue not only of his clear thinking, and his quiet courage, but no less of his sweetness and humor and debonair charm, one of the strong and triumphant personalities of our generation."

PREFACE

The purpose of this book is to describe the life and career of Randolph Bourne in the fullest possible detail. It is not the writer's desire to assail Bourne nor to write hero-worship, although he may appear heroic to some. Heroic or not, this man has evoked a kind of ongoing fascination and his writings are perhaps more widely read today than in his own time.

Unfortunately very little is known about this extraordinary man. Although much has been said about his writings and influence, the story of his life has remained essentially unprobed. Most of the relatively meager biographical literature about him deals with highlights and are repetitiously misleading; errors and unwarranted assumptions have been warmed up again and again.

While the present work does not pretend to be definitive, it is based upon painstaking research in the course of which the writer found much new material and learned a great deal from Bourne's relatives and friends.

The author of this book was born in Bourne's hometown, Bloomfield, New Jersey, and grew up there and in the adjacent community, Glen Ridge. In a sense this area was home to him almost as much as it had been to Bourne. During his research in its environs he was able to track down many elusive details and to locate some of Bourne's unknown writings.

The author has leaned heavily upon the archives of Columbia University where a large body of Bourne material was deposited in 1955; most of this material was not previously available. The Columbia papers and a small but very important group of letters at Yale University stimulated new and deeper understanding. Moreover, the writer also corresponded with or interviewed every person he could find who knew Bourne.

In these pages Bourne's writings are frequently quoted because he generally expressed himself better than any chronicler could explain him. As Van Wyck Brooks wrote of him in *Emerson and Others,* it is astonishing "the way in which like a ball of camphor in a trunk, the pungent savor of the man spreads itself over every paragraph. . . . One finds everywhere, interwoven in the fabric of his work, the silver thread of a personal philosophy, the singing line of an intense and beautiful desire."

Although spelling has not been made to conform with current usage, some punctuation and mechanical changes have been made to enhance readability. Moreover, footnotes have been greatly reduced from the original manuscript, copies of which are at the University of Virginia and available from University Microfilms, Inc., Ann Arbor, Michigan.

A word is necessary about three groups of letters. Generally, unless otherwise cited, all letters are from the Bourne Papers at Columbia University. However, unless otherwise shown, all letters to or from Alyse Gregory are at Yale. And unless stipulated, all letters involving Carl Zigrosser are in his possesion, although duplicates of many are at Columbia. Copies of some of the Gregory letters are at Columbia.

A list of persons interviewed is in the biblography of the original manuscript, as is a list of those with whom the author corresponded. Unless otherwise cited, quotations from persons who knew Bourne are from interviews and correspondence. Parenthetically it should be noted that the bibliography of the original manuscript includes an essay on Bourne material, notes on primary and secondary material used, and a list of works by and about him.

We are grateful for permission to quote from the following: *The End of American Innocence* by Henry F. May (Alfred A. Knopf); estate of Mrs. Ellery Sedgwick for *The Happy Profession* by Ellery Sedgwick; Alyse Gregory and Yale University for the Alyse Gregory Papers; Holt, Rinehart & Winston for *In the American Jungle* by Waldo Frank; Edmund S. Morgan for "The American Revolution: Revisions in Need of Revising," *William and Mary Quarterly*, January 1957; Princeton University Press for *The Little Magazine* by F. J. Hoffman, *et al;* Columbia University and Mrs. Ruth Bourne Branstater for the Bourne Papers; New York Public Library for the papers of Annette Rankin, James Oppenheim, and Amy Lowell; McGraw-Hill for *An Educational History of the American People* by Adolph E. Meyer.

And we thank the following friends of Bourne who helped the author: Dr. Lawrence K. Frank of Belmont, Massachusetts; Mrs. Agnes de Lima of New York City; Dr. A. W. Macmahon of Poughkeepsie, New York; and Roderick Seidenberg of Doylestown, Pennsylvania. We also are grateful to Dr. Merrill D. Peterson, Thomas Jefferson Foundation Professor at the University of Virginia, and Dr. Edward E. Younger, chairman of the history department there—friend and teacher.

JOHN ADAM MOREAU

Chicago

"I wish there weren't quite so many new ideas. Where do they come from? You seem to play with them and toss them aside, but I cannot. I try to think what is in back of them and speculation often disturbs my sleep. Why is everyone trying to break away from what we all know is sane and good? There is only one right way to live; there is only one right way to write and to paint. Yet all you youngsters seem to be searching for another way to do everything. What worries me is that you seem to be searching for an easier way and a pleasanter way. Nothing which is worthwhile is easy, nor in my experience is the actual doing of it particularly pleasant. The pleasure arises from completion and from the knowledge that one has done the right thing and has stood by one's convictions. Don't forget, John, that the only real satisfaction of life must be derived from this." —The father in John P. Marquand's *The Late George Apley*, writing to his son.

CONTENTS

"How shall I describe Youth, the time of contradictions and anomalies? The fiercest radicalisms, the most dogged conservatisms, irrepressible gayety, bitter melancholy,—all these moods are equally part of that showery springtime of life. One thing, at least, it clearly is: a great, rich rush and flood of energy."—Bourne, *Atlantic,* April 1912.

I

CHILD OF MISFORTUNE

The community in which Randolph Bourne grew up was the product of discontent and dissent. By the spring of 1666 some 30 nonconformists of New Haven colony had had enough of Congregationalist paradise. They were tired of quarreling with the authorities and they grieved over what they believed were religious harassments. Under their leader, the statesman and soldier Robert Treat, these Presbyterians from Milford and Branford—followed later by others from Guilford and the village of New Haven—sailed down the coast to New Jersey.

They settled and prospered in what is now Newark, and its surrounding area—a fertile plain eight miles wide, created by the Passaic River on the east and on the west by First Mountain of the Watchung chain. In 1691 a house was built in what now is Bloomfield, four miles west of Newark, and—once the threat of Indians subsided—more and more of these sturdy and predominantly English pioneers went there. Farms and small businesses increased, including a sawmill which furnished New York City cabinet makers with mahogany from Santo Domingo.

In the War of Independence the settlement of 150 dwellings played a small role in the insurgent cause. For a town which came to care much for tradition, it was thoughtful of Washington to have slept in Bloomfield the night of July 9, 1778.

The village grew steadily after the war and in 1796 the devout Presbyterians of the area began to build their church. They eventually completed a handsome brownstone structure which stands solidly today, its beautiful white steeple aspiring 150 feet into the Lord's air. In front of the church they laid out a large green. It was as if they had to acquire permanency and establish tradition before they became too busy with other things. Later the name of the temple was changed from Bloomfield Church to Old First, and today both the structure and the common appealingly dominate the center of the town.

The town's name honored General Joseph Bloomfield of Burlington, New Jersey, who was wounded at Brandywine Creek in September 1777, but fought a year later at Monmouth. In peacetime he was a lawyer, twice governor of New Jersey, the state's attorney general and a congressman. And he commanded troops in the Whiskey Rebellion and the War of 1812.

Before and during Randolph Bourne's childhood the town of Bloomfield seems to have been much like the General Joseph Bloomfield whom Charles Wilson Peale painted. He was attractive, but not handsome. Rather than dynamism or fervor, Peale's profile of the officer connotes stability, perhaps piety, and certainly an air of no-nonsense. If he appears humorless, there is nothing morbid or vapid about him.

The community hurried ahead in the 19th century, especially after completion in 1831 of the Morris Canal which connected the Hudson River with the Delaware River and the Lehigh coal regions, passing through Bloomfield along the way. Nineteenth century Bloomfield, so unremarkable in any single aspect, but so American in its totality, had by the Civil War sunk deep, stubborn roots. Home and church anchored life there. As Randolph Bourne observed as a young man, "The church seems to have been built with a rather rare spirit of co-operation and sacrifice, and under able pastors became a centre and nucleus of community life." [1]

Like many places, it aspired to sophistication, but the limits of its cosmos were pinched. When Randolph was growing up in the last decade of the century, the town still seems to have been producing mostly earnest folk like Charles M. Davis, one of the local first citizens, who had written to his wife from Europe in July 1867, "I would not allow my children to come here without both of us to watch and guard them, for all that Paris is worth. Nay, I don't think I would let them come here at all except for a few months, and then it would not do to let them go out without one of us with them. Sin here is open, unashamed, undisguised." [2]

It was into this quasi-Puritan atmosphere that Randolph, the first-born child of Charles Rogers Bourne and Sarah Barrett Bourne arrived on May 30, 1886. So horrible was Sarah Bourne's labor that it was as if her son immediately wished to state his case against the world. In a small neat house on Monroe Place, the family physician, Dr. William Bailey, wrestled with his forceps. It was, as Randolph later said, "a terribly messy birth." [3]

"Randolph's birth was the hardest," his mother later remarked.[4] The forceps scarred the child's face, setting his mouth permanently askew. The umbilical cord had been coiled around his left ear and the forceps may have done more harm. Consequently his twisted face was set off by a damaged, misshapen ear. It had been said that old Dr. Bailey was a quack.[5] This is only theorizing, for if the physician was incompetent, and that cannot be determined, he was loved and respected in Bloomfield and served the first families.

Sarah Bourne was not to be deprived of additional children, despite the difficult delivery. Natalie arrived on June 7, 1888, then Donald on February 22, 1892, and lastly Ruth on June 7, 1895. They were the descendants of a long line.

The forebears of Bourne's mother came to the New World in 1628, and later the Barretts moved from Cornwall, New York, to New Jersey. From an uncle, Colonel William Silliman, a Union officer killed at Gregory's Farm, South Carolina, in 1864, Randolph took his middle name. The paternal grandfather was Theodore Bourne, pastor for many years of the church at Sleepy Hollow, New York. His great-grandfather, George Bourne, was an abolitionist acquaintance of Ralph Waldo Emerson and William Lloyd Garrison.

The father, Charles Bourne, may have grown up in Bloomfield or some place in the town's county, Essex, for he joined Old First Church in 1878 when he was 19, and his courting of Sarah Barrett culminated six years later when they were wed at Old First. He was 25, his bride 24.

"They were always in love," sister Ruth recalled. But it was an unhappy affair in which one of the lovers threatened to pull the other down into a morass. Something happened to Charles Bourne, weakening the fibre which his father and grandfather appear to have had. Writers have contended nothing is to be known of Randolph's father. Yet the outline of his life can be traced. Ruth, later saw her father in uncomplicated terms. To her he was, "a handsome, gay blade who liked his fun. He drank too much and sometimes went on binges. He was charming with a good sense of humor; he even was a champion skater. But alcohol got the better of him and his business fell apart."

So there were failure and drink. Which preceded which is not clear. But it is obvious that Charles Bourne never got his head above water. Sometime before the turn of the century, a New York City trolley car caught his overcoat and dragged its wearer, permanently injuring his back. Ruth remembered her father as always on crutches, and a local resident who knew the family remembers the father's using two canes to walk with.[6] The accident may have happened in 1895, for that is the year the father's name last appears in the *New York Directory*. The tale the directory discloses does not suggest success.

Beginning with the 1880-81 edition, Charles Bourne is listed in five different undertakings at 10 different addresses. He was a clerk, printer, "disenfectant" (probably an exterminator), a stationer and a real estate agent. Whatever the elder Bourne was doing, he was not supporting the family. Evidently a break between the parents came within 10 years of their wedding, for Ruth, born in 1895, believed she was the result of one of several reconciliations. Finally, Sarah Bourne's brother, Halsey Barrett, a successful Newark lawyer who lived a block or so away, gave the parents an ultimatum: he would support Sarah and the children, but the father must get out and stay out. Charles and Sarah agreed.

Halsey Barrett was a stern man, competent and honest to his own lights. He also was tough. A story which may be strictly gossip suggests how it was possible for Randolph Bourne later to hate his uncle. According to a story ascribed to Bourne's father, he went to Halsey Barrett and asked him for $3,000. Barrett denounced him in scorching invective. Charles said he felt so badly he wanted to commit suicide. "If you go out and kill yourself," Barrett snapped, "I'll give the family $3,000 and have a huge monument put over your grave." [7]

If Charles Bourne was injured in 1895, it may have been 12 years before he could pick up even a few pieces of his life. There is no indication of what became of him. Then in the Bloomfield directory for 1903 and 1904 his name appears but without an occupation. He was living with his brother, Fred T. Bourne, a patent lawyer of nearby Montclair who commuted to his successful practice in Manhattan. Charles is absent from the 1904-05 directory, but in the next edition, that of 1908, he appears as a stationer and thereafter, until his lonely death in 1924 at age 65, as a "magazine agent" with business addresses first in Bloomfield, and then in Montclair after 1916. It must have been a depressing, demoralizing existence. His inconsequential advertisement in the 1910 directory announced, "All the Magazines and Books at Lowest Rates./ Charles R. Bourne,/Magazine Specialist./ Subscriptions Books,/Advertisting Specialties/Printing and Engraving/Lithographing, Typewriter Supplies, Account Books, Stationery/ Classical and Popular Music, 10 Cents . . ."

Such a spectacle of waste and ineffectiveness as his father's life may have shamed Randolph Bourne; a close friend of his recalls that he spoke of his father as a "disgrace." [8] Another friend, however, remembers that "Randolph always retained an attitude of lenience towards his father, and referred to him with pity, and even with affection."[9] As shall be seen, a student of Bourne learns that he said varying things about himself and his background.

The absence of a father in Randolph's household very likely had an unfavorable influence on him. The only other male there, brother Donald, six years younger than Randolph, left home for good when he was 19 for what was to be a successful career as a civil engineer in Oregon and California.

Randolph's sisters and mother hovered over him. "From early childhood," Natalie recalled, "I had an almost fierce desire to protect Randolph from hurts and insults and I can remember very vividly 'making faces' and sticking my tongue out at children who taunted him because his body was different from theirs."[10]

As an adult Randolph had more women friends who were his intimates than he did men, which in itself is insignificant except that as an adult he displayed a marked desire to be coddled and cared for. Indeed, he at times seems to have insisted on it. A more virile atmosphere in childhood might not have resulted in the severe artistically debilitating depression which periodically bothered him.

"Our household . . . ," Bourne later observed, "was innocent of current discussion,"[11] and his sister Ruth, concurring with his complaint, felt that this was "because there was no man in the house."

Sarah Bourne did what she could to compensate for the absence of a man in the family, and what she did was much, most of it anchored in an inexhaustible love. She was a slim, attractive, but not pretty woman, whose greyish eyes look out with a soft intensity from a photograph of her when she was young. Her almost black hair, her comely mouth, and strong nose adequately compensated for her lack of beauty.

Randolph may have been her favorite because of his affliction. She was immensely proud of his accomplishments and "My darling boy" was representative of her salutations in letters. She appears to have always been near if he needed her, and because she was in California when her son died and was buried, she grieved and reprimanded herself bitterly until her death in 1924 at age 64, four months before her husband's demise. She read, gardened, and occasionally wrote verse. She was, recalled a college friend of Randolph whose mother saw much of Mrs. Bourne, a naive and devout woman. She went regularly with her brood to services at Old First and when she died it was said that, "Her life was one of usefulness and kindness and she will be greatly missed by her large circle of friends." [12]

The house on Monroe Place was in the middle of a block along whose dirt street stood handsome, ample sugar maples, and graceful silver maples which spread through the neighborhood and mingled with proud, massive American elms on the green nearby. For one who was to lead the life of irony, as he called it, and whose affection for the established and traditional was sparse, it was paradoxical that Randolph's life began at the heart of so much of what he later would criticize harshly. Then, as today, the focus of Bloomfield life was that charming green where Bourne spent so many boyhood hours. Next to the green or near it were most of the town's main institutions—churches, schools, and business district.

Bourne was like any child who is loved enough—bubbly and happy. In a photograph he stands on the seashore with Guendolen, a Negro nursemaid, and shrieks with delight as a spent wave licks his feet. He was straight and pretty. When he was perhaps three or four he discovered the piano and improved quickly before formal lessons began.

At age four, however, he contracted a spinal tuberculosis which was to deform him, dwarf him, and make him a grotesque looking hunchback. Later several of Bourne's adult friends would testify that they forgot or overlooked his deformity in their relations with him.

But for him it was the cardinal tangible thing of his life. It is not clear whether his condition caused him considerable anguish or whether as a child and adult the deformity often played on his mind. Indeed, much of the time he was protected by a psychological wall he built around himself, permitting him to entertain the fantasy that he was no different physically from others.

From the house on Monroe Place, Sarah Bourne moved two blocks away when Randolph was nearly six. The new house on Belleville Avenue at Oak Street fronted on a wide, handsome, maple-shaded road which soon after passing the Bourne home went under the Erie Railroad bridge. The house, Bourne wrote, was an unremarkable three-story structure, "ridiculous, but . . . not despicable." [13]

"For your meals you went down into a dark basement dining-room, behind a blacker kitchen. And the outhouse, buried in Virginia creepers and trumpet-vine, was down along a path bordered by grapevines, where you went fearfully at night. [Randolph] was afraid of this dark, long after he was old enough to be ashamed that his mother must come with him and stand protectingly outside. In winter, the stars shone at him with icy brilliancy, and the vines made a thick menacing mass around him.

"Back of the house was a pump, painted very bright and green where the water came up cold and sparkling and ran suddenly out of its spout over your shoes unless you were careful. And when they had finished pumping, the well would give a long, deep sigh, whether of fatigue or satisfaction, [Randolph] never knew.

"In the dark kitchen, which you entered down a flight of stone steps, there was another pump, but it brought forth after long persuasion, only rainwater which to [Randolph] tasted uninteresting, and which he was not allowed to drink, but which they carried in zinc pails up two long spidery flights . . . so that you could wash your face in the morning.

"Only on washday was that pump interesting when the servant filled great wooden tubs out of it, and created huge foamy waves in them and beat and rubbed, and then filled long clothes-lines with damp white garments which coiled around you clamily and disgustingly if you ran too close under them when you were playing." [14]

The house belonged to Sarah Bourne's mother—known to the children as "Nonno". She was of average height with straight hair parted in the middle and brushed smoothly to form a puff over each large ear. With fascination they would watch her form the puff over her finger in order to make the hair stand away from her head. She faced them with a generous, full-lipped mouth and twinkling eyes as the youngsters climbed into her ample lap. Nonno's soft voice had no time for scolding, for there was something eternally placid about her. Somehow, while she had raised a family herself, she had read well and her mind continued active into her final and 79th year.[15]

Nonno kept plants growing on window shelves, and in the coldcellar stored fruits and apples grown in the yard. She looked wise and jolly in her gold spectacles as she rocked near the window and Randolph played at her feet; and he liked to have her all to himself. She gave him for his own a special compartment in her secretaire, and allowed him to puzzle over her papers and account books. On hot afternoons, as Nonno sat sewing in her bare arms, Randolph would lean over and rub his face against her cool flesh, and his head on her shoulder, listen to stories of when she was a girl. She was utterly composed. For his mother, however, "Every incident was a crisis," he wrote. She "did not seem to know what she wanted," and was sometimes "distressed and uncertain." Most of her time was "spent . . . with little brother, or, if he were asleep, she would be lying across the foot of the bed, with her face in her hands. Often there were tears in her eyes, and if

[Randolph] wanted her to do something for him, she would say piteously that she was not well." [16]

Sunlight poured generously into Sarah Bourne's upstairs room, nourishing her shelves of geranium, begonia, and heliotrope plants which she set out when spring returned. In the winter the children rushed to dress by her warm register before splashing cold water on their faces. It was a house with a porch across its front, a long, dark hall running front to rear, and back stairs. There was a horsehair couch, a banister down which the children sped when they thought the coast was clear, a deed sometimes rewarded with a walloping. There always was a young Polish kitchen girl with many skirts and a vast bosom, eternally peeling potatoes. It was a dark house, but Sarah Bourne left the door ajar after tucking in the children, so they would not be afraid. In the yard stood a barn filled with tools, but from which horses and carriages had vanished. Randolph played among lines of grape arbors, and tumbled into beds of myrtles and wisteria which climbed upon thick stalks and clutched the corner of the house.

Often his co-conspirator was Aunt Fannie, Frances Barrett, Sarah Bourne's youngest sister, who had been graduated from the Sargent School of Physical Culture and ran private gym classes in New York City. She was

". . . Very tall and very slender and very straight, and she had very black hair that came over her forehead in a kind of bang. She always wore black and white dresses, and she always had a fierceness about her that [Randolph] liked. She was several years younger than Mother, and she was very proud . . . . The long summer days were full of Aunt [Fannie]. She loved the garden, with its flowerbeds, and she loved to see the patches all clipped and weeded and raked.

"Once a week, a black man would come from somewhere and spend the whole day . . . mowing the lawn, digging the vegetable garden, and weeding the flowers. . . . They all seemed to be wrestling with the whole yard, to turn it up, to bring it to a bright, shiny newness. At the end of the day [Randolph] would walk about the garden on the gravelly paths, with Aunt [Fannie] to survey their handiwork.

"She would be immensely contented. Her bright black eyes would soften; she would be weary and her hands would be dirty, but [Randolph] would feel the peace that radiated from her at the sight of this freshly burnished garden. The grass would be smooth like a carpet, the flower beds and vegetable-garden all dark and tumbled with their upturned earth.

"The paths would be straight brown indented tracks, with the marks of the rake on the fine earth where George had worked it over. During the week the grass would grow longer, the weeds shoot up in the flower-beds, the paths become bedraggled at the edges, the grass grow up rank on the lawns. But soon Saturday would come with George, and the fine renovation would take place all over again." [17]

God also lived in the Bourne household, and Sunday was an especial day. Off to Old First Randolph would go with Mother, Nonno, and eventually Natalie, Ruth and Donald. He would have liked to put his head down on the pew rail in front of him like Mother and Nonno did, but he could not reach it. So, he ducked his head and shut his eyes tightly until he heard "Amen." When fidgetiness inevitably set in, he would cast his eyes about the handsome interior—at the galleries supported by slender white pillars and bordered by a narrow ledge; at the two enormous brass chandeliers; at the choir behind the minister; and then back to the noses and bonnets beyond the brass railing of the galleries. Then there was Sunday school, "a neutral, colorless event," where Miss Fogg, whose smile made Randolph uncomfortable, would horrify her charges with tales of the evils of drink.

Sin, "on the whole, was a very vague idea" and God "was a majestic old gentleman with a white beard, reclining on white cumulus clouds, and Jesus he knew equally well as a young man in an archaic blue robe, holding a lamb in one arm and followed by others. He had seen their pictures long ago, and whenever either of them was mentioned, these images popped into his mind, faintly colored by a sense of awe, as in the case of God, and of tenderness, as in the case of Jesus. But did he love them? The pastor was certainly a very poor caricature of God, and yet with his beard and square head and loud words, there must be a faint resemblance. [He] certainly did not like him.

"Much more nearly like God was his father's father, whom he had once been taken to see and whom he remembered now as a white-haired, white-bearded man, very solemn, and yet with something cold and repellent about him whenever [Randolph] touched him. [He] did not feel that he loved this God, and yet he knew he ought to, that it was the most important thing in life that he could do.

"So he would sit there and try to screw his heart into an attitude of loving. He would grow very serious and tighten his muscles, and fix his thoughts on the majesty reclining on the white cloud, and, pretty soon, he would feel that indeed he now loved God, and he would be kept from sin." [18]

In many ways Randolph's childhood was as normal as that of a boy who was not afflicted. But, he later emphasized, he did not feel kept from sin, especially when he tried to compete with his playmates. It was, he recalled, his fate to be just strong enough to play with others, and try their games and "stunts," without being tough enough to succeed in any of them. "It never used to occur to me," he wrote, "that my failures and lack of skill were due to circumstances beyond my control, but I would always impute them, in consequence of my rigid Calvinistic bringing-up, I suppose, to some moral weakness of my own. I suffered tortures in trying to learn to skate, to climb trees, to play ball, to conform in general to the ways of the world. I never resigned myself to the inevitable, but over-exerted myself constantly in a grim determination to succeed." [19]

Bourne's memories are not always consistent and sometimes clash or differ in emphasis from those of others. Natalie remembers that "Randolph was a real leader among the children who flocked to our yard," the largest in the neighborhood. She remembers his doing all the things the others did—skating, bicycling, tennis, tree climbing. He "had more imagination than the rest of us, so we usually followed his suggestions." [20]

If one can take Bourne at his word—and it is not certain one always can—he was precocious where schooling was concerned. In fact, he tells us in his "Autobiographical Chapter" that "school was an enormous joke," and that he could not take his teacher seriously. She was an intense spinster who had decided that knowledge could be bullied into children. Randolph had read so many books by the time he entered this school—apparently privately run—that it seemed absurd he should be taught to read. His subtle rebellion sometimes took the form of mimicking his teacher. Eventually her temper would break and Randolph would stand in the corner. "Drunk with power, [he] . . . would ride his high horse until the mill-whistle blew twelve o'clock and they all went home for the day."

Randolph's diary for 1901, suggests that by the time he was 14 he was not so arrogant as he sometimes pictures himself.[21] Indeed, his New Year's resolutions were cherub-like: "To be systematic in practicing and studying. To learn one Bible verse each day and read a few. To be more cordial." And Old First was something very special, as the January 4, 1901, entry shows: "This afternoon, Natalie and I went down to Mr. Curtis's to see about joining the church He talked to us very kindly and asked us some questions. Then he prayed for us. Nonno does not think we are fit for it, but he seems to. When she was young they had revivals, etc., and she seems to think that one must be almost perfect before he can join. Mamma wants us to very much."

Entries also mention the books he was reading, (one of which he calls "decidedly middle class"), the marks he was getting, an apology for wrongly accusing a boy elsewhere in the diary for a theft at school, remarks concerning his stamp collection, debates in school over whether China would be better off under Russian control, the school paper, and Queen Victoria's burial. And on January 15, 1901, he wrote, "It was something to be nominated, although I knew I wouldn't be elected. I'm afraid I am not very popular in the school and very little known. It pleased me though to be elected class president."

Even puppy love occupied Randolph. "I sent off my valentines for tomorrow", he wrote on February 13, 1901, "my finest to Grace Wade, a little card in the shape of an apple-blossom, with the inscription: "To my Sweetheart." Also four uncancelled Dominican Republic stamps which I think she will like. Next to Vanessa Furman, in Clifton, who, I think, is a very nice girl although I haven't seen her for months, and then only twice or three times. I sent one to Edna Jones for friendship and one to Peggy for the same reason. Two for love and two for friendship."

Grace Wade probably was the apple of his eye. From Baltimore, where she was in private school, she wrote in exquisite hand a letter professing her continued interest in stamps and her collection. "You have been in a pickle, haven't you? You were afraid I was going to keep your stamps, and that if you wrote asking their return, that it would look as if you thought I was stealing. I can understand your predicament and must humbly beg to be forgiven for having kept them so long."[23]

How much Randolph's affliction played on his mind cannot be said, but when girls and boys inadvertently shrank from him he must have felt the kind of anguish he records on February 9, 1901.

"I found that Mrs. Griffin had a ticket for Stanton for the Symphony this afternoon when I got up there, and that Aunt Fan wanted to see me and had one for me. I took a car down there and found that she wanted me to stay in, take lunch with her and then go up to Carnegie Hall. I did not like this thing. Right there before some of the gymnasium girls, she unbuttoned my coat, looked all over it, inspected my collar, to see whether it was clean, examined my necktie, made me hold out my hands to see if they or my nails were clean, made me open my mouth to see if my teeth were clean, and then brushed me off after making comments about things in general. I think it was one of the most disgusting, ill-bred, rude things to do. I am not going through it again, it is mortifying."

But the hurt was soothed in March, when he went with Aunt Fan to *Lohengrin,* an opera he found "glorious, glorious."

Bourne's diary shows a hungry reading and the purchase of books with pocket money. School records show that the fare was standard for the time; works by Goldsmith, Irving, Hawthorne, Chaucer and de Quincy were representative of the assignments. What Randolph had for nourishment outside of school books and the Bible ("a magical book that you must not drop on the floor") was what his playmates lent him—exploits of British soldiers in Spain and the Crimea, and death-defying adventures of young filibusters in Cuba and Nicaragua.[23]

"The classics [at home] were stiffly enshrined behind glass doors that were very hard to open—at least Hawthorne and Irving and Thackeray were there, and Tennyson's and Scott's poems—but nobody ever discussed them or looked at them. Miro's busy elders were taken up with the weekly *Outlook* and *Independent* and *Christian Work,* and felt they were doing much for Miro when they provided him and his sister with *St. Nicholas* and *The Youth's Companion.* It was only that Miro saw the black books looking at him accusingly from the case, and a rudimentary conscience, slipping over from Calvinism to culture, forced him solemnly to grapple with 'The Scarlet Letter' or 'Marmion.'[24]

At the same time, Randolph pursued his "unofficial" education. "The New York *Tribune,* lying freshly on our doorstep every morning, was gathered in like intellectual manna by my small and grateful self. It told me daily of a wide, fascinating and important world, and to it I reacted with never failing curiosity."[25]

If the Bourne household was lowbrow, it was lively in other ways. "We had open house," his sister Ruth recalled. "People were always there. It was a happy home, although it probably was hard on Mother because she always loved Father." Apparently it was Randolph's vivacity which did much to ingratiate him with his closest friend, Everett Benjamin, a dark-haired, attractive boy who lived nearby. The two often played chess until 3 or 4 a.m. And with the Hayes sisters, Marion and Helen, there was a running duel at the card table. Randolph's habit of losing these games failed to dull his humor, repertoire of stories or his teasing.[26]

His school records indicate that Randolph excelled in studies but did not outdistance his classmates. With the exception of a 79 one year in geometry, his marks for most of his courses—including English, four years of Latin, three of Greek, German, physics, and music—

ranged from the 80's to 99. From the way he wrote years afterward, however, the impression is of a tormented, frustrated boy.

"I was good at my lessons, and through timidity rather than priggishness, I hope, a very well-behaved boy at school; I was devoted, too, to music, and learned to play the piano pretty well. But I despised my reputation for excellence in these things, and instead of adapting philosophically to the situation, I strove and have been striving since to do the things I could not.

"As I look back now it seems perfectly natural that I should have followed the standards of the crowd, and I loathed my high marks in lessons and deportment, and the exhibitions of my musical skill that I had to give before admiring ladies. Whether or not such an experience is typical of handicapped children, there is tragedy there for those situated as I was.

"For had I been a little weaker physically, I should have been thrown back on reading omnivorously and cultivating my music, with some possible results; while if I had been a little stronger, I could have participated in the play on an equal footing with the rest. As it was, I simply tantalized myself, and grew up with a deepening sense of failure, and a lack of pride in that at which I really excelled." [27]

During graduation ceremonies on June 28, 1903, Randolph's "Washington's Campaigns in New Jersey" was one of seven orations at the exercises in Old First Church. He spoke well in public, and his effort on this occasion inspired a letter from a townsman who had been a college president telling him that he had "seldom heard anything better, if ever," from students at Bourne's age.[28] It may have been little consolation, for Randolph perhaps already felt he was not going to college, despite his passing Princeton's entrance examination.

Although the family house always seems to have had a yard man and a maid, this is not indicative of financial well being. Servants were inexpensive then. The main source was Sarah Bourne's brother, Halsey Barrett, and other help very likely came from comfortable relatives in Morristown where the Bournes often visited and where Randolph spent part of some summers with his maternal aunt, Mary Louise Silliman.

Randolph was embittered forever toward his uncle.[29] In later years he told a friend that his uncle thought college a waste of time for him and that he should support himself. "What! *you* go to college?" Halsey Barrett reportedly said.[30]

Halsey Barrett's daughter, Mary Barrett, recounted the situation differently. "I think Randolph resented father's not sending him to college, but father was carrying so many persons that he couldn't. Father gave the family money over the years; one year it was several hundred dollars." Later, Mary Barrett went to Wellesley, Ruth Bourne to Columbia, and Natalie to Pratt Institute.

Not going to college was a major turning point in Randolph's life; he dates the birth of a new intellectual awareness from about 1904 when he was 18. "My transvaluation of values," he wrote to a friend in 1914, " begun ten years ago when my Calvinism began to crack, has just about reached its completion." [31]

Soon after graduation Randolph began a new education—that in the school of the millions who lead lives of quiet desperation. Apparently he went through the frantic, humbling, and sometimes humiliating experience of job hunting. Judging from the way he commented about it later, it humanized rather than brutalized him. "Perhaps the bitterest struggles of the handicapped," he wrote, "come when he tackles the business world. If he had to go out for himself to look for work, without fortune, training, or influence, as I personally did, his way will indeed be rugged. His disability will work against him for any position where he must be much in the eyes of men, and his general insignificance has a subtle influence in convincing those to whom he applies that he is unfitted for any kind of work.

"As I have suggested, his keen sensitiveness to other people's impressions of him makes him more than usually timid and unable to counteract that fatal first impression by any display of personal force and will. He cannot get his personality over across the barrier. The cards seem stacked against him from the start. With training and influence something might be done, but alone and unaided his case is almost hopeless.

"The attitude toward him ranges from, 'You can't expect us to create a place for you,' to, 'How could it enter your head that we should find any place for you?' He is discounted at the start: it is not business to make allowances for anybody; and while people are not cruel or unkind, it is the hopeless finality of the thing that fills one's heart with despair." [32]

In large cities like New York the environment seemed worst for a disabled man. Here opportunities are so many that he is led restlessly on and on, his mind perpetually unsettled and depressed. His urgent need is repeatedly stung by failures, and inability to get a chance to fail. All the while he knows those at home cannot afford his idleness. Meantime, the dread of meeting people grows.[33]

Whether or how much Randolph supported himself during those six years before entering Columbia in 1909 is not clear. It seems to have been a bitterly demoralizing period. For an unknown length of time he worked in the Morristown office of a relative, evidently as a "factory hand." [34] He also gave music lessons. There are no known letters, diaries or writings for this period, but there is the much told piano roller story, sufficient to cause writers to think of Bourne as a kind of ground-down wage slave. The origin of this story was Randolph's piece in the November 4, 1916, *New Republic,* "What Is Exploitation?" Here he tells of working on a machine which cut perforated music-rolls for the mechanical players which were then popular.

"I was on piece-work, and everything suggested to my youthful self that it depended only upon my skill and industry how prosperous I should become. But what startled me was my employer's lack of care to conceal from me the fact that for every foot of paper which I made he received fifteen cents from the manufacturer with whom he had his contract.

"He paid me five, and while I worked, spent his time composing symphonies in the next room. As long as I was learning the craft, I had no more feeling about our relations than that there was a vague injustice in the air. But when I began to be dangerously clever and my weekly earnings mounted beyond the sum proper for a young person of eighteen who was living at home, I felt the hand of economic power. My piece-rate was reduced to four and a half cents.

"My innocence blazed forth in rebellion. If I was worth five cents a foot while I was learning, I was worth more, not less, after I had learned. My master folded his arms. I do not have to work for him. There were neighbors who would. I could stay or go. I was perfectly free. And then fear smote me.

"This was my only skill, and my timorous inexperience filled the outside world with horrors. I returned cravenly to my bench, and when my employer, flushed with his capitalistic ardor, built another machine and looked about for a young musician to work it, I weakly suggested to an old playmate of mine that he apply for the position."

Randolph's employer was Frederick A. Hoschke, a dark, swarthy, good looking Hungarian who was organist at Old First Church. He seems to have had a contract with "Ludwig and Co., Pianos," of New York City. A young woman, Helen Clark Hummel, whose husband was in California because of heart trouble, came to work after Bourne was hired. Working together in the parlor rooms of a house on Broad

Street, Bloomfield, Randolph and Helen "played" music on a piano which tore appropriate holes in the paper. As she recalls it, they had a good time, teasing and quarreling with each other, except when they "began to quarrel (mildly) because *I* had turned up my 'click' to sound louder which caused B. to turn up his 'click' so that we were trying to outdo each other."

If Bourne later decried the exploitation of the job, Mrs. Hummel did not. Indeed she felt that "Our pay was awfully good." Bourne "never showed any bitterness or anger for anything. Somehow his sense of humor and interest in all things made him above such things. I was quite mean to him in that I made him help in potato-peeling and dishwashing. . . . There was never anything in B. that savored of hate, bitterness, melancholy or meanness. . . ." Nor did she recall anything about the employer's composing, although she did remember that he lost his job at Old First for "cavorting with the soprano in the church quartet." [35]

After the piano job ended, Randolph worked as an accompanist in studios above Carnegie Hall. This was probably in the spring of 1906. One day Helen went with him to a song recital by a singer named Reed Miller in the studio of Francis Fisher Powers. Afterward Helen asked Powers to hear her sing. The result was that Randolph lost his job because she could trade her piano playing to Powers for his voice lessons!

Most likely it was during these interim years that he became estranged from Bloomfield. It is hard to tell because the recorded deprecating remarks made about Bloomfield occurred after his writing career began. What happened was that Bloomfield paled as Randolph's universe widened, as he devoured books, as he discovered a social misery which he never knew before. While he never rejected his family in the strict sense of the word, he grew in different directions, and so his people became in his eyes inadequate, inarticulate, and commonplace. He brooded about not being understood, and for this sulking there seems justification. As Natalie observed:

"Our family never understood Randolph nor me—we think in such different terms—the 'things' are essential to them, and they lose sight of the bigness of the spiritual things . . . .

"Our relatives did not understand Randolph, classed him as a '*Radical*,' decided he was *queer* and his writings such as to disturb their snobbish complacency.

"After his death, they discovered they had been related to someone who made a very real contribution to the thought of America and were proud to claim him then."[36]

Bloomfield in 1900 had 9,668 inhabitants and 15,070 by 1910. Bourne wrote in 1913—perhaps accurately—that he owed "most of my political, social and psychological education to that town." The only things he found to write about in essays, he said, were "generalized autobiographical data of my youthful life there." Moreover, "Its church, its social classes, prejudices, conservatism, moral codes, personalities—all furnish the background against which I throw all my experience, and in terms of which I find I still see life and suppose always shall."[37]

Bloomfield to him had a tenacious Puritan and religious quality. He felt its tone was a general mediocrity which repelled the artistic and the cultured. This was the way he reflected on his community after four years of Columbia University. By then it was the "town where I have so many thwartings to remember . . . ."[38] So interested in it was he that the place was the topic of his master's thesis at Columbia. The work is an appendage to his writing and thought—fascinating, at least for one who knows the region, dispassionate, fact-filled.

Most young men, Bourne wrote, left for the city for good. Local business fell to the less ambitious or less fortunate. The town languished in the orbit of New York City and Newark for "lack of efficient native leadership and the general mediocrity of the population." It was a community with an encrusted aristocracy, a suppressed working class, lethargic community undertakings, church jealousies, no social service, and where "Calvinistic religion was bred in the bone of the town . . . ."[39]

If localites were unaware how Bourne felt by 1913 about Bloomfield, they found out when his "The Social Order in an American Town" appeared in the February *Atlantic*. The piece, although the locale went unnamed, was based on the master's research, but in contrast, it thinly veiled two local leaders and called them feudal barons. These were (1) Thomas Oakes, head of the long established and successful Oakes woolen mill and president of the board of education, and (2) either Allison Dodd, an impressive aristocrat who was chairman of the board of Burns Brothers Coal Co. of New York and New Jersey, a bank president, and country club president, or John Newton, a successful coal dealer who had been staked to his business by monied men in town. Bourne discussed briefly many of the same things he later treated in his thesis, remarking: "This is the curious irony of aristocracies the world over,—that they can wield the ultimate power without bearing any of the responsibility, or doing any of the actual work. The ruling class in this town no longer assumes even political responsibility. The town committee is composed of members of the middle class, and all the political workers and henchmen throughout the town are equally plebian. Those good people who lament that politics are corrupt because the 'best men' will not enter public life, forget that this ruling class is behind everything that is done, and is getting its political work done at an extremely cheap rate. If the real rulers had any serious objection to the way things are run, they would soon enough be in politics. They remain out because their interests are well taken care of; another class bears for them all the burden and strife of the day."

Randolph had the misfortune to be home the Sunday after the *Atlantic* article appeared. Parishioners stared daggers at him as he entered Old First with his family, and later he probably was snubbed or dressed down by first citizens. Local stalwarts probably were angry not because of the accusation of parochialism, but because of that of profit-mindedness.[40] He most likely had no idea his essay would jolt Bloomfield, although after it appeared, he described the article as "a very bumptious analysis . . . calculated to rouse the ire of any stolid notable. . . ." [41]

Soon after, the Newark, (N.J.) *Sunday Call* took him to task. A headline read:

> BLOOMFIELD GRIEVED AND ASTOUNDED
> BY CITIZEN'S ARTICLE IN MAGAZINE;
> VITRIOLIC REMARKS BY FAVORITE SON.[42]

He told Ellery Sedgwick about it, and the *Atlantic*'s editor replied, "I'm sorry for Bloomfield but I rather think a passionate grievance lies in the bosom of the *Call* reporter. Of course, I could write to the Editor, but that seems scarcely worth while. I am sorry if you incurred any serious criticism, but if you have the injustice is preposterous." [43]

This experience provides an important insight into Randolph. By 1913 he had strong convictions and the sureness an indignant intellectual can convey when he is positive he sees things the way they indeed are. By this time, he was adamantly impatient with mediocrity. He was too hard on people and institutions, a notion he himself would reject. He did not understand Bloomfield so well as he thought he did. For example, a banker who knew the Bournes but disliked Randolph immensely—and a lawyer who also knew the family and liked Randolph greatly—recalled that Calvinism was not preached from the pulpit of Old First. Predestination was passé. [44]

And a woman friend of the family wrote Bourne a kind letter protesting that, "Several points . . . *are not true*." She quoted one of her husband's tenants who worked at the Oakes mill: The wages were the highest paid in any mill, there was "perfectly fair treatment," and the Oakes always were ready to adjust any reasonable complaint. Then she denied that Father Nardiella, the Catholic pastor, was neglected, looked on with suspicion, or never sought for advice by the first families.[45]

The rift was a local version of a widening chasm in America between the older and younger generations. More and more it was fashionable for youth to denounce scathingly both parents and the older generation. Each looked at situations differently. Where Randolph saw problems, implying solutions, his elders saw conditions, implying normality. Elders were hurt and puzzled when, perhaps for the first time, they were indicted. Where Bourne saw ". . . little dried-up men who have worked in the mill for fifty years" and observed that, "The most impressive thing about the working class, on the whole, is the profound oblivion of the rest of the population to them," [46] banker Biddulph expressed what the 'feudal barons' probably felt, a sentiment timely if unenlightened: "I never heard any complaints about the way the mill was run or what was paid. They probably paid no more than they had to. When the workers or their families were ill, Mrs. Oakes was there nursing them." [47]

If many Bloomfielders did not appreciate Bourne, there were those he drew to himself with the same magnetism that later attracted admirers. We know that while in many ways Randolph's life was arrested, it was not in a vacuum. He read rapaciously, and before setting foot in a Columbia class room, he was well informed. His closest friends were perhaps Francis and Helen Hummel. Francis was a sociable, dark-haired, temperamental Bloomfielder of about 30 who had returned recently from California. He had taught at Stevens Institute of Technology, but now was with a telephone company, perhaps as a researcher or technician. Randolph fascinated and charmed the couple and enjoyed the chance to have a sounding board.

The relationship shows Bourne alert and involved with ideas. The Hummels, Randolph, two friends of Francis, and two Yorkshire terriers padded off for two weeks at Indian Lake near Malone, New York, perhaps in the summer of 1906. In the morning, Francis and

Randolph would begin conversing at the cottage, ranging far, and often with the latter defending or advocating socialism. The arguments lasted until lunch and were resumed later. In the evening, the vacationers strolled to a nearby hotel where Helen and Randolph took turns at the piano, and guests sang. He appeared happy that summer, vital, and—except for Francis' need to chide him on his table manners—increasingly sophisticated.

Francis repeatedly insisted that no college would refuse him a scholarship. Finally he took the idea seriously and successfully applied for a Columbia University grant. Typhoid fever in the summer of 1909 was cured in time for him to enroll that September. He was 23.[48] In his characteristically self-deprecating tone Bourne wrote later of turning this corner. He solved his difficulties, he said, "only by evading them, by throwing overboard some of my responsibility, and taking the desperate step of entering college on a scholarship. Desultory work is not nearly so humiliating when one is using one's time to some advantage, and college furnished an ideal environment where the things at which a man handicapped like myself can succeed really count."[49]

Columbia was Bourne's redemption, for as he later wrote: "One's self-respect can begin to grow like a weed."

"From the apparently harmless and orthodox hamlet of Bloomfield . . . comes this tester of our staid, age-old, governmental traditions, this exponent of social experimentation, this doughty champion of the younger generation . . . . The great thing is that . . . he took up cudgels for the improvement of the human race—cudgels that he has learned to manipulate with unerring skill. Get into an argument with him on this, his chosen topic, and you are a converted or a ruined man. For back of his theories of revolution for the readjustment of society is a great mass of data that he has absorbed and correlated, and that comes tumbling about your head in an over-whelming and well-ordered deluge when you try to oppose him. History, philosophy and literature are at his fingertips. If you doubt this, look at the record."—*Senior Book,* Columbia College, 1912.

II

COLLEGE DAYS

Columbia University when Randolph Bourne entered in 1909 was a constellation crowded with scholars who shone in their respective galaxies or who were on the way to national and international distinction. From its founding in 1754, Columbia had plodded along with a passable reputation. Like most American colleges, it resembled a high-calibre preparatory school. At Columbia in the late 1880's, "there existed a state of things which is difficult to describe. There was no feeling of purpose, no agreement as to what was best for the future, no common interest in what was happening in the present. A prevailing unrest, a clash of opinion, and on every side a belief that everything went by chance or sometimes by favor—these were a few of the obstacles of good feeling and to harmonious effort." [1]

Johns Hopkins had been established in 1876, and some Columbia men feared that the times were going to sweep past the small college, located as it was on a block at Madison Avenue and 49th Street in downtown Manhattan. A whole post-Civil War generation had studied in Europe, many of them in Germany. They realized that no American school approached continental universities. Yet in Berkeley; Chicago; Ann Arbor; Madison, Wisconsin; Cambridge, Massachusetts; Princeton, and New York City, there were persons who believed that a nation so wealthy as the United States could create great universities.

At Columbia, two presidents—Frederick A. P. Barnard and then ex-Mayor Seth Low—worked toward the goal of a great metropolitan institution. Columbia changed greatly under Low and Barnard and later under Nicholas Murray Butler. Much of the work, however, was done by an educational pioneer, John W. Burgess, a longtime professor and dean. He was the key figure in the building of the graduate school, particularly political science, and the establishing of other graduate divisions; the great push came in the 1890's and in the first years of the new century.

From a small college with three loosely attached and professional schools in old buildings—regarded by the outside world as local, sectarian, and unpromising—a new university rose. The location was the spacious grounds of Morningside Heights in the area of 116th Street, previously the inauspicious site of the Bloomingdale Asylum, and—before the asylum moved there in 1859—once the home of the municipal Asylum for the Deaf and Dumb. The 1890's, then, saw the "sudden transformation of an old and weak college into a new and strong university." [2]

Bourne must have sensed the confident mood in September 1909, for by then Columbia had matured. Bright and distinguished men dominated the faculty. In the law school were Dean George W. Kirchwey, and the man who succeeded him in 1910, Harlan Stone. Franz Boas, a father of modern anthropology, and John Dewey in philosophy were equally noted. In the social sciences, James Harvey Robinson, John Bassett Moore, Franklin H. Giddings, John Bates Clark, and Felix Adler had unique reputations.

In literature, men like Brander Matthews, Charles Sears Baldwin, George Odell, Joel Spingarn, John Erskine, Carl Van Doren, and William P. Trent had crested the hill of distinction or were nearing wide esteem for excellence. While Michael Idvorsky Pupin was methodically inventing things which would affect society profoundly, the historian James Harvey Robinson was beseiged by a happy variety of competition. Charles Beard, Carlton Hayes, and James T. Shotwell were provokingly interested in man's political behavior, his past, and his present. And in mathematics Casius Keyser was locally and nationally famous in his field.

Many of these dynamos also were great teachers, men tolerant beyond expectation but for whom passivity was a sin. Columbia had been liberated from the sluggish routine of conveying official tradition. In its place came a restless encouragement of disagreement. In philosophy, the department chairman was the socratically contentious

Frederick Woodbridge, a widely, deeply read man who, although unoriginal, set minds ateeming with the eternal questions. Typically, one of his colleagues was a Catholic priest, a specialist in Thomism, a realm revived by the interest and solicitation of Leo XIII. Responsible liberty was the order of the day at Columbia.

"To the teaching staff it had attracted minds of an independent, vigorous cast: a strong tide of renovation was running in scholarship, the disposition to level the ancient barriers separating the academ-
Another factor likewise helped to invigorate the atmosphere. This was the disposition to level the ancient barriers separating the academic precincts from the workaday world.

"Columbia's metropolitan location furnished one incentive; even then the strenuous compulsions of New York were relegating ivory towers to antiquarian interest, among sedan chairs and snuffboxes. Perhaps, too, there was stimulus in the daily pressure of a miscellaneous student body, containing every cult—but as a group formidably suspicious of authority, dogma, and the example of the past." [3]

Columbia professors were ambitious, in touch with the world, ill-disposed to the cloister, leary of dry-as-dust scholarship. "You feel that they were attracted only by creative enterprize," a student later wrote.[4] As Bourne remarked, "It is becoming more and more common now that when you touch a professor you touch a man and not an intellectual speciality."[5]

Randolph studied under many of these distinguished academicians and was on intimate terms with some. Lamentably, however, it is rarely possible to know under which men he studied. His records do not indicate his teachers, and when the courses are matched with those in the catalogue, it is seen that almost always there were two or more men who could have taught Randolph's section.

For each of these men and for Bourne's fellow students the first encounter with him was unsettling; he was almost frightening. This "little, sparrowlike man, tiny, twisted bit of flesh," as John Dos Passos said of him,[6] rose up on spindly legs five disfigured feet from the ground—his unruly hair barely manageable—his head too large proportionally, his skin unhealthy looking.

Bourne had a fine head with a strong jaw, a massive forehead, and beautiful blue eyes; yet, he at first caused people to shrink from him in repulsion. He was, as Theodore Dreiser recalled, a major mind encased in a minor body. The lyrical quality of Waldo Frank's reaction was like the feeling of many others, once they were at ease.

"It was Randolph's eyes and hands that brought about the wonder.

The hands were exquisite, gentle, quiet. They seemed made for such clear profundities as playing of Bach: they bespoke his style—the caress of his ruthless understandings. And they flowered from his body with the inevitable irony of all his being. The eyes were penetrant, studious. There was a reticence in them, after the adventure, not before it. You knew from them that Randolph Bourne was wise, and that he had withdrawn some subtle spirit of himself forever from gross contacts: that he had learned to see and to experience without the ill-focused turmoil of too close contacts.

"So surely consonant were his hands and eyes with what he said, that the body became a sort of Christian *Lest Ye Forget*—a sign thrust into the humiliating coil of life, from the high freedom of his discourse." [7]

Combine these memories of Randolph's appearance with his impeccable manners and speech—unsoiled by vulgarisms, profanities or slang (although he liked a good Rabelaisian yarn)—and one has an approximation of the exterior Bourne from his college days to his death.

How long it was before Randolph felt at home at Columbia is not clear. Some remember him as a shy, withdrawn person, while others think of him as sociable and at ease. To Leon Fraser, a contemporary whose varied and brilliant career included the presidency of the First National Bank of New York, he gave the "impression of being a sensitive recluse" who "seemed to be resentful towards those who were in a better position than himself financially or socially," and who "did not wish to be bothered." [8] Yet publisher Alfred A. Knopf felt a dislike for Bourne because he was associated with a group Knopf considered intellectually arrogant.[9]

As a student, Bourne impressed his professors. In his first academic year, his marks included nine "A's" and five "B's". Subsequently even better marks assured his election to Phi Beta Kappa.

Although we know he probed socialism before entering Columbia, he still appears conventional and middle class in his first year. Little suggests a radical disgruntled with society. In his second year, on November 15, 1910, a letter from him in the college newspaper, *Spectator,* complained of difficulties in obtaining work. "It will seem to those men for whom the Employment Committee has secured work that it is performing its function with notable success, while those who have been left in the shuffle will take quite a different view of the matter." While he conceded that he was not "preternaturally able", he felt he offered a versatile list of specialties. He protested that in a great city like New York there should be work for all who wish it. The committee replied, without naming him, that Randolph could not get any of several possible jobs because of his "personality." [10]

The various reading lists which Bourne kept begin in 1912, but by the spring of 1911 he was evidently delving widely into radical literature. In the February 1911 *Atlantic* appeared an article by Cornelia A. P. Comer, "A Letter to the Rising Generation." The piece was a condescending and thoroughly denunciatory assault on youth—the way they spoke, their selfishness, agnosticism, lack of integrity, and flippant advocacy of socialism. Youth, Mrs. Comer charged, was shallow and irresponsible.

Meantime, Randolph had greatly impressed Frederick Woodbridge, whose history of philosophy course he was taking. Woodbridge suggested his class reply, and spoke to him individually about it. Randolph said he had written an answer already. The article appeared in the May 1911 *Atlantic* and set the tone for much of his writing thereafter. His piece, "The Two Generations," while ignoring Mrs. Comer's article, criticized elders and praised youth and their potential. The two generations misunderstood each other more than ever before, he declared. It is not surprising that the reactions of youth are unsatisfactory, for they find themselves in a world they in no way made and which displeases them. In fact, "the only choice for the vast majority of young men to-day is between being swallowed up in the routine of a big corporation, and experiencing the vicissitudes of a small business, which is now an uncertain, rickety affair, usually living by its wits, in the hands of men who are forced to subordinate everything to self-preservation, and in which the employee's livelihood is in constant jeopardy. The growing consciousness of this situation explains many of the peculiar characteristics of our generation." [11]

Moreover, the structure of the economy prevents youth's stamina from being unlocked so early or so automatically as in previous generations. Therefore, youth cannot be fairly charged with selfishness.

"We have an eagerness to understand the world in which we live that amounts almost to a passion. We want to get behind the scenes, to see how the machinery of the modern world actually works. We are curious to learn what other people are thinking, and to get at the forces that have produced their point of view. We dabble in philanthrophy as much from curiosity to see how people live as from any feeling of altruism. We read all sorts of strange philosophies to get the personal testimony of men who are interpreting the world . . . . We have, as a result, become impatient with the conventional explanations of the older generation."

Youth had found, Bourne contended, that they cannot keep religion, knowledge, and aspirations separate in water-tight compartments as their ancestors did. More and more youth see life's entities in a whole. The older generation is ever assertive, but "we . . . are becoming increasingly doubtful whether you believe in yourselves quite so thoroughly as you have us think. Your words are very brave, but the tone is hollow. Your mistrust of us, and your reluctance to convey over to us any of your authority in the world looks too much like the fear and dislike that doubt always feels in the presence of conviction, to be quite convincing. We believe in ourselves; and this fact, we think, is prophetic for the future. We have an indomitable feeling that we shall attain, or if not, that we shall pave the way for a generation that shall attain."

The *Atlantic* article, which made Randolph a minor celebrity on campus—as much from its contents as for having been published by a name magazine—was the ideological precursor of his essay "Youth" in the April 1912 *Atlantic*. In it he returned to the same theme, but in a quasi-mystical tone characteristic of much of his other writing.

In "Youth" he again exalted the potential of youth, that is, young adulthood. Youth, he contended, is a poignant flowing forth, a consciousness of being alive. As the world breaks in on an increasingly aware person, he has a feeling of expansion, of sudden wisdom and sudden care. In his tussling with the world, he does not accept ideas, ideas get him! Prudence is one of youth's enemies. It makes him prematurely old, and fatally weighs him down before he has discovered life for himself. It is here that youth's quarrel with the older generation occurs. "There is no scorn so fierce," he said, "as that of youth for the inertia of older men. The lack of adjustment to the ideas of youth's elders and betters, one of the permanent tragedies of life, is certainly the most sensational aspect of youth. That the inertia of the older people is wisdom, not impotence, is a theory that you will never induce youth to believe for an instant. The stupidity and cruelties of the world fill youth with an intolerant rage."

Old men, he argued, cherish the delusion that there is something mystically valuable about mere quantity of experience, but actually youth has the most experience. It is youth which constantly faces new situations, thus getting the "whole beauty and terror and cruelty of the world in its fresh and undiluted purity." But the ideas of adults are wrong, and grow more wrong as they become older, and youth, therefore, has no right to be humble. The ideals youth forms will be the highest it ever will have. Its insight will be the clearest it ever will have, and its ideas the most stimulating.

". . . More and more of the clear-sighted youth are coming to see the appalling array of things that still need to be done. The radical young man of to-day has no excuse for veering round to the conservative standpoint. Cynicism cannot touch him. For it is the beauty of the modern radical philosophy that the worse the world treats a man, the more it convinces him of the truth of his radical interpretation of it. Disillusion comes, not through hard blows, but by the insidious sappings of worldly success. And there never was a time when there were so many radical young people who cared little about that worldly success."

Bourne was not merely sending up a trial ballon from his ivory tower. There are letters in the archives at Columbia which demonstrate what a profound influence he had on many. While nothing he wrote was original, he did strike a deep vein of conscious and latent hostility and yearning. He got letters from persons his age, younger, and older, who had been moved by his vision of youth.

One thinks of the post-World War I period as that in which are found the beginnings of the America of today, although of course the stages of history are not sharp breaks. But as the historian Henry F. May says, one is puzzled when he looks at the period just prior to United States entry into the war and expects to find a peaceful and stable America. On the surface, he writes, dwell placidity and complacency; below the surface are the varied beginnings of the later change in American culture and society. In that prewar period a cultural revolution overlaps a Victorian calm.[12]

All Bourne's fervor could not change the fact that his civilization, however much youth might rave, still cherished long-trusted notions. These central doctrines included the certainty and universality of moral values, the inevitability of progress, and the importance of traditional literary culture. "Most Americans were still certain," May states, "that moral judgments applied with equal sureness in literature, art, politics, and all other areas. Second, it seemed clear that such judgment could be and must be applied not only to the conduct of individuals but also to the doings of trusts and labor unions, cities and nations. Finally, and this was perhaps the most stated corollary of all, the United States, as the leader in moral progress, had a special responsibility for moral judgment, even of herself."

Culture in America meant a particular heritage from Europe which included polite manners, respect for traditional learning, appreciation of the arts, and knowledge and allegiance to the standard literature—usually British. Randolph by 1911 was well on his way to rejecting that approach to culture and in later writing incessantly denounced what he felt was a dispiriting fawning.

Similarly, progressive leaders generally believed that American society did not need an uprooting. Thinkers like Wilson and Brandeis on the one hand or Roosevelt and Croly on the other wanted to repair the machine with different but not antipathetic methods; otherwise they would not have been so preoccupied with reform in government and the limits to which checks on capitalism might go. The problem was with the money lenders, not the temple. As May remarks, in the Progressive Era "people wanted to make a number of sharp changes because they were so confident in the basic rightness of things as they were. It may be defined as the time in which the leaders of the people believed in their own mission and also in democracy, and in which they were able to get the support, most of the time, of a majority of active citizens. It may be defined still better as the time when eternal morality and progress seemed to be joined together."

Bourne was part of this protest, but unlike most of the progressive mystique, he appears to reject American society as it fundamentally was. Yet he was a devotee of democracy and an exalter of America after the Whitmanesque manner. He *appears* to reject the United States but even that is not clear. He espoused a kind of socialism, but seems not to have made the kind of commitment which his socialism demanded. And he was always weak on alternatives when protesting existing systems. Regardless of his approach, it is clear from his early essays that he, like many of his ardent contemporaries, had a vision of a finer America. Like Americans since the Jacksonian period and perhaps before, he brooded about his country, and wondered what had gone wrong. In this respect he was typically American, for he was a David against Goliath.

By the time the first *Atlantic* essay had appeared, he had fallen in with a crowd which thrived on his company and he on theirs. His entree to friends at Columbia was the *Columbia Monthly,* the undergraduate literary magazine. He soon made himself known at the *Monthly* office. In his freshman year three of his pieces appeared in the review. In the first, "Some Aspects of Good Talk," in the January number, he seemed to articulate the tone of his relationships with close Columbia friends and acquaintances.

With an unstudied light touch, he denounced literature as compared to conversation because the former did not allow you to answer back. Conversation really is a duel. The good talker "takes the world quite seriously, but takes himself quite flippantly." The elder Holmes, Robert Louis Stevenson, and Anatole France, Bourne observed, found themselves tremendously interesting. They delighted in telling about it, but not in an egotistical, conceited sense. They simply found themselves the best evidence they could collect of how delightful and interesting human nature is. His friends tacitly accepted this notion, for—seen from one viewpoint—their college years appear a long, serious, frenetic, but sophisticated effort to soak themselves in life, paw over the ageless questions and often write each other urbane thoughtful letters.

There was Arthur Macmahon—one of his two closest friends—a tall, intense, handsome young man who would go on to a distinguished career at Columbia, and in non-academic enterprises connected with political science and economics. It was probably Macmahon's composure and practical, organized sympathetic nature which appealed to Randolph. Arthur probably was his closest sharer in interest in mundane affairs, for both were interested in socialism.

With Carl Zigrosser, a handsome, charming, shy blond Thoreauic youth from upstate New York, Randolph dwelled on the transcendent. Carl was a talented writer whose real interest and gift was art, and he later became curator of fine prints at the Philadelphia Museum. Although Randolph valued Arthur and Carl equally, it was with Carl that he poured out more of his inner self. Among these three was a love and confidence based on a supreme respect. It should not be assumed that Arthur and Carl were off in their own little enclaves, and that he tapped their resources alternately. It is clear from their letters that they were at home at a political rally or a chamber concert; that their serious reading ranged from the newspaper to poetry.

No less warm were other friendships. There was Simon Barr, a short, intense Jewish boy whose suits were far too big for him and whose dark eyes were too small for an already small head. He was deeply sensitive, refreshing, irreverent, and wrote mystical poetry which he got published in the *Monthly* (which he later edited), but not elsewhere. He went on to a career in technical journalism and then public relations. And there was Henry W. Elsasser, a brilliant bushy-haired student who, according to one story, in a few hours took Bourne through the basics of calculus. Elsasser later did advanced research in accoustics, but poisoned himself in 1921. Another friend was Lawrence K. Frank who became noted in education and for work with various foundations.

There also was Edward W. Murray, a New York Catholic boy, the son of Irish and Canadian parents. Murray was a charming, refined musician who later played violin under Eugene Ormandy of the Philadelphia Symphony, and who composed complex music which is hard to play and seldom tried. Another was a slightly built writer of love poetry for the *Monthly,* James Henle, later president of Vanguard Press and a writer and editor. Bourne also knew Roderick Seidenberg, an inquisitive future architect who had read widely and who was engrossed in beauty and the notion of the soul.

Randolph was considerably influenced by Charles Harry Chase and Read Lewis. Chase was 28 when he entered Columbia in 1909 after both hardships and a full life. As a boy he had worked hard on his father's struggling Colorado farm which blew away during a ruinous drought. As a secretary to a high executive of the Colorado Fuel and Iron Company, Chase saw bitter labor strife. Joining the Industrial Workers of the World, he eventually became national secretary of the organization's political wing. Immediately before entering Columbia he had been head of the publishing house of Daniel De Leon's Socialist Labor Party.

Chase was for Randolph a vivid contact with political action, and the two had in common a background of deprivations. Chase, a handsome, blue-eyed, athletic man of medium height—light of skin, hair, and voice—became fast friends with Bourne. Randolph particularly liked him for his charm, his mild persistence in argument, and for his considerateness. Later he was a researcher for the Brookings Institution, and for many years a teacher at Ohio State. In 1955 he had an office at the Library of Congress where he was trying to finish a study of how socialism can come to the United States without coercion and without losing political democracy. After Columbia, however, he did not return to the labor movement or to the party.[13]

Read Lewis arrived at Columbia in the Fall of 1909 after graduating from Wisconsin. He took graduate courses and then went to law school, getting his degree in 1914. Lewis was a nephew of a professor Randolph admired greatly—James Harvey Robinson—but what counted to Bourne was that Read was a highly individualistic person without straining for eccentricity. He was socially minded, tireless, uncomplicated, tenacious, yet unselfish, and loyal to friends.

Lewis began to practice law in New York, but in 1916 went to Russia for three years as special assistant to the American Ambassador. There he administered relief funds, and fom 1917 to 1919 directed American publicity in Moscow and Archangel. After the war he began a long career with the American Council for Nationalities Service —of which Lewis has been director since 1920—dedicated to integrate immigrants into American life and to promote international understanding. In the case of Read Lewis and Randolph's other college mates, the adage that one is known by his friends is meaningful.

With these and other acquaintances, Bourne went through four rich, if not always enjoyable years of university life. Clearly he needed these contacts; he craved friendship and idealized human relations. "My friends," he confessed in a sensitive essay entitled "The Excitement of Friendship," "I can say with truth, since I have no other treasure, are my fortune."[14] But the relationship was a two way street, and most persons who knew Randolph well carried for the rest of their lives small devotional altars in the back of their minds honoring his memory. A remark later by Arthur Macmahon expressed the impact Bourne had on those he touched: "To know him was one of the deepest experiences of my life." It is typical of other comments.

The relationship with friends at Columbia was held together by a counterpoint of social occasions. Often the scene was his house in Bloomfield, or a night-long conversation at school. His campus activities, aside from the *Monthly,* centered in the Philolexian Society, a literary group to which he belonged in his second year. There also was Boar's Head—from the name of the tavern which Falstaff and his companions frequented—organized by Professor John Erskine, and thus christened by Dixon Ryan Fox, the future historian and president of Union College, who preceeded Bourne as editor of the *Monthly,* and who admired him greatly. The group was supposed to discuss books and writing, but never could stay away from philosophical and current issues. Fox and Randolph usually took opposite sides. Inevitably Zigrosser entered the fireworks, usually on Bourne's side.[15]

Randolph very likely took greatest delight in an informal "Academy" which he and a few others established. Headquarters were in any available apartment and whenever someone had a paper to read. The Academy, he wrote, "had a brilliant meeting at Elsasser's Saturday. Springer was the event of the evening with a paper on Scholasticism. The idea was to give Springer who talks a good deal a chance to show what he had. As a showoff, he was a failure. We rendered him positively humble before the evening was over. Murray brought his violin and we played Beethoven sonatas together. Beer and lemonade furnished a fitting climax."[16]

And later he reported that, "The last Academy was very select. At Murray's house, on 'Religion'; Swain, Elsasser, Seidenberg and myself only." The Swain referred to was Joseph Ward Swain, later a scholar and chairman of the history department at the University of

Illinois. Swain said later: "The discussions usually centered about philosophical and social problems, socialism, religion, etc. [Bourne] dominated the group intellectually, and its sessions played a bigger part in my own mental development than anything the professors did for me. Those were the days when one's head bumped the clouds." [17]

Randolph was no more sophisticated than most of his friends, but it probably was he—with his flare for such things—who inspired many of the congenial dinner parties he went to while at Morningside Heights. He described for Zigrosser a dinner party attended by a new acquaintance, the aspiring poet Joyce Kilmer, and a friend, the then little known artist, Rockwell Kent. "Our dinner," he said, "was a fair success, Joyce Kilmer, sort of a frost, but R. Kent and Prof. Baldwin hit it up splendidly; talked art, while we listened spellbound. Kent quite mystical, and very fervent; Baldwin . . . excessively ethical; Elsasser was delightful because Kent seemed to attain a reduction ad absurdum of theories of art. It was after all, Kent said, an aesthetic feeling that was hard to define in concrete terms. Elsasser agreed and I told him he was a mystic!" [18]

So important was friendship to him that his ideas about it resembled a conscious theory, much like Aristotle's notion in the *Nicomachean Ethics* that friendship by definition is selfless and mutually strengthening. "A man with few friends," he insisted, "is only half-developed; there are whole sides of his nature which are locked up and have never been expressed. He cannot unlock them himself, he cannot discover them; his friends alone can stimulate and open them." [19]

But as there is a rhapsodic side to Bourne's relations with friends and acquaintances, so is there an unhappier, telling aspect. He could be devastatingly ironical; his invective was lethal. "Bourne," his friend Roderick Seidenberg later recalled, "was like a hard, fast tennis player in his thinking and conversation: hard serve, quick return, pressing game all the way. I loved it, although I could not match him—few could—but others didn't like to so much, especially if they were being demolished."

Moreover, not everyone, especially those who knew him slightly or not at all, grasped his irony. When one reads Randolph's correspondence, one realizes that there was constantly in his life the aftermath or memory of some quarrel, disagreement, or misunderstanding in which one or both parties had been hurt. At college he sometimes overstepped himself. Carl Zigrosser wrote him a letter telling him that his affliction never made any difference to Zigrosser and that he hoped he never tactlessly hurt him. The reply was revealing.

"Thank you very much indeed for your kind and really beautiful letter. None of my friends and certainly none of my Columbia friends, have the slightest cause to fear that they have ever hurt me. They have all been so good to me that I bless my good fortune for having them, and hope that I shall not lose them. The danger, I fear, is very much the other way.

"It is I who says cutting things and wound them, most of the time quite out of inadvertence, and through a diabolical weakness of trying to be clever. I had a reputation for a sharp tongue long before I had a reputation for anything else, and I am terribly afraid it flashed out on friend and foe alike.

"That is what gives me a guilty conscience to be praised for what I write, for I can write things that, while I believe I am sincere in saying them, are mighty hard to live to in concrete cases." [20]

Randolph usually decided instantly on meeting people whether he could and would like them, and they him—an imperfect use of intuition. He tended to look first at one's intellect, and not at the heart and soul. If the intellect pleased him, he was attracted to the heart and soul, too. But if he did not like the intellect, he discarded the person.

He expected too much of even his closest and unselfish friends. When he struck for the jugular, the move was like a defense mechanism reacting to a spot rubbed sore by the sense of aloneness he always carried with him. The sad thing about his friendships, a friend believed, "was that he seemed to give much more than he was able to receive. So many people disappointed him. They were less brilliant or competent or honest than he first believed. Or they did not have as much time for him as he felt their common interest required . . . Sometimes it seemed to me he detected a slight or an injustice or a lack where none really existed." Often "he seemed to become absorbed very quickly and deeply in a person and then suddenly to decide that here was less than he had at first thought." [21]

Another person who knew him well said: "He himself had fought so bravely, he thought everyone else should." [22] Even on the intellectual level where Bourne usually observed the rules of charity and dignity, he could strike what some might call a low blow. One Sunday afternoon he and perhaps a dozen others sat around the kitchen table of a Manhattan apartment listening to Vachel Lindsay read his "General William Booth Enters Into Heaven." When Lindsay finished, Randolph said to his face, "Great poetry—greater claptrap!" [23]

Nicholas Murray Butler also was an object of Bourne's acid. The president was unpopular with certain elements at Columbia. Some always alleged he elbowed from the faculty the esteemed composer Edward MacDowell. MacDowell had been appointed in 1896. It was a misadventure because although the composer was of recognized genius, he did not lecture well. So, only those well grounded and advanced profited much from him. In fact, when MacDowell could not communicate orally he played to his students. Justly or unjustly, he departed and fairly or unfairly Butler was blamed. One student remembered, "Butler was very much disliked, or at least, not liked. One never saw him." [24]

Butler loved Columbia as much as anyone. But he gave iconoclasts like Randolph and his acquaintances the impression that he was a prig. Sometimes he seemed to be talking down to students. "The world," he told them, "is full just now of persons who want to have everything done for them and to do as little as possible themselves." [25] A clear thinker, Dr. Butler said, sees the bright side of life; the sound character tries to make the bright side even brighter. "Among the greatest nuisances in this world are the persons who continually rise to remark, whether by voice or pen, that they 'emphatically protest' against something or other. If one must protest it is not usually good manners to protest too emphatically, and he will protest to greater advantage if at the same time he finds something to commend. Don't knock! Boost!"

It probably was this sort of thing which incited the devil in Bourne. On September 4, 1915, his "One of Our Conquerors" appeared in the *New Republic.* Although written two years after he left Columbia, it accurately reflects his feelings while a student. The man in the piece, Dr. Alexander Mackintosh Butcher, president of Pluribus University, was clearly Butler. Dr. Butcher was a vulgar Wall Street and politician type who fawned about, uttering clichés and tinny aphorisms. Dr. Butcher had spent his life on his treatise, "Why We Should Never Change Any Form of Government."

As easily recognizable was John Erskine, who was the model for the academic scholar in Bourne's "The Professor" which appeared in the July 10, 1915, issue of the *New Republic.* In it the professor is a naive pedant, out of touch with the modern world. Literature after Stevenson was anathema. While the professor is aware of the day's radicalism, he prefers the past. In short, he lives in a vacuum. It is not known why Bourne and—it appears from his correspondence—his clique were anti-Erskine. Apparently they not only disliked his literary tastes, but also thought him supercilious and jejune. Erskine deals so complimentarily with Bourne in his autobiography that one concludes Erskine understood his radicalism and aspirations, although the few letters from him to Bourne preserved at Columbia are chilling in their terseness, politieness, and stridently favorable remarks. After praising him, Erskine commented:

"In a partial sense he was, and would always have been a liberal, but never a young spirited or happy liberal. He was born world-weary, and even in his first papers, published in *The Atlantic Monthly* . . . he directed his lucid and provocative criticism against the elder generation without revealing precise hope or aspiration for his own contemporaries. Essentially he was a lover of tradition, an admirer of old cultures, and a critic of them only in so far as they had fallen short of what he liked to think they could have been.

"Early in our acquaintance I disappointed him because I had not read Masefield's "Everlasting Mercy" as soon as he had. I remember the day he showed me a copy of the English magazine in which the poem appeared. He criticized the way English was taught at Columbia, and in particular the way I taught it, and since his points were all valid, I reformed myself as much as I could. Yet I confess to a weakness, that I wondered why he felt called upon to be an indefatigable checker-up of other men's shortcomings." [26]

However, another Columbia English professor—Henry W. L. Dana, a friend of Bourne—remembered that although Erskine first exploited him he later could not stand his criticizing him, and turned viciously against him, saying savagely that in a deformed body the mind also is deformed.[27]

Randolph even lashed out in some ways at college life, generalizing from his Columbia experience. His "The College: An Undergraduate View," in the November 1911 *Atlantic,* argued that frivolity and Philistinism prevailed among large numbers of undergraduates. The fraternities, he wrote, are the center of a vast political system which fills the athletic managerships, selects members of the societies, officers of classes and clubs, editors and assistants of publications, and "performs generally all that indispensable public service of excluding the aliens, the unpresentable, and the generally unemployable from activity."

Athletics, he complained, had through the support of the American college become "a thoroughly unwholeome excrescence on college life. They have become the nucleus for a perverted college sentiment." If athletics were curbed, sentiment would flow into proper, that is, intellectual and cultural channels, Bourne contended. The final aspect of the essay was an optimistic assertion that the American college was thawing and awakening.

So encouraged was he that when he wrote "College Life Today" for the September 1912 *North American Review,* he maintained that the "solidest element in college was . . . the crowd of non-fraternity, non-influential, ordinary men . . . ." The college had become richly heterogeneous. Athletics was waning and scholarship was on the rise, although the "grind" and the prig were as rare as the "rah-rah" man. In retrospect, the article does not ring true.

A selective arrangement of details could show that Randolph soured on Columbia and his experience there. The contrary is true. He seems during his four years there to have felt the way he did after his second year. "After all," he opined, "Columbia is the best thing 'in the city of New York.' It may not be perfect, but its spirit is healthy, free and progressive; it smacks of the West as well as the East. One can breathe intellectually here, and the external beauty of the place grows on the spirit and makes one happy to be able to live among its buildings and along its Quadrangle." [28]

Besides his friends and a performance in studies so excellent that he was able to graduate in June 1912 a year early, Randolph had what promised to be an impressive career in letters. Beginning with his first article in the *Atlantic* for May 1911, his work appeared 18 more times until June 1917.

Bourne and the *Atlantic*'s editor Ellery Sedgwick formed a warm, trusting relationship. Sedgwick's letters to Randolph are full of tempered encouragement, and of fatherly guidance.

They met in New York in May 1911, and of course Sedgwick was shocked. "He was a dwarf in stature," he recalled, "without a redeeming feature. His shoulders were twisted and hunched, his face a mouldy brown, and the skin drawn too tightly over the jaw made his teeth stand out like fangs . . . . But in spite of my interest and my contrition, I could not bring myself to ask him to stay to lunch. That the Creator will hold against me. It is not the burly sins that will incense Him but the small meannesses. I make my confession now, but absolution I do not deserve and shall not receive." [29]

If Bourne sensed Sedgwick's initial uneasiness, he did not permit it to intrude on their relationship. Over the years until 1917, Sedgwick's letters were increasingly warmer. It is clear that he suggested half or more of the article topics on which Bourne wrote for the *Atlantic.* Sedgwick's blue pencil often caused him to revise, usually for the better.

Louis Filler points out that Randolph's indictment in the *Atlantic* of the older generation overlooked or tacitly dismissed very real and practical reform movements being carried on by elders, among them Robert LaFollette and Jane Addams. And muckraking publications abounded. He suggests that so far as the *Atlantic* articles are concerned they embodied radical thinking—nothing more—and it was this abstraction which made him stimulating yet still acceptable to his middle class readers.[30] His readers may have been tantalized, as Filler says, but Randolph was not merely going through mental gymnastics, as will be noted in Chapter III.

The *Columbia Monthly* editorship to which he was named in May 1911 also had brought Bourne prestige. By the time he resigned the next winter, 13 of his pieces had appeared in the review and four more followed. The *Monthly* was not of course the center of campus. Its staff was a small, earnest faction of articulate, sensitive young men, but there was no Big Man on Campus aura about being on the *Monthly*. As a writer, James Henle, recounted with tongue-in-cheek, "The subscribers would gather at the office to talk over each issue."

According to a casual acquaintance of Randolph, "There was a good deal of prestige to being a member of the editorial board of *Spectator* [campus newspaper] and little or no prestige to being a member of the editorial board of the *Monthly*. I would say that the prevailing atmosphere on the campus (among the students) was anti-intellectual."[31] And the publisher Alfred A. Knopf, who was business and advertising manager of the review, recalled that "the *Columbia Monthly* group and its editors probably were little known on campus."

It did not bother Randolph if popularity did not accompany prestige. Under him the *Monthly* reached the peak of its short life. Even today the issues he directed are interesting, and almost empty of sophomorisms. However, he welcomed his departure. "I am glad to be out. I have some hard courses this term, want to write some essays, and am getting just the least bit tired of the crowd. I feel sometimes as if I was growing up faster than they were. Now with a headquarters in Hartley [Hall], I am not so dependent on the *Monthly* office, and leave with real admiration for my good sense in not working a good thing to death . . ."[32]

When Bourne wrote those lines he was 25. Men's characters and outlooks of course are formed at different times. Some men perhaps are at 13 essentially what they shall be later. Some never mature. It was in Bourne's Columbia years and his postgraduate year abroad that his intellect became well-honed and during which he acquired a cohesive worldview. To that crucial development we now turn.

"In this lies man's true freedom: in determination to worship only the god created by our own love of the good, to respect only the heaven that inspires the insight of our best moments." Jotted down by Bourne the student from "A Free Man's Worship," an essay by Bertrand Russell

III

IRONIC INSURGENT

What Bourne became at Columbia was an implacable insurgent. As he wrote in the April 1912 *Atlantic,* "At twenty-five I find myself full of the wildest of radicalisms, and look with dismay at my childhood friends who are already settled down and have somehow gotten years beyond me in a day."

Radicalisms, however, were not all that he was full of at age 25. Some of the ideas he brought into focus at Columbia were conventional, or at least hardly radical. In these years he refined a style for confronting the world and himself, and for protecting himself—irony. He appears to have resolved what he thought about God or a god, while arriving at a notion of truth and a method for discovering truth which he would use for the rest of his life—pragmatism. And he became a socialist in a way which does not permit one to call him a Socialist. In many ways his worldview was representative of that of other radicals of his time.

Socialism was serious business in the United States at the turn of the century, although members of the various leftist parties and those who supported them at the polls were relatively few. In the 1890's the socialists united in the Socialist Labor Party. But the inflexible Marxist posture of its leader, Daniel De Leon, resulted in a revolt of the moderates, 1899-1900.

Disunity was characteristic of the socialist movement. As one historian has written,[1] the party before 1920 was a broad organization of all shades of leftist conviction. It was a coalition of regional groups with different and sometimes conflicting views. Diversity brought strength, and the success the prewar socialists enjoyed resulted because of the catholicity of the party.

While De Leon was organizing, Eugene Victor Debs in 1897 had founded the Social Democracy dedicated to achieving public ownership of railroads, industrial monopolies, and utilities. Then in 1901, Morris Hillquit of New York City and Victor Berger of Milwaukee joined their anti-De Leon faction of the SLP with Debs, thus forming the Socialist Party of America. The party had 41,751 members when it got 420,713 votes in the 1908 presidential election. It had 117,984 members by the 1912 election when the party polled more than 897,000 votes, or six per cent of the popular vote.[2]

The 1912 Socialist vote was an impressive increase over previous efforts, but in a nation which grew from 75.9 million people in 1900 to 91.2 million in 1910, and which gave 13.8 million votes to the three other presidential candidates in 1912, the party's following was slim.

If the nation at large was untouched by socialism, in intellectual circles there were pockets of the faithful, like Walter Lippmann and his fellow Harvard socialists. These men did not convert masses of Americans, but they influenced many. Bourne could not have escaped contact with the socialist element at Columbia where there was a chapter of the Intercollegiate Socialist Society. He was friends with an intelligent, experienced socialist, Harry Chase—with whom he roomed during the 1912-13 academic year—and he had entered school with a predisposition to socialism. He had once been seriously interested in Henry George's single tax theory, and was, as we have seen, talking socialism before the fall of 1909.

To Columbia, the catalyst in his thinking, he was indebted for the "making of my character."[3] Before years there his world had been one of "failure and deficit." He felt that he had accomplished practically nothing.[4] Prior to Columbia, he remarked, he had known the "bewildering, cramping" experience of not having anyone to talk with or understand him. "I don't really know what I should have done," he confessed, "if I had not come to college. Socialism was almost as tabooed a subject as liberal religion in the town where I lived. At college I met for the first time not only one person but many who thought as I did, and formed an interesting social group, in which the members constantly stimulated each other. Most of my education has come thus from talks and arguments here, with brilliant, interested young people."[5]

Although there is a drawing room quality about Bourne's socialism, it was not mere dilettantism. What he and his friends felt they were living under was "this awful capitalist system."[6] Randolph's reasons are not clear. We do not know that his affliction necessarily made him any more sensitive to misery than he would have been otherwise, but certainly his deformity was an influence in his turning to a kind of socialism. The impaired man, he observed, practically forms a world of his own, and "when he has been through the neglect and struggles of a handicapped and ill-favored man himself, he will begin to understand the feelings of all the horde of the unpresentable and the unemployable, the incompetent and the ugly, the queer and crotchety people who make up so large a proportion of human folk."[7]

A voluminous reader, Randolph threw himself more than ever into a study of socialism, although he did not turn away from other fare. It was a fervent experience but it cannot be said with Filler that the result was "an intellectual and heartfelt conversion to socialism."[8] The fascination of socialism to so many of the rising generation, he declared in 1911, "is . . . that scientific aspect of it, its claim of historical basis, and its very definite and concrete organization for the attainment of its ends. A philosophy which gives an illuminating interpretation of the present, and a vision of the future, with a definitely crystallized plan of action with concrete methods, however unsound it may all be, can hardly be said to appeal simply to the combination of 'a weak head, a soft heart, and a desire to shirk'."[9]

Socialism to Bourne perhaps inevitably would have an aspect connected with youth. He liked to think of it as most natural to youth and to youth's marriage with social justice. The passion for social justice indeed was the "most splendid of the ideals of youth." It could keep alive all the other virtues, and it stimulated life, giving it new meaning and tone. It furnished a *leit-motiv* so lacking in many lives, and without which youth perishes. It keeps youth alive even after one has grown older.

A relish for right and wrong must be one of social right and wrong as well as individual, Bourne contended, and in this respect the charge to youth was evident. "The first concrete duty of every youth to whom social idealism is more than a phrase is to see that he is giving back to society as much or more than he receives, and, moreover, that he is a nourisher of the common life and not a drain upon its resources." The reason for this was that "the very food we eat, the clothes we wear, the simplest necessities of life with which we provide ourselves, have their roots somewhere, somehow, in exploitation and injustice. It is a cardinal necessity of the social system under which we live that this should be so, where the bulk of the work of the world is done, not for human use and happiness, but primarily and directly for the profits and masters and owners."

Bourne thought the solution was within reach. After visiting Europe, he wrote that the "stench of proletarian poverty" hovered around park and palace. It was "a very good thing for the world to smell that stench. For if our directing classes and our democracy can only once feel that evilness strongly enough, they will find it intolerable, as they have found it in Germany, that classes should exist below a minimum standard of life. And if we once find it intolerable we shall set to work to make it unnecessary."[10] In other words, he knowingly or unknowingly apparently had accepted Marx's theories of surplus value, exploitation, and class conflict. Doing so was a departure from his inclination to talk of socialism in humanitarian rather than political and economic terms. He was more an Owenite than a Marxist.

In America, he believed, the political system was an outworn traditional shell which no longer expressed society's needs. What had happened was that in the 19th century the center of social gravity shifted from the political field to the industrial. This industrial hierarchy was what had to be attacked. Trust prosecutions were farcical, he argued, because they did not strike the core. Socialism must be approached as a movement, not a definition.

"It is true that the Socialist party in this country, trained in the . . . school of false intellectualism . . . has tended to think in political instead of industrial terms; much of Marxism is doctrinaire and static in its concepts, and yet the three cardinal propositions of Marx,—the economic interpretation of history, the class-struggle, and the exploitation of the workers by capitalistic private ownership of the means of production—if interpreted progressively are the *sine qua non* of Socialism. Indeed, they are Socialism itself rather than any pedantic definition . . . .

"Any one who accepts these three propositions as an interpretation of history, a philosophy of society, and the basis of a collective for reform, is a Socialist.

"The means by which the exploitation is to be ended is to be worked out progressively and experimentally in the light of our advancing sociological knowledge. The old solution of State ownership and control was valid when and where the State was actually stronger than the industrial hierarchy; it is thrown over when and where the industrial is the more powerful, and the substitution is made of a complete *industrial* (not political) democracy."[11]

The tyrannical state which might come from socialism is "a suggested but purely tentative and now abandoned means of realizing Socialism," but "It cannot be too often repeated, that such questions of Socialist *tactics* are purely relative to the country and industrial advance in which the movement is taking place." Tactics may vary, but they are aimed at the same thing. For the uneasiness that something is wrong with society "is no longer the uneasiness aroused by the clash of class and individual, but by the conflict of class and class . . . . The days of innocence are forever gone; the life of the modern world has become conscious of itself; social introspection in earnest has begun." [12]

Despite these intriguing passages it is not clear whether Randolph embraced what he labelled cardinal propositions of Marxism. In 1912 he contributed to the *Monthly* a brilliant article entitled "Socialism and the Catholic Ideal," but that article provides an even less adequate picture of where his heart left off and his mind picked up. It is clear from it, however, that he rejected 19th century individualism, and believed that greater social consciousness and stickier or at least less tolerable problems than ever before demanded collective attention.

It is revealing that Bourne suggested in his *Monthly* piece on "The Next Revolution" such readings as E. A. Ross's *Social Psychology* and *Social Control* and W. J. Ghent's *Mass Psychology*. Bourne's known reading was heavily in sociology, psychology, anthropology, philosophy and history. He emphasized courses in these areas in college. His reading, sentiment, and interest took a sociological rather than a socialist path. Economics was not his strength, or so it appears from his writings which almost never touch economic problems, and then only briefly. He did read Veblen and other economists, but an economist colleague on the *New Republic* recalled that "Randolph was not strong in economics." [13] Randolph, as shall be shown eventually, did not like the kind of attention to scholarship and facts which economics demands.

The fact is that he never was sure what he felt about socialism, although his humanitarian concern, his role as a reformer, and his attachment to socialism cannot be denied. "Courage demands exposure to assault," [14] he had written; but while he was fearless in many ways, his activism did not take him into the arena. Some things suggest his unflagging interest in American socialism. He belonged to the Intercollegiate Socialist Society and paid his dues. The organization in 1914 named him a delegate to the Second International at Vienna. In Europe he spent much of his time at socialist meetings talking with socialists and reading the literature.

But there is missing a deep personal identification with the formal movement. So far as is known, he wrote almost nothing for socialist publications. If a person of his gifts were truly committed, then he probably would have devoted some time to the movement. There is nothing in the Columbia archives to suggest that he ever joined the party. As one knowledgeable source said: "Mr. Thomas does not know if Randolph Bourne ever was a member of the Socialist Party . . . . He was certainly very close to the Party." [15] And in 1912 he supported Roosevelt out of enthusiasm for the reform platform of the Progressive Party.

Bourne himself questioned the solidity of his feelings: "I get in perfect despair over the sincerity of my revolutionary sentiments when I think of my perfectly humdrum conventional life, my irreproachably bourgeois connections, my lack of real knowledge of the workers, their thoughts, ambitions and feelings, my personal enjoyment of comfort and taste, my interest in art, my personal complications of character, and the disgusting spectacle of the enormous contrast between my overweening ambitions and both the figure I cut in the world and the [hazy?] way I am taking to realize my ambitions." [16]

At one time, when more certain of his position, he admired Kropotkin. His Columbia friend, Carl Zigrosser, was a disciple of Kropotkin, and the charming old gentleman's ideas seemed ideally suited to Bourne. While Kropotkin favored abolition of the wage system and eventual production in common and free employment of goods, and although he wanted the destruction of government and believed these things would be obtained by a feeling of solidarity among men, he did not advocate bomb throwing and violence as customary devices.

According to a friend of Randolph who also was much swayed by Kropotkin, in the context of the times advocacy of the Russian's ideas was not so much a plea for an anarchistic solution of social problems as a reaction against Social Darwinism. Advocates of undiluted competition, it seemed to Bourne and others, were the anarchists in action. To them Kropotkin appeared to be an advocate of the naturalness of social control as well as cooperation in the evolutionary process.[17]

In addition to Kropotkin there was another who inspired Bourne: "Nietzsche! I must have convictions for I read him without a tremor, and I read him in company with Tolstoi, the latter not as an antidote, but as supplement, each speaking their half of the gospel of the great ideal of personal humanity, stripped of all the professional, official, misunderstanding barriers that divide people now, and make this world, in spite of its riches and verities, so narrow and limited a place for the individual soul, shut out from communion by the cruel senseless machinery of society, which kills the personal, the imaginative, and the sympathetic in all but the more gifted and sensitive. Nietzsche stands for the splendid liberation from alien codes, the smashing of inequalities and cowardices; Tolstoi for the positive interweaving of understanding and love." [18]

Ten weeks after he wrote those lines in December 1913 he seemed even more sure of himself. His social philosophy, he announced, had arrived at a paradoxical desire for Tolstoyan ends through Nietzschean means—"socialism, dynamic social religion, through the ruthless application of scientific materialism." [19]

The truth is that like John Reed, Randolph thought mostly with his heart rather than his intellect where socialism was concerned. As his socialist friend Harry Chase said later, "I doubt very much that Randolph ever read Marx or Engels. We didn't have to talk socialism per se. We usually talked about conditions of exploitation and oppression."

Bourne had suffered, he was sensitive, and he had a middle class guilt about glaring inequalities in America. He couldn't understand "how anybody with a social conscience who has once had his eyes open to things can ever get adjusted to things, without feeling like an accomplice in great crimes." [20]

". . . I have not lost the first glow of enthusiasm," he declared in 1912, "nor my belief in social progress as the first and permanent interest for every thinking and true-hearted man or woman.

"I am ashamed that my experience has given me so little chance to count in any way either toward the spreading of such a philosophy or toward the direct influence and action. Nor do I yet see clearly how I shall be able to count effectively toward this ideal. Of one thing I am sure, however: that life will have little meaning for me except as I am able to contribute toward some such ideal of social betterment, if not in deed, then in word. For this is the faith that I believe we need to-day, all of us,—a truly religious belief in human progress, a thorough social consciousness, an eager delight in every sign and promise of social improvement, and best of all, a new spirit of courage that will dare." [21]

One wonders where Randolph got the ingredients which produced the apparently balanced and hopeful adjustment reflected in the above quotations. He found in another writer an explanation of his predicament and a justification for his existence. The writer was Alfred Adler (1870-1937), the Austrian-born disciple of Freud; he came upon Adler at a time when Bourne was trying to make sense of so many things, including himself.

One of Randolph's closet friends, Lucile Deming, recalled that Randolph once remarked at dinner, perhaps in 1915: "Adler wrote the story of my life."[22] Another friend recalled: "Veblen, Freud, and Adler we read at the same time, and I remember Randolph coming into my room with a copy of Adler under his arm, and saying with a look both grim and rueful, 'He has described me exactly.' "[23]

For Freud man's main drive is eros. For Adler the will to power and the drive towards superiority and self-assertion comprise the central drive. In 1907 Adler published in German a work which in 1917 was translated as *Study of Organ Inferiority and Its Physical Compensation.* Bourne read German and surely his professors discussed or mentioned Adler.

Adler asserted that when a specific organ inferiority is a bodily defect—such as a hunchback—the person usually suffers scorn, mockery, pity, compassion. This causes not only the normal feeling of inferiority which each person has to some degree, but a pathological inferiority complex. The complex arouses a strong reaction in the form of an urgent drive towards superiority. The reaction may take the form of compensation wherein a Demosthenes conquers his stuttering, or a short Napoleon becomes a great leader, or a Randolph Bourne becomes an accomplished pianist, conversationalist, or writer.

But if talent or energy lacks, Adler believed, compensation is impossible. (While Randolph frequently took walks which lasted for hours, he at times complains bitterly of lack of energy.) "Compromise" or "arrangement" occur—mechanisms intended to overcome an unbearable feeling of inferiority. Compromise may take a negative attitude. The individual withdraws from life and society, and becomes a mere spectator, a critic, a scoffer. He may rejoice in the failures of others, belittle their efforts, or profess a cynical and blasé attitude toward everything. And it may be, Adler said, a positively anti-social attitude, when the person who has been unable to assert himself through positive achievement attracts attention by means of anti-social or criminal conduct.[24]

It has been seen and will be seen again that Randolph fits this description in some respects. What is important is that through Adler he saw himself for the first time in realistic perspective, thereby reducing a confusion and anxiety about himself and his sometimes almost misanthropic actions; and not only justified to himself his existence, but at the same time paradoxically became aware of something to overcome.

Bourne concluded that there was no place for him in politics, although much of the time he convinced himself that he was physically no different from other persons. Deciding that there was no role for him in public life was a long step, and was perhaps the point at which formal advocacy of socialism was no longer realistic. What he would be, he resolved, was "a prophet, if only a minor one." In Adlerian overtones he added that "I can almost see now that my path in life will be on the outside of things, poking holes in the holy, criticizing the established, satirizing the self-respecting and contented. Never being competent to direct and manage any of the affairs of the world myself, I will be forced to sit off by myself in the wilderness, howling like a coyote that everything is being run wrong. I think I have a real genius for making trouble, for getting under people's skin; I have proved it in my various assaults on things [here at Columbia]. Between an Ezekiel and an Ishmael, it is a little hard to draw the line; I mean, one can start out to be the first, and end only by becoming the latter."[25]

The cue, then, is from Bourne. He seldom called himself a "socialist." He did not use any other particular term, but he thought of himself as a radical. "Socialist" was too political. He wanted a radicalism which ran through all American culture, of which politics were but parts.[26]

To his radicalism he brought a religious posture derived from the rejection of his Presbyterianism and Christianity in general. As a youth he had been excited by Thomas Wentworth Higginson's *Sympathy of Religions,* and, as he put it, had slipped away to Unitarian services whenever possible. But Unitarianism was too bland for him; although he usually went to Old First services when he was in Bloomfield—probably to please his pious mother and out of interest for sociological phenomena—he wanted no part of organized cult. Orthodoxy, he asserted in a youthful, illiberal essay, was the bane of modern life and thought.[27]

In this respect he was like many of his generation. Despite the social consciousness of thinkers among the clergy like Walter Rauschenbusch of Rochester Theological Seminary and of Father John A. Ryan of Catholic University, the iconoclastic intellectual radicals of the day generally declared themselves out of harmony and patience with Christianity. Bourne in some ways personified this mood, for his "religion" was man and society oriented. And yet he is refreshingly free of anti-dogma clichés. Man, he acknowledged, naturally yearns to something inexplicable and beyond himself, and in the 20th century it would be a perfection of society—a kind of Beloved Community of Josiah Royce by whom Randolph was swayed.

For him the question never was settled completely. He remarks in his essay "Some Thoughts on Religion" that once one thinks he has the world bedded snugly away in a box of materialism or idealism, something always upsets the assurance of his conviction. The world, he said, was not suffering from an excess of idealism. "It is sick rather with the thorough-going and plausible scientific materialism with which our philosophy and literature seem to reek."[28] A numbness had "stolen over our religion, art, and literature, and the younger generation finds a chill and torpor in those interests of life that should be the highest inspiration."

What was needed, Bourne contended, was a return by science and philosophy to their proper domains. He called it the "crucial intellectual dilemma that faces us today." One cannot be satisfied with the "dreary" conflict between religion and science, the former so often allowing the latter to make it look foolish. The only satisfactory view of religion and science is one in which each contemplates a different aspect of the universe. One considers the quantities and relations of the universe, the other the qualities, ideals and values.

"Truth for truth's sake is an admirable motto for the philosopher, who really searches to find the inner nature of things. But the truth of science is for use's sake. To seek for physical truth which is irrelevant to human needs and purposes is as purely futile an intellectual gymnastic as the logical excesses of the schoolmen. The scientist is here to tell us the practical workings of the forces and elements of the world; the philosopher, mystic, artist, and poet are here to tell us of the purposes and meanings of the world as revealed directly, and to show us the ideal aspect through their own clear fresh vision."

For Bourne religion was not to be service and adoration of God, but a system of faith and worship, a devotion, a fidelity, a consciousness. A new idealism was being created, he wrote, in which religion will have the same place in the spiritual life of man as before. But now, "religion is our sense of the quality of the universe itself, the broadest, profoundest, and most constant of our intutitions.

This, then, was a way for him and contemporaries to commit themselves to causes and ends in a universe which—looked at from one aspect—was senseless.

Because men are alive, Randolph reflected, men reinterpret the world as living. In all religions men interpret the world in terms of personality. This is called the "divine personality," the "cosmic quality," and—particularly in times of personal stress—the "Great Companion." "This is the religion of ordinary people to-day; it has been the heart of Christianity for nineteen hundred years." His point is not—as incidentally he seems to believe—that man creates this divine personality, but that it is essential: it brings beauty and sensitivity into men's lives.

For Bourne the transition from abstraction to reality was a personal and natural one. Socialism, he had decided, "was really applied Christianity, in all the best sense of the latter." [29] "Your spiritual man," he wrote to a friend, "is my social man, vibrating in comaraderie with the beloved society, given new powers, lifted out of himself, transformed through the enriching stimulation of his fellows,—the communion of saints,—into a new being, spiritual because no longer individual." [30]

In this way he found personal identity, for as has been noted, he looked at socialism as a straining up to a great consciousness; and youth was demanding a definite faith. Youth's spiritual center was shifting from the personal to the social. Life, he testified, "will have little meaning for me except as I am able to contribute toward some such ideal of social betterment, if not in deed, then in word." [31]

Bourne, then, was—like such radicals as Max Eastman, Floyd Dell, Louis Untermeyer—not religious but reverent. Being an atheist was not contradictory to his notion of religion. His friend, the writer Herbert J. Seligmann, recalled that when Seligmann declared himself an atheist, Randolph remarked, "There is a man after my own heart!" In the Columbia archives is his "The Prayer of a Materialist," in which he rejects the spiritual.

And one who knew him well and who was present when he snapped at Vachel Lindsay who had been reading his "General William Booth Enters Into Heaven," recalled that, "anything savoring of orthodox religion made his hackles rise. I think he resented the fact that the poet's reading of it had stirred him profoundly, in spite of its theme and its Christian imagery.[32]

Regardless, he deserves to be taken at his word concerning the settlement he made with his conscience:

"Really to believe in human nature while striving to know the thousand forces that warp it from its ideal development,—to call for and expect much from men and women, and not to be disappointed and embittered if they fall short,—to try to do good with people rather than to them,—this is my religion on its human side. And if God exists, I think that He must be in the warm sun, in the kindly actions of people we know and read of, in the beautiful things of art and nature, and in the closeness of friendships. He may also be in heaven, in life, in suffering, but it is only in these simple moments of happiness that I feel Him and know that He is there.[33]

"This then is the goal of my religion,—the bringing of fuller richer life to more people on this earth."[34]

Randolph was greatly influenced by the religious ideas of William James. It was an ironic affiliation, for James' thought was permeated, as Lewis Mumford has written, with the ideas of the Gilded Age, whose essence Bourne rejected. Getting along and cash values certainly were not what James cherished, but given the times, his ideas re-enforced the ways of those who valued his philosophy. For him, however, the thought of James was a path out of stifling tradition.

Bourne's identification with William James was a recent development. Two years before in 1913 he had written, that "when I was studying a philosophy course with a wonderful teacher, the best we have here [Frederick Woodbridge] . . . I was a rank materialist and took great delight in lacerating a rather tender and green young man whose delight was in Emerson and Plato, whom I despised. But my readings of James and Bergson since then and my studies in primitive psychology have led me to give the feelings and aesthetic perceptions a much higher place in the world than I had, with a corresponding reduction of the intellect and reason."[35]

James, like a different kind of pragmatist, Charles Peirce, asserted propositions which were fundamental to the history of pragmatism, and which one finds in Bourne's writing.

What he welcomed besides James' theory of knowledge was the way pragmatism reinstated a theory of faith and at the same time discredited all conventional institutions, authorities, theologies and creeds. James and Dewey rejected the "block universe," and looked at religious experience as something emotional, immediate, mystical, perhaps only understood in terms of psychology or anthropology. This was not to deprecate religious persons. God became not a fact, but a folkway. In humanism God becomes experience of the widest actual conscious span. This gets rid of agnosticism by refusing to entertain the idea of non-emperical or trans-emperical reality.

James excited Bourne. His books were "the most inspiring modern outlook on life and reality."[36] James "settled so many of my own worries that I preach him as a prophet."[37] Pragmatism appealed to him because it was a method and not a theory of reality. James thought of it not as a solution, but as a plan for more work: not results, but orientation. Pragmatism looked away from first things, principles, categories, supposed necessities. What concerned it was last things, fruits, consequences, facts.

He noted that James observed certain phenomena—religious experiences, psychic experiences, occuring through all time—and asked how to explain them. They cannot be dismissed as pure illusion. What must be done is somehow comprehend a world in which the cold mechanical facts accompany an emotional life of desires, ideals, and hopes. These latter are as real as physical truth. "Now this means," he believed, "that the rigid distinction between the Supernatural and natural breaks down, and becomes of less importance. Human experience is now what we have to study, and out of that we have to form our values and ideals. . . . The point is not, Is there another world? but What are we to think of a world where amazing regenerations of the vital and spiritual forces of man take place, and which in spite of all analysis remains so incorrigibly alive and so incorrigibly mystical?" [38]

From Dewey, under whom he studied, Bourne got many notions of the mind and society. While, as shall be seen, it is in the field of education that Dewey most influenced him, Dewey had a concern with politics and daily affairs which James did not. Like James, however, Dewey contended that ideas or universals can be found in experience as plans or habits of decision. Similarly, Dewey did not want religion tied to cosmology or supernaturalism. Instead, it should be just part of human experience, and shared by men in common.

Dewey developed his ethics in terms of the economic and political issues of his time. He seems much less concerned with the individual than was James. Yet his social philosophy is built on an ethic of self-realization, elements of which are evident in Randolph's writing. It is a "new individualism" but also a belief that the latter can come only through collective action. Dewey was perhaps the chief American exponent of democratic socialism, and the world from which he always starts and to which he returns is not *a priori,* but that of everyday experience.

For Dewey—and Bourne—all existence and reality itself are in transition. Nature is a process. To declare a finality is to cut off the work of intelligence. But even if one accepts absolutes, whether God or a law, doing so does not solve the problems facing man, nor does this suggest how to attack problems. Since we live for the future, a practical thing is a reference to the future. Thinking, then, is a natural response to environment—literally something to do. The intention or value of particular ends is gauged by how well they satisfy particular lacks.

Dewey's philosophy commonly is referred to as instrumentalism—the theory that the function of thought should be instrumental in controlling environment and that ideas are valuable according to their function in human experience and progress; it greatly appealed to Bourne. Not only did he esteem Dewey personally, but he placed him with James—and, perhaps for a time, Bergson—in his gallery of patron saints. By his last year of college Bourne was saying that "we are all instrumentalists here at Columbia. Thought is a practical organ of adaptation to environment; knowledge is a tool to economize this adaptation, rather than a picture of reality." [39]

In brief, then, Dewey's desire was that philosophers directly confront the problems and beliefs of society, thus clarifying society's values and the alternatives of social behavior. The flaw in the practical world is that actions often are unintelligent routine, the results of unreflective behavior. There must not be a divorce between action and ideas, believed Dewey.

The connection from Dewey's ideas to Bourne's actions was in what Randolph called the experimental life. In his essay "The Experimental Life" he rejected both action which comes from rigid, unreflective habit, and also from slovenly anarchistic deportment.

Maturity, he suggested, involves seeing that the belief in the power and the desirability to control everything is an illusion. Life is too much for one person to control. Man's gifts are not given him for conquering life, but for being alert, ready, resourceful and keen. Indeed, the great interest in life is its adventurousness. "The world," he remarked, "is too full of people with nothing except a will. The mistake of youth is to believe that the philosophy of experimentation is enervating. They want to attack life frontally, to win by the boldness of their attack, or by the exceeding excellence of their rational plans and purposes. But therein comes a time when they learn perhaps that it is better to take life not with their naked fists, but more scientifically—to stand with mind and soul alert, ceaselessly testing and criticizing, taking and rejecting, poised for opportunity, and sensitive to all influences." [40]

If one does not adopt the experimental life, he is—said Bourne in positing one of his few absolutes—in bondage to convention. Experimental life is not like a laboratory exercise: the laws of personality and life are too complex. Each experiment reveals something really novel and unique. "The old rigid morality, with its emphasis on the prudential virtues, neglected the fundamental fact of our irrationality," he asserted. Man does not do what he wants to, but what is easiest and most natural. Instead of correcting this by experimentation, man has established objective benchmarks to indicate how he should or should not have behaved. This is the rational ideal, the result of which is an inflexibility of character, and a "deadening conservatism."

Conservatism does not adapt to circumstances, nor make allowances for the chances and ironies of life. It has "riveted" moral life to logic, when it should have been yoked to sympathy. "The logic of the heart," Bourne insisted, "is usually better than the logic of the head, and the consistency of sympathy is superior as a rule of life to the consistency of the intellect."

It was the liberating aspect of the experimental life then, which he found in the philosophies of James and Dewey that attracted Bourne. Such a life does not look on nonconformity as irritating and suspicious but as pleasurable, as grist of understanding and developing a philosophy of life. The world has never favored the experimental life. The world despises prophets, poets, fanatics, and lovers. It admires physical courage, but has small use for moral courage. Yet it was those who led the experimental life and who formed their philosophy from it who were "the light and life of the world." Causes have triumphed finally only when rational or "gradual progress" advocates were overwhelmed. Such men do not see deeply into the ways of the world.

In being a humanist, a pragmatist, and a kind of socialist, Randolph Bourne was at the center of insurgent American life. It was, however, the way he as a wordsmith combined humanism, pragmatism and socialism which best reveals the mood of young radicals. He refined an irony with which he confronted both the world and himself and which he also used as a shield. This is important because his irony was much like that of Anatole France whom he admired and who influenced him. France's irony, it has been said,[41] was a spirit alien to an existing society. The vitality of France's irony was a sign of an outworn aristocratic tradition.

The same was true of Bourne whose time was trying to break from an earlier epoch. But irony for him was not, as it may be for some, the last phase of disillusion. His irony was predicated on hope and vision. It was, as Aristotle said in the *Nocomachean Ethics,* a pretense tending to the far side of truth. In fact, it was mostly from the

Greeks that he developed his notion of irony, which he summed up in a brilliant sally, "The Life of Irony." [42]

Socrates electrified him. The method in which meaning is concealed or contradicted by what is said seems to have appealed to something fundamental in his makeup. He had read Plato and in the Socratic manner he loved to assume ignorance in an exchange with someone. It was to the Greeks, Bourne said, "an incomparable method of intercourse, the rub of mind against mind by the simple use of simulated ignorance and the adoption, without committing one's self, of another's point of view. Not until I read . . . Plato did I fully appreciate that this . . . was a life, and a life of beauty, that one might suddenly discover one's self living all unawares."

Irony for him was not a method, but a way of life. It was almost a religion. He found in Socrates an irony with an "inherent nobility." Such irony lacks the spur of religious emotion, and its sweetness may be harder to maintain than the mood of faith: but for that reason irony is superior to religion, if only for the intense aliveness it bestows. At its best, irony is an exquisite sense of proportion, the *mesure* of Greek civilization, spiritual tact in judging the values and significances of experience.

For pragmatist Bourne, irony was "the science of comparative experience," which compares things not with a fixed standard but with each other and with values that result from process, personal experience, and the constant re-thinking of them. A life of irony has the values of the religious life without its defects, he contended, because it expresses aggressive virtues "without the quiescence of resignation." It even has a democratic virtue becaue it knocks down pompousness. Irony was what he called the "truest sympathy," for "It is no cheap way of ridiculing an opponent by putting on his clothes and making fun of him. The ironist has no opponent, but only a friend. And in his irony he is helping that friend to reveal himself."

Randolph prized irony because it was an assault on "outworn ideas . . . skulking in dark retreats. . . ." The tabooes, the things never mentioned, the prejudices and basic assumptions underlying men's lives thrive because they never are transplanted to the lips of others, to the ironist. Irony must not be dishonest, however. The ironist must show another idea in its own light, not distorted. The deadliest way to annihilate the unoriginal and the insincere, he felt, is to let it speak for itself. That is what irony does, thus becoming the "photography of the soul." The ironist's vision throws things as they are against a background of things as they should be. All good satire, he once wrote,[43] is "searingly" true.

Therefore, nothing for the ironist is "too sacred to touch, nothing too holy for him to become witty about," and in rooting out monstrosities one must look for the inflated in the lofty, and the significant in the trivial. But the ironist is no cynic, satirist, or dealer in burlesque and ridicule. Irony, Bourne stated, should not make fun of people but "give their souls an airing." As in Anatole France, any malice is urbane, gentle and indulgent. Unlike the satirist, the ironist is not brutal or overbearing. Any wounding comes from the fineness and delicacy of the attack, and is incidental. The ironist must be that way because he himself is under criticism, and has a personal interest in each case.

If the ironist is destructive, it is his own world he destroys; if he is critical, he criticizes his own world. This is his defense against the charge that he has a purely aesthetic attitude toward life. His aestheticism is only skin deep. The ironist is ironical not because he does not care, but because he cares too much. He feels "the profoundest depth of the world's great beating, laboring heart, and his playful attitude towards the grim and sordid is a necessary relief from the tension of too much caring. It is his salvation from unutterable despair. The terrible urgency of the reality of poverty and misery and exploitation would be too strong upon him. Only irony can give him a sense of proportion, and make his life fruitful and resolute."[44]

It is thus the function of the ironist, Bourne affirmed, to puncture windbags and stimulate thought and action. He must bully and challenge people to a self-respect, and get them to air the dusty rooms and oil the creaking doors of their minds. He is "the great purger and cleanser of life." Irony is essential to any real honesty: in fact, "the ironist is the only perfectly honest man."

Bourne's irony is reminiscent of Dr. Johnson's irony. Johnson could be as personal as he pleased because he could be as impersonal as he pleased. Randolph introduced his own experience; like Dr. Johnson, he blended his imperfections into his writing without affronting classical decorum. His broad impersonal view of himself and of the world prevented one's attention from shifting from the subject to the person involved with it.[45]

Irony is the key to understanding Bourne. He just does not always mean what he literally says, not even in the essay on irony, for one of his tools is exaggeration—usually done skillfully and tastefully. One cannot satisfactorily study his writings and his letters without understanding how important irony was to him. As he himself revealed, "I put so high a value on irony and such a low one on conventionality. . . ."[46]

Often he expressly makes one's having a sense of irony or using irony the criterion for deciding what he thinks about a person or thing. Unless carefully read, he sometimes may seem to be exaggerating and nothing more. The truth, however, is that intellectuals, loving the play of the mind, sometimes indulge in grotesque situations, feeling that if the recipient does not catch on, too bad for him! Sometimes in Randolph such grotesqueries take the form of a mirthful irony, other times of a vicious denunciation which balances uncertainly on the line of dishonesty about which he warned.

Bourne's letters demonstrate how carefully he must be read and how easy it is to mistake him. He often wrote to intimates, pouring out the troubles plaguing him. When he bared his soul most nakedly, he did so in irony: he portrayed himself as a silly goose for feeling and worrying as he did. In such cases, his words said, "I don't really mean what I say," but the impact was the contrary. Moreover, one must observe that what he felt was the truth, expressed ironically, was sometimes *not* the truth. Late in his life, as shall be seen, in a brown study of irony he announced an impending destitution, but in fact he was solvent. His friends were aware of the aura of irony about him. As one acquaintance recalled, "It is strange to think that Bourne, who was the ardent poet of youth in America, was rather mordant and tough in his expression—at least in conversation. It is easy to lay this to his deformity: I believe, however, that it was far deeper and was an expression of a profound irony. That was the salt that made Bourne stand far above his affliction. . . ."[47]

"The Life of Irony" and essays of like calibre attracted a following to Bourne. Shortly after the piece was published in *Atlantic* for March 1913, it appeared the same month in a collection of his essays, *Youth and Life*. Correspondence preserved at Columbia indicates his wide appeal. For example, sad, beautiful letters came in response to his article on the handicapped. His attraction, as was remarked, was a synthesis of needs he answered for certain of his contemporaries.

He had become a symbol of rebellion, and his readers perhaps vicariously participated in the strife he had known. The mystery of words also was involved. His style, although not often elegant, was clear, streamlined, close packed with ideas one on the other. He stripped away wordiness, redundancy, and baroqueness, although he was never satisfied.

Randolph would have someone read his work to him, first entirely, then every sentence, and sometimes by word. "He wrote and rewrote," a friend recalled. "I am sure I have seen him work over a sentence twenty times before he was satisfied, or, at least, willing to let it alone. . . . I have known [few] persons who write with such pain and anxiety."[48]

Prose is not enough, however. What distinguished his style then as now was the inevitability of much of what he said, a mark of grand writing. He was like Caesar who conquered Gaul more with his words than his legions. He had a convincing way of generalizing to all people his personal beliefs, in this case an effective ironic device. He relied seldom on marshalled data but instead on a subjective expression of his experience and opinions. There were finer contemporary stylists, yet he nevertheless was a superb writer.

He has been accused of being naive. Some always will find him so, although such judgment may in part be based on taking him too literally. In 1913 and for much of the rest of his career, what his admirers found so refreshing and inspiring about him was that while he was not naïve in mind, he was unashamedly, unapologetically naïve in heart.

If Randolph was pleased with his career and accomplishments, he also was worried about his future. A scholarship had allowed him to pass the 1912-13 academic year earning a master's degree.[49] But he brooded about what he would do, and job overtures to the New York *Post* and to the then conservative *Nation* magazine were apparently unfruitful.

Ellery Sedgwick, his *Atlantic* editor, had encouraged him to consider a career in some editorial capacity, but warned that such positions were few and seldom open. He approached publishing houses, but nothing turned up. Sedgwick queried President Lowell of Harvard as well as a professor there about the scholarly life. They told Sedgwick that this was perhaps Randolph's brightest possibility: trouble would arise from his deformity if he let it stand in his way, but most likely not from student reaction.[50] Letters of introduction to editors which Professor Odell gave Bourne apparently led to dead-ends also.

He was increasingly depressed, largely perhaps because Columbia seemed uninterested in hiring him. He had no idea, he wrote a friend, where he would be the next year.

"It will be difficult for me to obtain a teaching position and the literary jobs seem thoroughly occupied. The *Atlantic* is a dubious support and life on the whole presents almost the same forbidding front that it did when I broke the ranks and came to college. To be sure,

I have now more philosophy and a tenuous literary reputation, which my college superiors amuse me very much by cudgeling their brains in an effort to capitalize for our mutual benefit.

"They are very slow, however, about offering me any job here, and perfer to speak optimistically of a 'far-off divine event.' If worst comes to worst perhaps they will give me a scholarship again. But I am becoming a bit restless after four years of leisurely study, and would like to do something direct and useful in the world, occupy some steady position where I could get back some habits of persistent work.

"Academic study is a little too much of an invitation to dawdle, and every now and then it strikes me as an ineffective waste of time in a world where there are so many things to be done and done at once." [51]

He was as much worried about losing contact with friends as he was about not getting a job. "I have been living here in such a kindly sheltering circle of friends," he wrote, "that it chills me, especially in the nighttime, to think of exposing myself to a foreign world and putting my friendship-forming capacities to so cruel a new test. The experimental life calls, it is true, especially when the sun is bright and warm, and I comfort myself with the feeling that my friends will be here when I come back, and they cannot change very much in a year." [52].

The reference to returning concerned Columbia's having made up Bourne's mind for him by awarding him the Richard W. Gilder Fellowship, which provided for the study of political and social conditions in the United States or abroad. He sailed in July 1913 on the *Rochambeau.* He had by then acquired a world view, but there were worlds he had not yet seen.

"There's the threatened war, which has already damaged the Socialist Congress that I anticipated attending at Vienna, and which seems about to set the world crazy. It made me very blue to see the crowds of youths parading the streets long after midnight the other night, cheering for Austria and the war and singing *"Die Wacht am Rhein"* [The Watch on the Rhein]. It will give these statesmen who will play their military pawns against each other such a splendid excuse for their folly, for they can say that they were pushed into it by the enthusiastic demands of the people."—Letter from Bourne to a friend (Dresden, 7-30-14).

IV

EUROPEAN EXPERIENCES

As Randolph gazed over the bow of the *Rochambeau* and watched flying fish disappear headlong beneath the surface and fat bellied porpoises, with great fins, shoot from wave to wave, he was exceedingly happy. The passage was one of those interludes of serene contentment which he rarely enjoyed. He moved easily and effervescently about the ship, pacing the promenade deck as though it was "a great street where your friends were at home."[1]

After initial awkwardness on the *Rochambeau,* Bourne became immersed in the ship's cosmopolitan and predominantly European social life. He delighted in the types abroad, particularly "old women from the middle west who are trying to act up to what they think an ocean trip should be like, and making it obvious that it is not their realm of imaginativeness."[2]

Randolph was perhaps as much an attraction to the voyagers as they were to him. Professor Single, the president of Davidson College —a scholar with a "raw, aggressive, Southern accent" and "usual lack of subjectivity"—bid for his time as did the Rev. Lawrence Skinner, an earnest, much-travelled Universalist minister. They were rivaled by Dr. Joan Sohan, a stocky Hungarian Jewess engaged in psychiatry in New York, and, as he liked her immediately, she tried to monopolize him.

From group to group moved a huge irrepressible multilingual French priest with an ugly weather beaten face. There also was Catherine Hackett, the young sister of Francis Hackett, who had become nationally known as literary editor of the Chicago *Evening Post* and who later would join the *New Republic* when Bourne did. Randolph and Catherine, a delightful Irish girl who was uncertain about life, spent hours talking.

If Mary Eaton had been the only other person aboard, Bourne would have been content. She was a lovely St. Louis widow with two children. To her Randolph confided his craving for deep companionship. Together they gave a benefit concert for seamen, and the next night put up with an atrocious song recital arranged by a genial Chicagoan. Her letters to Randolph later from Paris and Ireland hinted softly of some dark tragedy in her life, and harked back to the passage. He and Swain, she wrote, were in her prayers each morning at Mass. "I will always remember your beautiful music." [3]

For Randolph the crossing was a succession of lyrical vignettes. He was immensely happy aboard ship and during the first weeks ashore. In these moods he produced some of his best work. Part I of his "Impressions," for example, is outstanding. It caught the eager wistfulness of a full heart. Passing from his account of the Chicagoan's silly song recital, he wrote:

"The next morning, how different the scene! It was Sunday, and on that same piano, and with the same persons, though this time they were kneeling on the floor, was being celebrated the holy sacrament of the mass. The great, thick voice of the French priest, interspersed with curious snuffles, rolled through the salon; before him gleamed the candles and the golden vessels, and at the piano a graceful French girl sang a soft prayer to the Virgin for safety at sea, while all around knelt the adoring people.

"Through the windows could be seen the passing steamers and low dark coasts of England, for we were in the Channel, and inside, the gorgeous vestments of the priest shone with the flickering rays of sunlight that shone down from overhead." [4]

It was not to the *Rochambeau* that Bourne clung as he neared Le Havre and an uncertain year. It was to happiness. "I was quite sad when it was all over," he wrote home, "and we were thrown again on our own resources." [5] But he nevertheless plunged into the adventure, believing as he did that "he must have a callous soul, indeed, whose first hour in a foreign country is not one of the most romantic experiences." [6]

Bourne and Joseph Ward Swain, a college friend, rushed pellmell across Europe. Belgium was especially captivating; there Randolph found dazzling towns contrasting with primitive medieval peasant life. Bruges, a lovely town little changed from its 15th century form, charmed him. Holland seemed "hideous," but Switzerland he adored for its "democracy and a good standard of life and divine beauty of scenery and artistic charm of houses and villages and towns." And in Verona Randolph needed a sense of humor. "There was," he related, "a delicious fat old rogue at the baggage room who was systematically swindling everybody he could, picking what seemed like a personal quarrel with every one who presented his baggage to be weighed, and attending to no one else until he had said all he wished to say. He charged me double price for keeping my bag for the day, although the tariff was plainly printed on the ticket, and was so full of outraged virtue when I pointed it out to him that I found myself objecting no more."

In Paris, where Swain remained for a year at the Sorbonne, the companions parted. Randolph went for a visit at the Welsh country estate of Stanley M. Bligh. Bourne had been so impressed by Bligh's books—*The Ability to Converse, Social Therapeutics,* and *The Desire for Qualities*—that he began a correspondence which produced an invitation. The setting appeared perfect to him.

Bligh's house at Builth Wells was filled with visitors, down for a a session of riding, hunting, fishing, and talking. Randolph was awed. He had walked into a sophisticated London crowd—novelists, critics, journalists, conservative lawyers, nobles, and businessmen. They were "not the big people, but very English," and their charm, brilliance, and sophistication sparkled. "Sexual passion and moral indignation are alike absent . . . . The talk is very free, spades are called spades and then there is a sort of triumph in coming out with a real shocker." [7] And shock—he wrote in long, dazed letters to friends— was just what he did and the result was "one of the most piquant and dislocating experiences of my life." [8] It is a strange event, both revealing and unclear, even when Bourne's irony, exaggeration, and sensitivity are considered.

To Randolph, Bligh was a pushy Philistine, large, with a brown beard, funny little spectacles and shabby clothes. Bligh listened incredulously to his ideas, passionately defended capitalism, and portrayed his guest as a wide-eyed visionary, with fuzzy, baseless notions. As Bourne told Carl Zigrosser, "I got talking on Socialism and antimilitarism, etc., and they began to treat me as if I was a harmless lunatic. Even Bligh could hardly conceal his disgust and amazement . . . ." [9] But, he confided to Alyse, he "was delighted to find that my real faith didn't waver an instant before the deluge; it only served to bring out more clearly,—indeed more than ever before,—the contrast between my Socialism and the old ideals, and make me want to crush the latter all the more completely."[10]

The result was that after four days Bourne had to leave. He was told (although he had been invited for a fortnight) that his room was needed for the aged parents of Bligh's wife. At first he was chagrined and chilled; he "could not see how I had not behaved with dignity and all the good manners I possess .... Mr. B. gave me a lot of good advice about becoming strong and decided and definite and rich like him, and my general childishness did show up in striking contrast to him."[11] This sort of treatment, he told Alyse Gregory, "one might give, you know, to a Zulu chieftain who obviously had no feelings and whose utterly alien standards of conduct would make such rough and ready utilitarian treatment quite consort with the honorable traditions of an English country house."[12]

It is curious that in other letters Randolph was not so pained and emphasized different aspects of the experience. That he may have been indulging in an intellectual grotesquerie—a frosting to cover up his going too far out on a limb and not holding his own—is suggested by a remark which puts most of the blame on himself: "Then I came to Wales, on my long-expected visit to my literary and psychological affinity, which proved to be a flat failure owing to my childishness and inability to negotiate what I take to be one of the smartest and most sophisticated sets in London. I have always been appalled at the vastness of the world, and what I was not understanding about it or getting from it, and have never known how to limit myself to what I could handle. And now I feel what a mess I am making and shall make of my opportunity."[13]

It also is noteworthy that Bligh and Randolph corresponded after their separation. Bligh wrote warm, complimentary letters, suggesting things to do in London and recommending friends to meet. Bligh's comments about socialism are those of an open-minded dissenter. In fact, he admits he might be wrong: "I am an ardent individualist probably soaked in prejudices due to my life history and personal surroundings."[14] Moreover, the tone Bligh used in letters discussing socialism and religion is that of one who respects and esteems his reader.

What one sees, then, is an impulsive Bourne who not for the first time enters a situation with fine intentions, only to jam hard upon a reef. His disaster was best summed up by a niece of Bligh who saw through both the uncle's defects and the eagerness of a visitor she liked very much. "You seem to be over sensitive," she wrote to Bourne, "and to expect rather too much of our reserved unsociable English nature. We are as a nation suspicious of our fellow men; and you will, I'm afraid, never get on well with us if you expect us to overcome our distrust of strangers in the course of *one* luncheon party. Give us time, and you will find us worth knowing . . . ."[15]

The aftermath of the Welsh nightmare was that, although he did give the British time—or, rather, the English, for he spent almost all his time in London or nearby—and found many worth knowing, he ended by disliking and damning England. His letters reek with contempt for English society and intellectual life. British political democracy was a fable, institutions were old and weary, and despite London's greatness Britons lacked continental charm. The government, he asserted, flippantly condescended to the needs of the oppressed. It was encrusted with a visionless, frequently retread, and smugly ruling class which ran the country for selfish purposes.

England in 1913 was in the last stage of an intellectual mediocrity which originated in the Victorian era. Bourne did not arrive at an auspicious time. What he found in the press and popular books, he said, was an exuberant irrelevance and a vivacity of interest about matters alien to what he considered the personal and social issues of life. One never knew whether an Englishman "cared" or how much. Intellect seemed permanently detached from emotion. Nowhere was so much literature a mere hobby of gentlemen whose cares were elsewhere. Intellectual life, he declared, was "hobbyized." Ideas were taken as sports, and sports considered serious issues.[16]

After an initial downcast period following the Bligh affair, and after being lonely for New York friends, Randolph recovered. He combined the making of acquaintances with a busy probing of London, which he soon loved. He met scholars, dined with Jewish barristers, and ingratiated himself with professional people. When he did not haunt the British Museum, or university and public lecture halls, the various art collections and architectural jewels, he read widely—the press and books. And occasionally he entertained at his quarters at 8 Gordon Street. The lodging was in a boarding house run by a pleasant Swiss woman whose cooking, Randolph rejoiced, was superb. It was a four-story Queen Anne structure from which double windows looked out on a small backyard garden.

Political rallies particularly attracted Bourne, and on one occasion he was rewarded by a hysterical demonstration at Royal Albert Hall in protest against the imprisonment of the Irish labor leader, James

Larkin. Another time a large meeting addressed by Winston Churchill erupted in fist fights which were ended when bouncers tossed out the hecklers.

The Fabian Socialists intrigued him because they made socialism respectable and were not violent. He was not very impressed, however, when he went to the residence of the Fabian leaders, Beatrice and Sidney Webb. Webb "talked as he lectures, with the patient air of a man expounding arithmetic to backward children. . . ."[17] But Bourne was enthusiastic about the non-Fabian middle class socialists. He found them hard-headed men grounded in history and economics; they were not patronizing to their working class audiences and they spoke and wrote on a high plane.

Randolph also attended big, restless suffrage meetings at Knightsbridge addressed by Christabel Pankhurst while enthusiasts cried "shame!" as the evils against womanhood were enumerated. As much to his liking were gatherings in the East End packed by swarms of cheerful, begrimed, stodgy workers.

Similar meetings were taking place throughout Britain in that fall of 1913. England was uneasy, for Ireland was nearly out of hand, and strikes were widespread. Bourne agreed with those who suspected that civil war was highly possible. The rub, he wrote, was in exploitation, and "our fond theory of the triumph of orderly trade unionism slowly levering up the working class to a position of comfort and influence is daily knocked into a cocked hat. The same rising of the unskilled to demand a share, and the opposition of the aristocracy of the skilled, that we see at home, is taking place here; and the country looks at starving Dublin quite unmoved, while a ruthless band of employers, assisted by English federations, announce their intention of crushing out unionism in Ireland. We might be 1813 instead of 1913."[18]

Despite preoccupation with social issues, interest in literature did not wane. Although John Galsworthy was away and Shaw could not be bothered, Bourne read their books. Shaw's works he imbibed as if he personally had discovered him. "I heard Shaw the other night and the next night Chesterton and the contrast was most instructive and impressive. Shaw, clean, straight, keen, fine all the way through,—Chesterton with the repulsive looks of a glutton, shifty, insincere, as disgusting a figure of a man as Shaw was distinguished."[19]

It was an evening like that with H. G. Wells which sent him home skipping on air. Wells' lodgings were crowded with Indians, some in London on political business, a few studying at Oxford. There also were William Archer, a translator of Ibsen; H. W. Nevinson, a correspondent and rebel who had exposed modern African slave trading, had seen most of the world, and who had earned the antipathy of the Czarist government; and Sir Sydney Oliver who recently had jeopardized his government post by denouncing armaments.

"I spent my time," he reported, "in a group of Wells and the Indians and we went over art, religion, the caste system, East and West, for all of which the Indians supplied the facts while Wells played around them with his most luminous and beautiful mind. It was a great adventure: there were no discoverable humiliations and though I heard later that Wells had a reputation for fierceness, nothing could have been more genial than his manner toward everybody that night."[20]

Randolph finally succeeded in meeting Havelock Ellis, but the event was not satisfactory because, "These Englishmen don't know how to flow genially, and you have to conduct a cross examination as if you were a newspaper reporter. I asked him some questions, which he answered as if he was afraid his anwers would offend me, and he would therefore have to be very guarded, and then I found myself expressing my own views on the subject, and then we stopped."[21]

Such lightness and drollery as in the description of the Ellis meeting may have been what enabled Randolph to draw in people. He liked persons like Mrs. Edward James whose husband was a Boston James and a "sort of utopist international republican . . . expected back soon from the orient." Although Mrs. James struck Bourne as a rather silly, frustrated woman, he liked her and enjoyed discussions with her and visiting public works projects and model housing.

Another time he walked along the bank of the Thames with Walter Lippmann, whom he had met the previous spring. They dined at the Cheshire Cheese, once a favorite of Dr. Johnson. Over pigeon pie, beer, and Cheshire cheese they talked, perhaps of the *New Republic* which was being planned. Afterward they walked to Chelsea, saw Carlyle's house and Whistler's studio, and idled over tea at a quaint place along the river.

The security Randolph had come to feel in London, however, could not keep him from moving on. He liked Britons, but he did not admire their society. But, he confided, "This spleen of mine does not mean I do not like individual Englishmen; I have met many charming people, luminous and splendid; but it all goes to the support of my sociological theories of the enormous power of institutions, and how little the quality of the *individual* character counts in them. This is why I am a Socialist and want brand-new institutions, and why I think the Webbs are a bit behind the times, and not using their enormous knowledge in the best direction."[22]

Bourne's social consciousness was sharpened in England. He was convinced that a rise in the standard of living was the great fulcrum for improvement in taste. Before there would be social betterment, people must "really *hate*" ugliness and poverty and disease, instead of merely pitying the poor and sick. "I am immensely interested in civic art, town-planning and kindred movements over here, and shall use all my opportunities to study them. Architecture, commercial art, landscape gardening, etc. I am almost ready to believe is the king of the arts because of its completely social nature . . . ."[23]

Randolph probably was sincere when he wrote home that he was sorry that Montcalm lost the battle of Quebec and that British culture before and since Quebec had formed American culture. Britain was a wonderful nation, he said mischievously, "and all the more wonderful for the nauseating hypocrisy about itself which it has got imbedded in literature and in the minds of most of the moulders of public opinion on both sides of the Atlantic."[24]

But as he crossed the Channel, raw in its December gloominess, he felt a critical, indirect gratitude toward England. London had done one thing for him: "immensely strengthened my radicalism. The old institutions, though they may have a glamor from afar, are so cruel and unlovely on closer acquaintance that I am no longer assailed with the doubts that did strike me occasionally at home whether I was assailing the best possible established order of things. But I am heartened by finding girls and youths . . . who are going through the same crises that some of us are in America, though how the social compulsion ever reached them in their sheltered circles and lives I don't know."[25]

The return to Paris had a cruel overture. Swain went with him to a pension arranged by mail. The landlady gasped and refused him. Swain argued her into letting him stay the night and Randolph was consigned to the annex. Next day, Swain's own landlady said she had a hunchback lodger and that another would be bad business. A two-day hunt at Latin Quarter boarding houses produced the same results. Swain finally got him a place on the rue St. Jacques—a dirty hole of a hotel, "full of vermin which caused him to scratch himself most of the time he was in Paris."[26]

Randolph probably knew what the landladies were saying, although his spoken French was sadly inadequate; he was used to being stared at and experiencing the reflex repulsion of persons meeting him for the first time. His Goyaesque blemish accompanied him everywhere. At times such as when he traveled entranced through southern France—cluttered with Maxfield Parrish valleys and castles and bright colored houses rioting toward the horizon—it was as if he never knew he was deformed. "I never heard a single morbid remark," a friend recalled, "though I walked with him in Italian hill villages where women crossed themselves as we passed and a train of staring children sometimes thronged behind, so that I found myself hating children for their unmeaning cruelty . . ." [27]

But Paris pushed the deformity to the back of Randolph's mind for much of the six months there. He became an almost unrestrained Francophile. This fervor was nourished with the customary round of encounters with scholars, students, lectures and meetings, professional and common folk, exciting books, and the arts. Bourne read and then met Jules Romains and became interested in the *Unamist* literary movement which Romains and Georges Duhamel, the Albert Camus of the period, seemed to lead. The movement was a Whitmanesque concern with and devotion for the new man, the man who was part of and caught in mass society. It suited him well, as he reported to Carl Zigrosser:

"My observations over here lead me to the belief that, if, as I see it, the path of progress is *away* from Christian civilization, and all it implies, *towards* a Socialistic civilization, and all it implies—then France and Italy are the most advanced countries today, with less complications and impediments to the forward march . . . America lags woefully behind, hardly yet conscious of the situation, as they are so clearly conscious here.

"And with our deep-seated distrust of social equality, our incapacity for political life, our genius for race prejudice, our inarticulateness and short sightedness, it seems highly probable that we shall evolve *away* from democracy instead of towards it." [28]

He rejoiced over what he found to be a nation where the distinction between the intellectual and non-intellectual appeared to have broken down. Class differences, it seemed, were blurred compared to England; the French remained pure, simple and "usable without the triteness and vulgarity which dogs the English, and which constitutes the most subtle evidence of our inherent Anglo-Saxon snobbery." [29]

There also was that mysterious composure of the French and the impression they gave of ample reserves of emotion, intelligence, and humor held in careful check and handed out most carefully. The Columbia experience—during which the influence was strongly pro-

French as against German—had predisposed Bourne to French intellectual life, and perhaps it was a logical outcome that he could write: "The French mind is very congenial to me, but I do not quite 'get' the personality. As others have told us, there is always something withheld, a reserve which is combined, however, with a frankness of speech and interest of manner. It is very curious this touch of inscrutability; it is the immortal Latin touch of the Jaconde in contact with the Anglo-Saxon." [30]

Admiration for the French intellect had broadened to include political life. It was not that French government was necessarily more efficient: it had uproarous sessions in the Chamber of Deputies and periodically tumbling cabinets. But there was a healthy dialogue which constantly excited national politics. If there was among the many political parties an intellectual violence which occasionally spilled into the streets, there was also a tacit political tolerance. Nobody tore down the royalist posters which went up beside the Socialist and Republican placards. Adversaries were thought of as opponents, not enemies. He was all too aware of backwardness and brutish inequities in France, but where in Britain he saw a mighty Tory selfishness, in France he felt the supports of injustice were well on the way to being undermined.

Randolph probably spent much of his time convincing his widening circle of acquaintances of these things. Mrs. James had come to Paris for the winter, and together they inspected model tenements. To be a character was sometimes the best way to have him warm to you. He had an instinctive interest in oddities, and "Mme. Martin," an American divorcee with a scarlet past, was one. With both her ignorance and frankness, she fascinated Bourne. Mme. Martin was several years older and rather mothered Randolph. To some students of the Latin Quarter, they were Quasimodo and Esmerelda from Victor Hugo's *Notre Dame de Paris*.[31]

And then there was Madeleine—or Yvonne.

She was a 19-year old convent educated girl who "belonged to that France which Jean-Christophe found in his friend Oliver, a world of flashing ideas and enthusiasms, a golden youth of ideals." [32] The girl answered a request Randolph left at the Sorbonne for someone with whom to exchange conversation. What he found was a tender, critical, strong-willed rebel who had kicked over church as well as social mores—a person truly master of her conscience and soul.

Yet she seemed so conventionally French in other ways, principally her femininity. They strolled and talked in the Luxembourg, along the quays, stopping occasionally to rest in the Parc Monceau or the Trocadero. The friendship "became a sort of intellectual orgy," [33] and soon he became deeply infatuated with her or fell desperately in love. He talked to Swain about her, but never granted his request to meet her. To Swain she was "Madeleine," and Swain believed Randolph loved her.[34]

On the other hand, she may have been Yvonne, two of whose letters are in the Columbia archives. They are not love letters, but they are moving in their tenderness, concern, and esteem. And in them she calls Randolph "Mon cher ami" and sends him the warmest thoughts of a "disciple and friend." Whoever she was, she was perhaps his first romance—however tiny and one-sided—and she became the "Mon Amie" protrayed thusly in the March 1915 *Atlantic*:

"She adored her country and all its mystic values and aspirations. When she heard I was going to Germany, she actually winced with pain. She could scarely believe it. I fell back at once to the position of a vulgar traveler, visiting even the land of the barbarians. They were her country's enemies, and some day they would attack. France waited the onslaught fatalistically. She did not want to be a man, but she wished that they would let women be soldiers. If the war came, however, she would enlist at once as a Red Cross nurse. She thrilled at the thought that perhaps there she could serve to the uttermost.

"And the war has come, hot upon her enthusiasms. She must have been long since in the field, either at the army stations, or moving about among the hospitals of Paris, her heart full of pride and pity for the France which she loved and felt so well, and of whose deathless spirit she was, for me, at least, so glowing a symbol."

It was a year before Randolph could write Dorothy Teall: "You are right about Mon Amie: she is eclipsed, abolished." [35] Yet it was a Madeleine or a Yvonne he wanted more than anything else in the world.

Bourne was a constantly thwarted man, the more so because he had so much to give. While he valued his European experience, it showed him how very little security he had and how precarious life was. A friend recalled that he was in a "constant turmoil of emotional upheavals and frustrations—devotion, disillusionment, anger, misunderstanding." [36] Consequently he at times withdrew into a troubled silence, complaining that it often seemed no one understood what anyone else was trying to say.

Bourne had long seen himself a jumble of desire, optimism, and melancholy. At Columbia he spent many of his days brooding, chiding himself about his egoism, comparing his writing to himself, and not liking the way the latter came off. Was he, he asked, the "puny, timid, lazy, hypochondrical wretch" who wrote the words in *Youth and Life?* "I have been unhappy," he confided to Prudence Winterrowd, "for so many hours of my life over my weakness of will, and inhibitions, and melancholy even over my melancholy itself, that sometimes the privilege of chanting a lay of the ideal and presenting that it is you seems a just revenger for all the low-lying days." [87]

Platonic friendships with men and women would seem for a time a beautiful ideal. Then suddenly—where women were concerned—up would spring "eternal, insatiable desire, the realization of which, inhibited in me, sets the old problem recurring poignantly . . . ." It was particularly unbearable that there should be no solution, for he was "a man cruelly blasted by powers that brought him into the world in a way which makes him both impossible to be desired and yet—cruel irony that wise Montaigne knew about—doubly endowed with desire."

"Give him an extreme fastidiousness of idealism, and you have a soul that should satisfy the most ironical of the Gods. Encase that soul, which is myself, in Puritan morality and you produce a refined species of spiritual torture, which is relieved only by demands and appeals, fortunately strong, of philosophy and music and heaven-sent irony which soften and heal the wounds.

"But to complete the job, make him poor and deny him the thorough satisfaction of the higher appeals, deny him steady work and thus make easy the sway of desire, and you force all his self-impelled action, all his thinking and constructive work to be done in hampering struggle with this unrealized desire, which yet—another irony—colors all his appreciations, motivates his love of personality, and fills his life with a sort of smouldering beauty. This is a complete, if perhaps too dark picture. But like many things in life it and the other side are true." [88]

No bones were made about wanting to marry. When another's intimacy touched him, Bourne was cut to the quick by longing. His Columbia poet friend, Simon Barr, wrote a long and lyrical letter while Randolph was abroad. Barr described the girl with whom he had fallen in love, and she with him, and how this love changed him and became his life. In his reply Bourne confessed:

"You make me feel suddenly very old and bitterly handicapped and foolish to have any dreams left of the perfect comrade who is, I suppose, the deepest craving of my soul. It is her I write to, meet casually in strange faces on the street, touch in novels, feel beside me in serene landscapes and city vistas, grasp in my dreams. She wears a thousand different masks, and eludes me ever.

"In half a dozen warm friends the mask is very thin, but it is always a mask. To touch it chills my blood, and I am touching it constantly when my eager exasperated curiosity about all her goings and comings, my jealous desire to envisage all her life, meets nothing but cool, friendly response." [39]

Loneliness tortured him even more than this apartness from romance. He could not stand to be alone, and when he must, the bottom threatened to fall out of his world. In a way it almost seems that life revolved around the making, keeping, and cultivating of friends. Consequently, he worried about losing them. "Friends in quantity seem less attractive than they used to be," he noted. "I seem always to be pursuing them, and this grows monotonous." [40]

Randolph gently complained how no sooner was he in a movement or group than he was "thrown off by the roadside." He would give up clamoring to be in things and doing things, he said, and assume the role of a "lonely spectator." He would, he remarked at one point, enjoy the present, and not look to the future. "I must always expect to be poor and unloved and obscure. I shall probably have enough to be thankful for if I am warm and fed, and may creep into the Public Library now and then to read with other . . . poor, unloved and obscure."

It was being abandoned that Randolph particularly feared. "Please don't leave me in the lurch, and make me feel like a precarious incident," he told a friend. "Too many of my friends make me feel that way, and I have horrible moments of littleness and panic, when it seems as if all my friendship with them was merely a constant asserting of myself upon their good-humored tolerance. My pressure relieved, they would not follow. I need them, but they would light-heartedly never feel the need of me. All these personal urgencies, so largely disguised in college, and forgotten abroad, come back to me now with almost too much force, with demoralizing frequency. Yet, as a hermit, I should die."

Such personal problems felt like encumbrances, blocks to accomplishing anything. Bourne did not know how to liberate himself, he lamented, for "strength and money would do it, I always think, and I let the lack of them inhibit me. It is so terrifying to plunge out alone. It would be all right except for the evenings. *Mon Dieu,* the evenings! No wonder the human race invented alcohol as an antidote to evenings. My sense of control suffers a steady diminuendo from break-fast time. This is the real horror of living alone."

One trouble was that he was always looking for the "one perfect person or that one perfect group," and then became disillusioned when he thought he had found them. "The big people that you meet are all so busy that they can never permit themselves those long hours of talk which are necessary if you are really to know them." This always was a dilemma for Randolph for almost all his friends and acquaintances—in and out of the arts and intellectual life—worked regularly. Randolph always was a free-lance, following his own schedule, always trying to fill days and hours with something. It was for him a disagreeable irregularity.

Beyond the irony, exaggeration, and intermittent melancholy, there is a basic truth to his view of his problems, and his work suffered. While it shall be remarked again in connection with his career with the *New Republic,* it can be noted here that Bourne went through moods of loss of confidence in anything he might try. Often he complained how hard it was for him to write; how he doubted he ever could write well; how surprised he was when a magazine accepted an article; how he worried that he would run out of ideas or already had; how he was unsuccessful in trying to write journalistically; and how he feared there was no audience for him.

Youth and Life seemed hypocritical to Randolph because it purported to represent him, but only represented his ideals: he was not on the firing line, for example, of social and political movements. "If I only had some confidence in my ability to persuade by writing," he said, "but I lack that; after I have written a thing, suddenly all the other points of view come trooping before me and jeer at my puny, exaggerated one sided ideas until I turn almost sick within me. So that some of my theories which should be bold are really written with the most shame-faced timorousness, and sent off to the editor with a forced and desperate bravado. Now this is no attitude for a would-be man-of-letters, a would-be man with a message who wants to be a preacher, and even a prophet."[41]

Being a preacher or a prophet involved a problem never completely resolved: the pain and discomfort a writer inflicts upon himself by producing for public consumption. As he told Prudence Winterrowd:

". . . In writing I am much more courageous if I think I *am* going to have a public . . . I cannot bear to think of the individual personal disapproval, while on the other hand I rather thrive under public abuse . . . I fear my own self-criticism most of all. My own contempt for the work which I feel unable or too lazy to improve, is the bitterest pill I have to swallow in writing. I don't know quite what to call it except my over-critical sense, my 'perfectionist' standpoint, turned inwards upon myself.

"This last essay, 'The Life of Irony,' I hurried off to the publisher without reading over and slunk around for a day or two, feeling what a fool and incapable I was and sure it would get summarily rejected, and with such scorn that I should never get another hearing. . . .

"The fact is, each of my essays has expressed an aspect of me, horribly idealized I must admit . . . But all together . . . they sound like many different personalities, or like many insincere aspects of one personality. I would have great difficulty in convincing anybody that they were all thoroughly and almost uncannily autobiographical . . .

"I don't mind abuse, but I don't want to be laughed at, and some of the naive confessions of my heart, I'm afraid, will sound awfully silly to the academic people here. I am afraid both of that, and that some of it sounds like the preaching of a prig." [42]

In Europe Bourne spent a part of his time wondering whether he would get a chance to do any proclaiming at all. He wanted to teach at Columbia, but nothing was offered him. Moreover, he declared himself so out of touch with the style of the "supposedly radical" magazines like the new *Harper's Weekly, Outlook,* and *American Magazine.* He feared his articles would not suit them. Yet, he said, "I wish there was to be some forum, when I get back to America, from which I could preach disagreeable truths to my countrymen." [43]

The time to act was now if he were ever to become a professional scholar or a university professor. But Randolph disliked scholarship. In a way, he had a bias against the academic life solely because so many of its practitioners seemed to him to be indifferent to social issues and needs. He saw the trouble in many instances as stemming from the gap between the younger and older generations. Classics, for example, were to him "dead classics." Research and scholarship, he asserted, were "esoteric." American universities still produced hard working, patient, but mediocre scholars, or clear sighted skeptical critics instead of intellectual leaders; this, he maintained, was partly because the United States was so inarticulate a nation. Randolph admitted that he was "restless over details" and indignant over the way academia went about its task.

Although one cannot generalize infallibly to other disciplines, it is pertinent how he felt about the study of literature. Warning a young friend, about to enter Barnard, against literature, he announced that "nothing seems to me more deadening than the University study of literature for its own sake, and the 'scholarly' research which consists of pouring over Chaucer or digging up some obscure poems or facts that the world does not need at all. I find most of the teachers of literature curiously narrow and childish in their philosophy of life and outlook on the world, and much more so than any other department, and so I have always kept away from them." [44]

This was a supportable position for one who would spend his career—as Bourne predicted—poking holes in society. But as his friend Harry Dana advised Randolph, scorn of scholarship was anathema to university life. Said Dana:

"If I didn't want to hurt both your feelings and Erskine's at the same time, I should say that you were too 'Erskinian.' I say your 'scorn for scholarship' and not for 'pedantry,' for nothing could have been more 'pedantic' than your attack on the English Department bulletin board. It is almost as hard to think of the English Department offering you a chair as to picture the Roman Catholic Church offering Voltaire a bishopric. . . .

"When I imply that you have bitten the hand that fed you, I mean to raise the question whether you do not owe something to the very institution and the very individuals whom you criticize.

"Yet all these prejudices against your apparent ingratitude would melt, if you could only once show the world that you cared for ideas based on facts, in other words, for scholarship—that you care for something, that is to say, beyond mere impressions." [45]

Randolph did, of course, care for ideas based on facts, but not with the enthusiasm of the dedicated scholar. Looking back, it seems university teaching—if not scholarship—would have been the happiest choice. It would have given him a reasonable, steady income and forced on him the routine he desired. College teaching could have placed him in a metropolitan area with the conviviality he craved. He would have had time to write and to open doors which continued to seem so irrevokably closed to him.

Something always came along at the right time, however. Professor Charles Beard wrote in May that Herbert Croly had agreed to take Bourne as a contributor to the forthcoming *New Republic* and guarantee him $1,000 a year. A warm correspondence began between Croly and Bourne. Croly had been reading some of Randolph's material, and asked for more. The general idea, Croly explained, "is to start a new journal of political, social, economic and literary criticism. It will be something like the *New Statesman,* only we shall not emphasize social reform and evils as much as the Webbs do and we shall try to make it rather livelier and more readable. We shall be radical without being socialistic and our general [liberalism?] will be pragmatic rather than doctrinal. We are seeking to build up a body of public opinion behind a more thoughtful and radical form of progressivism than that which ordinarily passes under that name." [46]

Here possibly was a chance to howl to his countrymen that everything was being run wrong. As Walter Lippmann wrote to Van Wyck Brooks: "We have an opportunity of focussing the young men in America, and if we succeed we ought to do something that America needs very badly. We may be able to define the issues on the robust middle plane." [47]

Randolph left Paris April 29 for Naples where he met his Columbia friend, Arthur Macmahon. They traveled in Italy, Switzerland, and were in Berlin when the war began. Only after a dash to the station, an uncertain train ride, and a boat crossing to Malmo with several hundred refugees, were Randolph and Macmahon safely out of the war zone.[48]

The layover in Scandinavia was a composite of Bourne's constant methodical firsthand study of institutions during his year in Europe. Garden cities, municipal housing, civic centers, and city planning were much discussed then, but were not to be found in guide books. Not only was he systematic and selective about seeing the great galleries, churches, and architecture, but about new innovations.

Typically, when he was in the German walled town of Rothenburg, he went to city hall. There he studied the building ordinances, the yearly building program, and inspected properties. Then he and Arthur Macmahon visited a group of New York University students who were in Europe to study planning, and upset them by the amount they knew about Rothenburg's system.

A similar routine was followed in Scandinavia, and it was in Sweden that one sees him conversant with European politics. After Jean Juarés and the Belgian Emile Vandervelde, Europe's most distinguished socialist possibly was Karl Kjalmar Branting who later became the first Social Democratic prime minister of Sweden and winner of the 1921 Nobel peace prize. The war had just broken out and what Randolph found in the little parlor of Branting's Stockholm residence was a momentarily crushed man whose international hopes were in ruins and who confessed he was first of all a Swede.

In Denmark Bourne spoke with public officials and made first-hand inquiries about the people's high school system. Then after interviews, he spent a memorable evening at one of the high schools in nearby Roskilde. He was immensely taken with both the Danes and their way of life. "I especially recall," Macmahon later said, "his sense of civilization in Copenhagen. You could see it entering and spreading in him as one sees a watered plant lift and brighten." [49]

Even Denmark was disturbed by the war. The Germans—it was widely rumored—had given the Danes an ultimatum to dismantle forts, but life seemed normal in Copenhagen, except for the crowds about the public bulletin boards. During supper at a little inn the news of Danish mobilization reached Bourne. He hurried to leave for Christiana, now Oslo, where he sailed for home.

After a year of denouncing the behavior of and the type of American tourist in Europe, Randolph "never expected to be so glad to come back to America. . . ." [50] Europe suddenly had gone all wrong, particularly in the "utter defaillance" of the European Socialists in supporting their respective nations.

"The wheels of the clock," he brooded, "have so completely stopped in Europe, and this civilization that I have been admiring so much seems so palpably about to be torn to shreds that I do not even want to think about Europe until the war is over and life is running again." He was hurrying home eager, yet distrustful of the future. "I want so much to turn my experience to some useful purpose, but have always the demons of choice and feebleness of spirit to fight. New York always scared and confused me a little."

With him he carried a set of complex impressions. He had acquired a sense of national culture and of its value and importance as a course of spiritual power, even in a world of political and economic internationalism. Moreover, he still carried his notion of youth, particularly that of the role of the young student class in purifying the nation. No student, wrote Van Wyck Brooks, ever returned from Europe with a more fervent sense of the chaos, spiritual stagnation and backwardness of his own people and of the responsibility upon himself and others touched by the modern spirit.[51]

Part of Randolph's awareness of America's needs came from greater sophistication. He had been, he suspected, too snobbishly utopian, and he had missed good things and good people because he labeled them "bourgeois"—which he was himself. The war would be a holiday, Bourne said, in which to "try to understand more sympathetically what other kinds of people are doing".[52]

Ostensibly, but meaningfully, it was to his friends that he was returning. He had told his mother: "That is what I want—not change while I am gone, nothing that will make me alien on returning." [53] And to an intimate he confided: "I hope I have not been away so long as to lose touch with my friends, for I think of them as the real home to which I am returning." [54]

In the America to which Randolph was returning, movements and ideas were stirring. The iconoclasts and radicals were encouraged because there were indications big business was nearing the end of its once lightly challenged power. For many the concept of service was more meaningful than any success which business could bring. Young men and women, helping the luckless in asylums and factories, thought they glimpsed an American culture of unprecedented richness. Many previously satisfied members of the middle class preached the dogma of responsibility and social justice. The efforts of these and like groups would fail to a large extent, but meantime they insisted on a nation-wide house cleaning. Randolph came home to join this effort to force open the ears of America, update the nation's mind, and send new blood careening through its arteries. His influence would be strongest in culture, in education, and then in his shrill dissent from United States participation in the World War.

A temporary red beard covered Randolph's face, and he wore an ankle-length black cape he obtained in Europe and would wear for the rest of his life. Bourne was 28, anxious, and comparing himself to his beloved Whitman, who did little of consequence before he was 33. He appraised the situation thusly: "It is this wanting to do beyond one's power to do or opportunity to do, or courage to try to do, that makes all the trouble . . . . Perhaps there is some spirit that makes every person with the gift of articulation say more than he is, speak clearly and authoritatively what he but dimly strives to reach, describe the heights seen by him in moments of penetration, though from a point far down the mountain side.[55]

Other Americans felt this wanting to do beyond the power to do. It was a time—the Irish painter John Butler Yeats, father of the poet, once said in another context—when fiddles where tuning up all over America.

"The difficulty in getting people to think is in convincing them that there is anything worth thinking about."—Bourne, *New Republic,* 9-14-15.

V

GADFLY OF THE NEW EDUCATION

The fiddles tuning up all over America in late summer of 1914 as Randolph Bourne approached a new career had been painfully strung during previous decades. Perhaps Americans always had been dissatisfied with their past. Possibly they habitually railed against precedent, so much so that—as Lord Bryce said ironically—there is a new generation in the United States every four years.

If Bourne's time was distinctive in rejecting the genteel tradition, it also was the product of the stirrings and achievements of earlier malcontents. There had been a frenetic restlessness in the reform era of Samuel J. Tilden, the unlucky presidential candidate in 1876. This mood was followed by the protests of the Populist movement, and then by the golden age of journalistic muckraking, a time of considerable social reform. In September 1914, Woodrow Wilson sat sturdily in the White House, and the nation—as befit a dynamic society—was as usual at the crossroads.

Recent social legislation had confronted the problem of harmful medicines and adulterated food. Reform in state and municipal government had accompanied laws against deceitful business practices. Legislation had attacked the plight of labor but worker unrest was felt from Paterson to West Virginia to Colorado. Theodore Roosevelt with his New Nationalism had been arguing for a larger and beneficent role for federal government in the workings of society, while Woodrow Wilson with his New Freedom had been advocating the efficacy of smallness in business. Income tax, tariff revision, currency reform, and greater regulation of business would be accomplished, but many still were dissatisfied with the state of the nation.

Progressives and radicals thought all of American society needed looking at, and that much of it should be changed. Two persons who shared the reform mood were Willard and Dorothy Straight. In the course of his career, Willard Straight had been the intermediary in

China for American financial interests, a State Department official, and an important Wall Street figure. He had married Dorothy Whitney, an heiress to Standard Oil millions. The Straights, who returned to the United States in 1912, wanted to establish a newspaper of the moderate left. Williard was 33 in 1914 and had ahead of him new worlds to conquer.

The Straights read Herbert Croly's *The Promise of American Life* (1909), and after meeting him they dropped the idea of founding a newspaper. Instead, they enthusiastically agreed to back Croly's hope for a magazine like what the *New Republic* became. It was an undertaking which Dorothy Straight continued after her Army officer husband died in Paris in December 1918 of influenza.

Willard and Dorothy were among those in 1914 who believed a marvelous renewal of the nation was at hand, and that therefore the country was at a crossroads. The feeling was that while a good deal already was accomplished there was so much room for hope; with intelligent behavior, there was no reason why America had to become involved in Europe's war. The corporations were not yet so strong that they could not be brought under surveillance; because the nation was wealthy a different distribution of abundance could heal social and economic cankers. Furthermore, as the United States never had had an age in culture comparable to the Golden Century in Spain, the epoch of Racine and Corneille in France, or of Shakespeare in England —but as Americans clearly had genius for other things—there were indications that America would stumble out of the brambles and create its own Elizabethan age.

To these ends, the Straights established the *New Republic,* "A journal of opinion which seeks to meet the challenge of a new time," as the cover of the first issue of November 7, 1914, proclaimed.

Its editor-in-chief was the brilliant, efficient, practical Herbert Croly, author of *The Promise of American Life* (1909) from which Roosevelt is said to have patterned his New Nationalism,[1] and of *Progressive Democracy* (1914). He was the kind of editor who made people want to work for him and win his approval. Under him were editors with almost as much power, including Walter Lippmann whose *A Preface to Politics* (1913) had attracted wide notice and whose *Drift and Mastery* (1914) increased his reputation.

There also were Walter Weyl whose *The New Democracy* (1912) established him as provocative commentator on America; Philip Littell whose "Books and Things" column exuded enthusiasm and learning; and the literary editor, Francis Hackett, who sometimes wrote circles around the rest of the staff. He already had become nationally known as literary editor of the Chicago *Evening Post.* Following in train, often leading Croly and his colleagues, were distinguished contributors. Their efforts were processed in a cramped office on West 21st Street—in historic Old Chelsea north of Greenwich Village, next door to a girl's detention home, and opposite the General Theological Seminary.

Bourne was a *New Republic* contributor from the beginning to his death, or 120 published pieces later. His becoming a collaborator thrust him as close as he could get to the world of action, doings and involvement. His youth had been prolonged by Columbia and then by an Indian summer in Europe. But he now was on his own. Randolph knew he was in danger of becoming one of the youths whom Benedetto Croce once described—youths whose lives are comprised of sitting in beer gardens, making fun of men and teachers, but without showing themselves capable of creativity, in sterile revolt against the established order. Of the *New Republic* Randolph told a friend, "It seems like just the opportunity that I have wanted to get myself expressed, and I am only hoping to be able to be really big enough for the opportunity."[2]

The *New Republic* was equally enthusiastic about him. Croly wanted him connected with the journal as closely as possible. But if Bourne hoped or expected to be an oracle on national affairs, he soon understood that Lippmann, Croly, Weyl, and the contributors had the area to themselves. He told Croly he wanted to handle the fine arts. But Croly felt that because of the "present chaos of artistic standards and practices," the only authoritative writing on the subject would have to be done on a basis of social standards. And the review already had made arrangements with a friend of Walter Lippmann, Lee Simonson, to cover the fine arts.[3]

However, there was room in other areas, Croly said, particularly "your own special topic of Town Planning," and two topics Bourne suggested, religion and education. Prophetically the first issue of the *New Republic* carried Bourne's "In a Schoolroom." Croly had advised: "I believe . . . that a certain amount of conscious patriotism is necessary. . . . We have got to be thoroughly critical, but there must be also a positive impulse behind our criticism. That means, translated into practical terms, that we have got to discover and try to develop the beginnings of sound work whenever they appear in this country."[4]

For many, "sound work" included progressive education. The movement was as much a part of a changing America as the railroad, anti-trust laws, and urbanization. The new education was but one aspect of the response to industrialism, and in its way represented the increase of public responsibility and the crumbling of laissez-faire. As more and more educators pondered the social implications of school training, the individualism expressed in works like Rousseau's *Emile* seemed out of place in the new era. Some thinkers like the sociologist Lester Ward declared flatly that inequality of distribution of information and knowledge resulted in exploitation of one class by another.

Clearly, many felt, education had prepared the American to guard his personal interests and selfish ends, but not to live in a cooperative society. The theme now was that environment could change man at least as much as man could alter environment. A true individualism nourished itself with the wealth of all, it was argued. Democracy is the best way to live, but it must be consciously cared for and passed from generation to generation. If in an aristocracy only the upper class is important, in a democracy all people are precious; and a good society was one in which interests and cultural goods are shared.

Progressive education was "part of a vast humanitarian effort to apply the promise of American life." [5] It was what the name suggests, the educational side of the progressive movement. Schools were to be used to better the lives of Americans. Health, vocation, and family and community life now were part of the school's concern. Principles derived from research were increasingly being tested in the classroom. Education was changing to meet the different classes of children flooding schools, and primary education was fast becoming universal. If everyone was attending school, methods and curriculum would have to change, progressives believed. The movement implied that learning and culture could be democratized without being debased.

But progressive education was so varied as to be indefinable. It was a movement of moderates aware, as the educator W. T. Harris said, that an ignorant people can be governed, but only wise people can govern themselves. Its practioners were caught up with the problem of how to both free a child and yet shape him, for education—as Cardinal Newman said—is by definition an arduous process.

It was indeed an ancient problem which Bourne and enthusiasts of progressive education faced—that of the tabula rasa. In the riddle of the tabula rasa, one has a blank slate on which there must be writing before one can himself write. Yet the slate must be his very own to write on and what he writes must be his own. It is the riddle of the individual in society, and in a political democracy the problem had to be solved for great masses of men.

Progressive education protested against a narrow view of the school.[6] It inveighed against harsh discipline, and the tendency sometimes to confuse punishment with discipline. It criticized the time-honored custom of classroom drill and memorization. The school room, the progressive educationist generally felt, should be a laboratory in the practice of democracy, a project—carried to completion in its natural setting—in which children would learn to live together and learn to do by doing. In a way it was a dissent from emphasis on reason, the classical or humanist subject matter, and bookish intellectualism.

Randolph probably shared the views of new education long before the *New Republic* made him an evaluator of American education. At Columbia he had criticized aspects of lecture hall presentation and of his childhood schooling. Of the younger generation, Bourne asserted, "Our enthusiasm for what seems to be in store for the next generation, and for what is already the fortune of the children in many advanced schools, scarcely overcomes the poignancy of what we have missed ourselves. Probably our country has seen no generation so miserably educated as we have been."[7] Behind his sentiments were the theories of John Dewey. He was Dewey's rapt admirer. At Columbia he had taken at least one course, "Psychological Ethics," with Dewey and had read many of his works.

More than any other thinker, Dewey (and his disciples and advocates) influenced American public education in the 20th century. In dozens of writings he argued—in harmony with other progressives—that industrial society had profoundly changed American life, and therefore its educational needs. The household and rural community had once provided sufficient education for life, but that was no longer so.

In pre-industrial America daily work engaged the imagination and provided knowledge of natural processes and materials. Children shared the work which went into subduing a new country and were thereby disciplined. Under such conditions bookish education was fitting because almost all children learned outside the school the other things they needed to know.

But conditions had changed, and what children now got in school was antique, of no useful relation to mass and increasingly specialized industrial civilization. The worker did automatically what he was assigned instead of using a personal knowledge of materials, tools, and methods. Previously the duties in the home had disciplined the child morally and practically. Now, however, thousands of children were involved with irksome industrial tasks or they were idle. Both situations were debilitating.[8]

As the formulator of instrumentalism, Dewey argued that the very character of American society was a constant beginning anew and therefore there was a comparative absence of tradition and *a priori* principles. The advantage of instrumentalism was that it supplied practical wants as they arose. The way to prepare a child to meet practical wants was to make school as close to society as possible, an embryonic, organic community life. Strongly denouncing traditional education, he saw the school as the source for improving society at large: now the school comes to the front and the child is made the center of it.

The approach was derived from the idea that American democratic society had a basic constant: change. The implications reached far beyond political democracy. Democracy to Dewey also was a way of living, a communal experience. Such a society must arrange for its members to be "educated to personal initiative and adaptability. Otherwise, they will be overwhelmed by the changes in which they are caught and whose significance or connections they do not perceive."[9]

To Dewey education was the ordering of phenomena so as to add to the meaning of experience, thereby increasing one's ability to control future experience. He defined education as growth: in addition to making members of society—workers, citizens, parents—it should encourage people to continuously reach for their potential, that is, live to the fullest. This process involved both maturation and learning. At the same time, learning was dependent on maturation.[10] Ideally, society would not merely reproduce its habits, but form better ones.

It was because of the desire for fullness that he denounced the traditional division between labor and leisure, man and nature, thought and action, individuality and association.[11] To split culture and vocation was not only false, but unnecessary, even if the historic reasons for the divorce were evident. In a democracy there must be a reworking of culture, he believed. Vocational subjects were to be introduced into the schools not just to build utilitarian skills, but as ways to enrich life in industrial society.

Vocational education, of course, was older than John Dewey. But now he tied it to culture, and his view of culture went far beyond the arts. For him any discipline was cultural to the extent its possibilities were followed: "There is perhaps no better definition of culture than that it is the capacity for constantly expanding the range and accuracy of one's perception of meanings." [12]

For Bourne the meaningful implication in Dewey's thought was that the most valuable knowledge was that which was social. In a changing democracy, a narrowly utilitarian education for one class and a broadly liberal education for another were anathema.[13] In Bloomfield, his hometown, the massive new high school dwarfed the handsome brownstone Presbyterian church built a century before on the other side of the street. The physical relationship symbolized what he believed to be the nation-wide eclipse of the church as a community source of enlightenment and authority: "We are becoming used to the impressive schoolhouses that tower over the unkempt and fragile houses of our American towns. The school already overshadows the church. If this means that the school is the most important place in the community, then it is a hopeful sign." [14]

It is thus not surprising that the themes of needless waste in American schooling and of what the future held pervade most of Bourne's writing on education. He expressed the sentiments—if not through facts and specifics, then in general terms—of progressive educationists and their supporters. The older generation, he felt, had always hidden the unpleasant things of life and had preserved a conspiracy of silence about them.[15] Education had been no exception. It had encouraged a rigid and therefore useless morality unrelated to real life. The older generation was as responsible for the need and growth of progressive education as were population increase and industrialization. For, as Randolph said in another context, "educated men still defend the hoariest abuses, still stand sponsor for utterly antiquated laws and ideals. This is why the youth of this generation has to be so suspicious of those who seem to speak authoritatively. He knows not whom he can trust, for few there are who speak from their own inner conviction." [16]

As one who cherished the Socratic method, he maintained it was just this speaking from conviction which was crushed by traditional education. His first school article for the *New Republic* was based on a visit to his hometown high school. Only the year before, a shiny, expensive building was completed in Bloomfield. Inside, however, he found an unreality of curriculum and a cranky rivalry between teacher and student which he supposed unfolded daily in thousands of American schools. Although the business at hand presumably was ideas, an artificial silence was imposed on students.

Only when class adjourned did the pupils show interest in anything.

Socrates would have been amused by this training school for incipient legislators, he commented. The only thing the Bloomfield classroom resembled, he said with Mencken-like dismay, was a state legislature. It is a platitude, Bourne observed, that those who succeed in life are those who express themselves and whose minds are flexible and responsive to others. Thinking cannot be done without talking. But the classroom shuts off such intercourse.

Randolph admitted he might be overly intellectual about the matter, and acknowledged the problems of cost, equipment, time, and space. Still, the difficulty was that—unlike cotton looms—massed children compose a social group, and personality can be developed only by free stimulation of minds. "Is it not very curious", he asked, "that we spend so much time on the practice and methods of teaching, and never criticize the very framework itself? Call this thing that goes on in the modern schoolroom schooling, if you like. Only don't call it education." [17]

He believed he knew why the school was out of harmony with 20th century America. To him pedagogy was just learning that you can put a child in school but he will not profit unless he is fed well, his physical defects cared for, and particularly unless he grows naturally. The child's energy must be harnessed to interesting and fruitful activity. Indeed, the case against the conventional school was blacker than the worst muckraker could conceive. The next generation, he predicted, "will rank the pseudo-pedagogy which had directed the physical conditions of school life with the black magic of the Middle Ages." [18]

American education had become a morass because the nation's educators traditionally had seen the world divided into two radically different groups, adults and children. While adults went about their work, off in a separate sphere, children idled, waiting to take their places in the world. Book knowledge, because it was a badge of success and seemed the key to achievement—it was the sign of the enviable leisure class—had become the stock of the school. "We came," he said, "to think of ourselves as cupboards in which were laboriously stored bundles of knowledge. We knew dimly the shape of the articles within. But we never expected to see the contents until we were grown, when we would joyfully open our packages and use them to the infinite glory of our worldly success and happiness. But it was a slow child who did not begin to suspect, long before his shelves were full, that most of his adult friends had lost no time, when their schooldays were over, locking their cupboards and leaving their bundles to the dust and worms." [19]

If parents and teachers now recognized this they generally still insisted that discipline is the ability to do painful things. Adults still distrusted a world in which children do joyfully what interests them. This doing the interesting was the trend of the new education, Randolph contended. It was the transformation from the unconscious school to the self-conscious school. That change was the very kernel of the excitement of the new education.

What had happened in American education, it appeared, was that a democratic education had been achieved in the sense that common schooling was practically within the reach of all. But in another sense education was not democratic because it did not give equal opportunity to each child of finding in school the life and training he peculiarly needed, that is, of finding himself. Such education still had to be worked for, and this meant transforming the American school from an institution into a life-like situation.[20]

Education had presumed, he said, that children were empty vessels to be loaded with knowledge. They are neither that nor machines for the teacher to wind and set running. They are "pushing wills and desires and curiosities." As growing things, they need places to grow. Children live full lives more than older people do; and they cannot become minds and only minds for four or five hours a day without stultification. It was clear, Bourne continued, "that education has grown up in this country in a separate institutional compartment, jealously apart from the rest of the community life. It has developed its own techniques, its own professional spirit. Its outlines are cold and logical. It is far the best ordered of our institutions. Its morale is the nearest thing we have to compulsory military service. There is something remote and antiseptic about even our best schools. They contrast strangely with the color and confusion of the rest of our American life. The bare class-rooms, the stiff seats, the austere absence of beauty, suggest a hospital where painful if necessary intellectual operations are going on." [21]

Compartmentalizing of American education had resulted in "puzzle education," Bourne maintained. This constituted a rote memorization of facts, seldom related to the main current of life. This was nothing more than a "riddle-curriculum," and one's genuine education, that is, his familiarity with the world, came after getting out of school. He declared that such a system was demonstrably futile, and with relish he cited a then widely discussed study made in Springfield, Ill., by the

Russel Sage Foundation. Presumably-educated participants from many walks of life failed miserably on a simulated school test which involved the need to know many facts. If they ever memorized such trivia in school, Randolph said, they quickly forgot it.[22]

Foolishness in education or elsewhere always was fair game, but he had an un-Menckenesque approach to his carping, and he believed his criticism just.[23] He admitted that education resented outside criticism, and that there were few able administrators who did not believe they were doing the best with the resources they had. Naturally pedagogues felt that criticism should come only from the profession and were resentful and hurt when arraigned in the light of the product turned out by the schools.

Yet, an almost pathetic confidence in "expert" overhauling had not been justified, he argued. Alleged experts really did not have the magical power attributed to them, and as much as educators complained that their problems are financial, a student of the subject could not be convinced—in a wealthy nation like the United States where the prestige of education was extraordinarily high—that money was the crux of the matter. The problem was one of more intelligent use of resources, less ostentatious concern with buildings and frills, and higher teacher salaries.[24]

The difficulty, in short, was to Bourne not predominantly mechanical, but psychological; and the public in sensing that it was psychological, was demanding more and more that as much attention as had been given to orgnization and system be given to the conscious and spiritual side of learning and teaching. The result of preoccupation with organization and system, he said, was an unnecessary emphasis on routine which created the "wasted years." This was the period of intellectual leakage. The child first learned the basics of the three R's, but instead of using them to move into other disciplines and awaken intellectual curiosity, he rehearsed from primary school to high school. Paradoxically the more excellent became the primary methods, the poorer became the schools' product at the end of the system.[25]

The question facing Americans who wanted to create effective school systems before population overran buildings and swamped trained personnel was, to him, evident. The nation was pushing against old barriers which had thwarted it in leading the full life it was capable of. The issue was, What kind of school do we want? To decide that would determine the kind of society Americans wanted. About the future of American education, he was both guarded and hopeful. All the revolutionary strivings of the past, he said, were away from institutional authorities toward greater freedom.

"But in spite of all the freedom we have won," Randolph commented, "society was probably never more deeply unhappy than it is to-day. For freedom is not happiness; it is merely the first negative step towards happiness. Happiness is control, and society, now intensely self-conscious of its imperfections, is still very helpless towards controlling its destiny . . . It is in showing the unity of all the democratic strivings, the social movement, the new educational ideals, the freer ethics, the popular revolt in politics, of all the aspects of the modern restless, forward-looking personal and social life, and the applicability of all of them of scientific method, with its hypotheses and bold experimentation, that Professor Dewey has been the first thinker to put the moral and social goal a notch ahead." [26]

Bourne might have continued theorizing abstractly about education, had the *New Republic* not sent him in March 1915 to inspect the Gary, Indiana, school system, then famous for its innovations. The Gary Plan convinced him that the embryonic community life type of school had been effected. Followers of Dewey, he wrote, saw in the Gary system, as the master himself did, the "most complete and admirable application yet attempted, a synthesis of the best aspects of the progressive 'schools of tomorrow'." [27]

The father of the Gary plan was William Wirt, a Deweyite who already had attracted attention for similiar pioneering innovations as superintendent in his native town of Bluffton, Indiana, before Gary hired him in 1907. Wirt had tried 50 different programs for what he called "work-study-and-play" schools, but Gary was a special challenge. The town was recently established and a school system had to be formed from scratch.

In 1906 the United Steel Corporation began building a giant lakefront complex 27 miles southeast of Chicago. At first there were 300 villagers. In 1909 the population was an estimated 12,000 and it reached 35,000 by 1915. Thirty different nationalities were said to be represented in Gary. In 1908 the foreign population was an estimated 56 per cent, although it dropped to 40 per cent by 1912. There had been only 350 students in one standard type school building in the early months of Wirt's tenure, but in March 1915 Bourne found 5,000 students assigned to five buildings. What impressed him was that there were only 2,500 seats for those 5,000 youths.

Wirt was convinced of the efficacy of developing in school the full child, but he denied it could be done by sitting him at a desk all day. So he developed a four-fold unity of interests, or, as progressive educators would have said, he *recognized* them. They were (A) intellectual study, (B) play and exercise, (C) shop and laboratory specialities, and (D) expressive activity in the auditorium or in outside community activities.

Strictly speaking there was no such thing in Wirt's mind as "outside" community activity. For besides wanting to win the public's confidence, Wirt wished to open the school and make it an intimate part of community activity. His ambitious plans for shops, play areas, and auditoriums would be expensive, it was charged. Not any more and perhaps less than a traditional school, Wirt replied. How? By rotating classes, so that groups of students always were doing something different. While some were in class studying traditional subjects or in shop or laboratory, the rest either were in special activities such as gym, playground, or gardening. According to Wirt a 12-class school would require eight rooms and 12 teachers. A 72-class school needed 43 rooms and 64 teachers. The Gary plan became known by such names as the platoon system, rotary, shift, duplicate school, and work-study-play. Bourne was just one of hundreds of American and foreign observers who visited Gary.

To enthusiasts the Wirt plan was no mere tinkering, nor a fad, nor an experiment. It was a new kind of education and it worked. More important, it could be adapted to any situation, although it was specifically designed to meet the challenge of increasingly crowded urban areas and high costs. For while Wirt had built two large schools, Emerson and Froebel, which included grades 1-12, he also had applied the system to small schools in Gary.

However, it was believed more economical and more enriching for the students if all grades were under one roof. Bourne agreed, and began calling the Wirt plan the school of tomorrow.[28] In articles for the *New Republic, Scribner's,* and in a book, *The Gary Schools* (1916), he explained how Wirt used every crook and cranny, thereby using what previously had been considered waste space.

Also described was how the school related study to real life. The print shop produced the office supplies. The commercial course worked on the school's financial records. Home economics prepared the meals and served them at cost, and the chemistry class—taught by the municipal chemist—analyzed local food, candy, and water supplies. The session was lengthened an hour to 4 p.m., but teachers and students had no homework. Classes were designated slow, normal and rapid, aimed at graduating students in 10, 12, and 14 years. Voluntary Saturday classes were packed, 6,000 adults attended night school, and a long summer school, intended to keep children off streets and creatively busy, had proved its worth. In fact, Gary authorities believed they could not afford to have their schools idle. Randolph also depicted how teachers of manual courses were craftsmen who incidentally were good teachers. Part of their salary was for keeping the buildings and grounds in shape, tasks at which their students assisted.

The Gary system could have been the most stupendous laboratory in creation, yet if it lacked social pertinence he would not have looked twice. But in a nation where perhaps only one-fifth of school children reached high school, here was a chance to change the situation. The special activities were not mere trimmings on the three R's, but neither was the latter neglected in favor of the former, Bourne explained.

"The ideal of the Wirt plan is that the child should have every day, in some form or other, contact with all the different activities which influence a well-rounded human being, instead of meeting them perfunctorily once or twice a week, as in the ordinary school. This does not mean, of course, that every child is expected to develop into a versatile genius, equally able in science and music and shopwork and history.

"Most children are sternly limited in their capacities, and . . . unable to assimilate more than a small part of what the school offers them. But the Wirt school definitely offers the opportunity. If there are capacities, they have the chance to develop, while no child need lack that speaking acquaintance with the varied interests of work and study which now the old traditional type of school so tragically denies." [29]

When antagonists charged that the system was an intricate method of making things easy and encouraging unruliness Bourne became angry. On this major point he cited Dewey. It was wrong to consider that an interesting school with little formal discipline like Gary unjustifiably simplified things. The point, he contended, is that interesting things are not necessarily easy. They may be hard, but when there is interest, the difficulty is overcome or at least lessened and prepared for a later effort. It is in the overcoming that the moral value lies. Moreover, there is an implicit geometic progression: interest means more and more acquired skill and therefore a more intense effort. Bourne called it "willed skill." A side effect was that interested busy children seldom were troublesome.[30]

In the February 10, 1917, *New Republic,* writer Edith Hamilton —then head mistress of Baltimore's Bryn Mawr School—in an article entitled "Interesting Schools," criticized Randolph, the new education, and progressives' ideas as to what was good discipline. Let the old-fashioned educator ask himself, he replied in the same issue, "whether the child gained the statisfactions of accomplishment *because* he went through the discipline, or whether he was willing to go through the drudgery *because* his temperament liked the satisfaction of accomplishment. If you admit the latter, then you have admitted the case of the new education. Temperaments, impulses, interest—or, if you like, in the feeble, the *lack* of impulses and interests—will insist on dominating, on determining the way each child takes his experience. All education can do is to provide experience, stimulate, guide, organize interests. Anything else may produce, at its best, a trained animal. It will never produce men and women."

As much moral value lay in what he called the democracy of the Gary plan. The school not only had become intimately part of the lives of Garyites, but had destroyed traditional barriers separating book learning from vocational training and manual work. Nothing seemed more delightful about the Gary schools than the absence of cant.

"Most of the current educational problems, the books and ideas on pedagogy, educational psychology, administration, teaching-methods, class-room management, discipline, etc., which fill the attention of the current education world, are here as if they were not. It is a school built up outside the influence of the professors of education, the teachers' colleges, and the normal schools of the land.

"It is true that there is probably not a single idea operative that is original with Mr. Wirt. Probably there is not a single idea that is not being applied in some school in the country. The novelty is the synthesis, and the democratic spirit that motivates it." [31]

Randolph also viewed the Gary school as a combination preventative and rescue operation where the child's development was concerned. Previously and still in 1915, the vocational school touched the child too late in life, sometimes not until high school, he complained. By then the child's interest very likely was dulled. When the student was then put to work, he often found pure drudgery. The Gary plan, however, tried to lead the student early to what suited him. Neither books nor tools was paramount. More important, machines were not ends, but means.

The public school in the United States generally turned out low-grade specialists, despite a fancy liberalized curriculum, Bourne maintained. Industrial training had made no effort to produce the type of mind most needed—the versatile machinist, the practical engineer, the mind that adapts and masters a mechanism. Such resourcefulness, inventiveness, and pragmatic judgment of a machine by its product—the sense of machinery as a means, not an end—are precisely what society demands of every profession and trade in the 20th century. "The Gary school," he remarked, "is the first I have seen that promises to cultivate this kind of intelligence. It frankly accepts the machine not in the usual sense of the vocational schools, as an exacting master that the child is to learn docilely to obey, but as the basis of our modern life, by whose means we must make whatever progress we may will. The machine seems to be a thing to which society is irrevocably pledged. It is time the school recognized it. In Gary it is with the child from his earliest years. It is the motive of his scientific study." [32]

When Bourne visited Gary in March 1915, William Wirt had been retained by New York City to study its school problems and experiment with the Gary plan. Many schools there were decrepit and construction had fallen disastrously behind the demands created by immigration, natural growth, and urbanization. Of 800,000 school children, 150,000 received only part-time schooling. In one borough, the Bronx, only 25,000 of 35,000 children could be accommodated.

After Wirt first tackled Public School 89 in Brooklyn, and then other schools, it appeared that the board of education would commit itself to the Gary plan. Then the problem became a political issue. Conservatives, in and out of education, doubting educators, opportunistic politicians, and advocates of the Gary plan joined the melee. The opponents of the Gary plan viciously attacked reform Mayor John Purroy Mitchel who supported Wirt.

To Bourne the New York City situation was fraught with forebodings. Six of his articles from June 1915 to June 1916—aside from those he wrote specifically about the Gary schools—dealt entirely with vocational education and the Wirt plan. Calmly, he castigated those who for selfish reasons would set New York education back even farther than it was. He discussed the political, economic, and social background of the city's public school conditions, and begged the city to commit itself to Wirt.[33] Bourne wrote that "Popular tradition tries to make us glow with the belief that this world is a ladder up which virtue and industry will automatically ascend. But unfortunately the ladder of opportunity rarely reaches down so far. The lowest rung is beyond their reach. The gap between it and the ground is often too great even for initiative and character to bridge. The employed minors fourteen and sixteen years of age become the nucleus for that partly employed, sodden and anemic mass of drifters which drags down labor everywhere and clogs social progress." [34]

Progress and kindred issues eventually became tangled in partisanship, and discussion of the Wirt plan passed beyond the realm of what was good for the city. In the 1917 mayoralty campaign John F. Hylan, the Tammany candidate against Mitchel, charged that the Wirt plan was an attempt to economize on the education of slum children rather than a genuine pedagogical advance. Religion also became involved in the wrangling; eventually Hylan charged the Gary system was backed by Rockefeller interests on behalf of the wealthy. Hylan's landslide victory buried the Wirt plan in New York City.

To Randolph the fate of the Gary plan demonstrated how the vicious narrowmindedness of public officials and demagoguery could confound and cheat the people. But even had politics not become tied to the Wirt plan, there were level-headed, dispassionate New Yorkers who would not have been sorry to see the school board reject it. His articles on education were generally temperate, and he consciously tried to make his writing sober in *The Gary Schools*. But if his articles on the new education were felicitous in style, they also were occasionally marked by a characteristic intemperateness toward what he rejected. And he forgot that reform sentiment could run ahead of the community.

What stands out in Bourne's writing about the new education, particularly the Wirt plan, is his unquestioning espousal of it, although he did realize that no prudent person could declare that the Gary plan was a panacea. And he was keenly aware of practical problems ranging from politician educators to a lethargic citizenry. His *The Gary Schools* was well received generally, but it gave many the impression expressed in a sympathetic reception in the December 1916 *Education Review*: "He thinks the problem solved."

Wirt welcomed an independent study of the Gary system, which was published in seven volumes on various aspects of the plan, and an eighth which summed up the other seven. The summary work highly praised the system, particularly its imagination and courageous innovation, and declared the Gary plan a major pioneering effort. But inspectors found discipline not so pervasive as it was reputed to be, competency in the three R's less than what had been claimed, and skills in the vocational and special activity courses poorly developed. Moreover, all that was asserted about the financial benefits of the Wirt plan either could not be substantiated or were discredited.[35]

Years later Abraham Flexner—one of the collaborators on the summary volume, and a distinguished educator—wrote in his autobiography that, "The general effect of the report was disastrous to the exploitation of the Gary system."[36] If Flexner was correct, it may not have been the report alone which hurt the system. The world war also played its part. As the historian Louis Filler remarked about progressive educationists, the conflict turned the education reformers into war propagandists and distracted the public from the needs of the school.[37]

In the next 14 years two serious books treated the Wirt plan as a contemporary fact. One was Charles L. Spain's *The Platoon School: A Study of the Adaption of the Elementary School Organization to the Curriculum* (1924) and Roscoe David Case's *The Platoon System in America* (1931). In 1929 there were 1,068 schools in 202 cities which used the Wirt plan, perhaps the peak time, and Wirt continued to refine the method until his death in 1938 while he was still superintendent in Gary. Such figures[38] suggest that Bourne did not commit himself to an unreal, faddish pipe dream.

Although the Wirt system—or what it became—took a beating in a special report published in 1955 for the Gary board of education,[39] there is no denying its extensive influence on American schools. Although progressive education as a movement was passé by mid-century, a qualified critic could nevertheless observe:

"The Progressivists' claim that their favorite principles have penetrated the public learning is not merely vainglory. Our better schools, taking one with another, certainly bear more likeness to their progressive rivals than they do to their public antecedents of two or three generations past . . .

"The Progressivists were the first to declare themselves for the new ideas, and their schools were the first to nail them down into practice. Nevertheless, the New Education, whether public or private, is as much the product of the era, with its changing values, as are the transformations of business and industry. . . .

"Historically, the role of the Progressive School seems to be essentially that of the gadfly. This, at any rate, has been the case wherever it has appeared . . . . As a result of its example, the best of its ideas have been adopted by the slower-moving public school. In this sense its work, though frequently at odds with the common beliefs, is nonetheless necessary—nay indispensable."[40]

Bourne, too, consciously acted as a gadfly, bringing the tidings of the new education and often trying to sting the public into concern for something he believed vitally important to the welfare of America. Mindful of the relatively few persons, even among the articulate, informed, and educated whom the *New Republic* reached[41]—and mindful of widespread reaction against the Gary Plan—one must not claim too much for him. He and the Gary plan had opponents as evidenced by a piece such as Paul Shorey's "The Bigotry of the New Education" which appeared in the *Nation* for September 6, 1916. Yet his *The Gary Schools* was generally well received. So was his *Education and Living* (1917) in which all but one of 28 essays were *New Republic* contributions.[42]

Max Lerner wrote[43] in 1940 that, "It is hard for us, in these days when John Dewey's reputation is embalmed in jubilee volumes, to think ourselves back to a time when his educational ideas were living and—it seemed—revolutionary weapons. Yet that was true, and to no small measure as a result of Bourne's ardent discipleship." Lerner overstated the case for Bourne. Most assuredly, it was the force of Dewey's ideas which was responsible for the impact Dewey had on American life. Had Randolph never appeared on the scene, Dewey's ideas would have had their hearing.

As one historian of education has pointed out,[44] Dewey's *School and Society* (1899) was a best seller, going through seven printings in the next 10 years. Schools like Caroline Pratt's famous Play School, established in 1914, predated Bourne's various writings on Dewey and education. *Schools of To—Morrow* (1915) by John Dewey and his daughter, Evelyn, preceded Bourne's serious output.

He certainly acknowledged his allegiance to Dewey.[45] In fact, as one reads Dewey's *The School and Society, Schools of To-Morrow*, and *Democracy and Education* it seems that all Bourne's major ideas on education came from Dewey, or in fairness, coincided with Dewey's. There is nothing significant in *The Gary Schools* about the Wirt plan which was not covered in *Schools of To-Morrow*.

Dewey was the original thinker; Bourne's significant effort, principally aimed at the literate informed public, was as publicist. For he took Dewey's—and Wirt's—ideas and phrased them in meaningful, human, day-to-day terms. So well did he write, that the new education under his treatment took on fresh mundane significance.

The Reader's Guide for the years 1910-21 lists 105 articles about Wirt or Gary schools or by Wirt. A sampling gives the impression that no article or combination of articles surpassed his handling of Dewey's ideas and the new education. For Randolph realized that the new education was not only the pedagogical ramification of progressivism but also of efficiency innovations in American life, especially those initiated and encouraged by Frederick Taylor. As Bourne saw it, science had jumped the barriers of subject matter and spread through the school system.[46]

"Science means that nothing must be wasted," he had written,[47] and now he understood perfectly that efficiency was what industrial America wanted—the best use of time, space, and all other resources of its schools. Randolph saw Taylorism in the Wirt plan and it was that insight which contributed to the vividness of his writing on education.[48] He was publicist of the new education.

The new education meant a firmer America. A public school, Bourne said in words which struck the heart of the progressive education movement and which ring true today, "is a mockery unless it educates the public. It cannot make the rarefied and strained product at the top the test of its effectiveness. And the public is not ideally educated unless its individuals—all of them—are intelligent, informed, skilled, resourceful up to the limit of their respective capacities. Life itself can no longer be trusted to provide this education; the school must substitute. The Gary school deliberately sets such an ideal."[49]

"People with that inner command of moods do not need friends so keenly as I do; they are more self-sufficing. What would seem to me a prison with a life of penal solitude is to them simply the four walls of their own home, where they dwell among their interesting moods and ideas. I lack this, and I generalize far too sweepingly on my own poverty of inner resources."—Bourne to a friend, 1-16-13.

VI

IN SEARCH OF A GOLDEN PERSON

As a *New Republic* writer, Randolph settled easily into a way of life in Manhattan. His days had an exterior routine and the four corners of his intellectual world became the New York Public Library (where he studied the latest writings on education), the office of the *New Republic,* Russel Square, and Greenwich Village. Many of the glimpses we have of how intimately connected was his personal life to his career are from his days in the city.

In the fall of 1914 Bourne and his Columbia friend Carl Zigrosser took an apartment in a Phipps model tenement at 335 East 31st Street. Their quarters overlooked the East River. In the kitchen, largest of the rooms, an India print table cover and a row of books braced by brass bookends cooperated in hiding the gas range. Gradually a collection of friends and acquaintances gathered as an informal salon.

The focus of Randolph's life was Greenwich Village, where most of his circle lived. The Village was then a refuge where hundreds came to denounce Victorianism and pursue professional or artistic careers. From the little Indian hamlet of Sappocanican—which became the 17th century Dutch settlement of Bossen Bouwerie and then the English village of Green Wich—the area, huddled near the southwest side of the island, had been reconstituted as a 20th century oasis of individualism. Once an aristocratic English place to which the well-to-do adjourned for pleasure or in fear of the plague, the Village was now peopled with folk from the Middle West, New England, and elsewhere who found in its cramped domain a wider world than they ever had known.

The village was known nationwide but had not yet been commercialized. Rents were low and one accepted inconveniences as part of the romance. The oldest houses—beautifully proportioned by architects of the Federalist period—gallantly bore their colored window frames, flower boxes, and ivory-white doors. Here a dormer window perked out of patched, slanted roofs, there a cluster of old houses bordered cobbled streets and leaned against one another, each certain to topple should it be left alone.[1]

Many Villagers were radicals, particularly about sex and marriage. Some flouted wedlock and assumed an open conjugal "bliss," the most notorious examples of which, recalled one resident, were often more tyrannical than blessed unions.[2] Tucked midway between the canyons of lower Broadway and the flats of West End Avenue, and unbothered by gaping college sophomores, out-of-town buyers, or Babbitts, the Village all but institutionalized "free love"—which to one contemporary poet was a contradiction of terms.[3]

When Bourne and his friends walked the Village's tangled lanes and crisscross streets in pre-war years, the quarter was not for them an exotic escape or an erotic utopia. It was instead an informal commercial convenience populated by immigrant laborers, a few geniuses, some hard-working artists, and some professional people. At Mama Bertelotti's on 3rd Street under the elevated tracks, "the long-haired men and the short-haired gals" took fifteen cent lunches—a nickle for thick minestrone and bread and butter, a nickle glass of red wine, and a nickle for the dirty-aproned waiter.

In better times Randolph and Villagers breakfasted at the old Hotel Brevoort at 8th Street and 5th Avenue, and lunched or dined at the Hell Hole, at Mori's on Bleecker Street, or at the Hotel Griffou on 9th Street where a baby bear was chained to one of the trees in the yard: the proprietor was afraid of wasting a $300 inheritance so he bought the cub.[4] Often they ate at a little place called Three Steps Down or at Polly's on MacDougal Alley. Polly Holiday, the proprietress, was an anarchist from Evanston, Illinois, who "looked very madonna-like, presided with benignant serenity over the wild noisy horde of young people who began to collect in her restaurant, seeing to it that these truants and orphans were properly fed."[5]

Her right-hand man—cook, waiter, dishwasher and chief conversationalist—was Hippolyte Havel, a poet anarchist who sported fierce moustachios and a goatee. Those who earned his disfavor became "bourgeois pigs!" Such targets occasionally included the editors of the Socialist *Masses*, to which Havel contributed, for voting on the merits of poems submitted.

Persons like Hippolyte also were at ease in nearby Washington

Square, originally a Potter's Field and hanging ground, more recently a center of fashionable life, and in 1914 increasingly the domain of soapbox orators. On the east the Washington Square branch of New York University gazed down on starchy-white nurses pushing expensive perambulators, and on chattering ragamuffins. Here Gertrude Drick, named the Golden Bird by the then famous poet James Oppenheim, held a party one night on the top of the Washington Arch. Here Randolph Bourne strolled, brooded, and conversed.

The Greenwich Village of his time sprouted organizations like the Heretics Club, which he joined, and another group to which he belonged, the Liberal Club, remembered for its annual ball, the Pagan Rout, and its way-out speakers. The Village was more than cutting-up, more than low rents and arty people. It was also "a place where people were free to 'be themselves.' It was, among other things, very conspicuously to an outsider, a place where people came to solve their problems."[6] It resembled the *Masses* which "stood for fun, truth, beauty, realism, freedom, peace, feminism, revolution."[7] More than anything it was a state of mind. Like a gentleman it was hard to define but recognizable.[8]

Randolph—with his ankle-length black cape and his droll appearance—became part of the ongoing carnival of the Village where he eventually settled and lived until his death. His acquaintances increased more rapidly after he moved into the Village but they were just one of his entrees. People began to know him not only as a writer for the *Atlantic* or as author of *Youth and Life* but because of the *New Republic.*

As indicated, he confronted his writing with that agonizing anxiety characteristic of persons desiring success, lacking self-confidence, and hungry for esteem and affection. His *New Republic* articles on education had a self-sustaining verve about them. But during these years he wrote also for the *Dial, Seven Arts,* as well as *Atlantic* and an occasional esoteric publication. His interests ranged from Tolstoi to love and from city planning to culture. Each effort had at least a few good ideas. But he constantly underestimated his work and his ability. His exaggeration does not prevent one from recognizing an essential unevenness about his craftmanship. The cause, as has been seen briefly, was more from his personal life than shortcomings of skill. In the first place, relations with the *New Republic* particularly distressed him.

Croly's support contributed greatly to the impetus of his best work. But at times Randolph despaired "at the puniness of my outlook and activity, which is at present sitting around this pathetic apartment and attempting to hammer out with great pain ideas for the *New Republic,* most of which never see the light. I don't want to drift into peevishness, as I seem to find myself doing, but it would be so glorious to be 'in' something, making something go, or at least connected with something or somebody to whom you were important and even necessary."[9]

Freelancing for the *New Republic* was not demanding enough of his abilities, although it was time-consuming, he told Alyse, "and so anybody who has no work grip him except what he will initiate laboriously himself, and finds no one to take and marry him, gets slowly beached high and dry, out of touch of everything but the amiable conventionalities of his de-inspired friends, and the new conventional people he meets in the world."

Randolph came to feel like a nobody where the *New Republic* was concerned. After the journal published articles timed with the end of the first year of the European war—thereby eliminating ones he was doing (apparently without the editors' knowledge)—he complained that he had no voice in policy. He declared himself an insignificant retainer, but then admitted nothing had been done to deserve a high place. The problem was an "old sore," not worth pursuing.[10]

One cliché is that the *New Republic* persecuted Bourne and then shut him out when its editors disagreed with his opinions on United States participation in the war. However bitter he may have become it is unlikely Randolph would have argued that a magazine could not reject writing contrary to its position. Croly encouraged him to attend the weekly Tuesday luncheon meeting at the *New Republic,* and Randolph's date book shows he went often. The scene of the luncheons was the *New Republic*'s headquarters, a four-story yellow-brick house which had been done over to resemble as much a gentleman's club, as an editorial office. A French chef turned out elegant meals for the staff and their weekly guests.[11]

Although Ellery Sedgwick had urged him not to be disheartened about the *New Republic,*[12] Randolph imagined he had enemies on the publication. Referring to a division made by H. G. Wells of people into those who still expect to lead a noble life some day and those who have given up the idea as priggish and unnatural, he put Philip Littell, writer of "Books and Things," in the latter group because of his style and "that suave and discreet disapproval which I feel him to be shedding around the more fervent things which I sent to the N. R. I thank God every day for Croly . . . ."[13]

Later he complained that the *New Republic* was getting restive paying him $100 a month for work it could not find space for. His job was "trembling," he reported, but he did not seem surprised. "I really thirst for fame, but the minute I begin taking steps for it, it seems so absurd to imagine that I am likely to do much more than I've done." [14]

As usual, he spoke ironically, but he clearly was worried. The *New Republic,* he said, paid starvation wages, and he felt trapped by the gloom and solitude syndrome. What he probably would have to do, he declared, was to take himself austerely in hand, live a Spartan life alone, deprive himself of his piano, and turn himself into a journalist trying to cling to the *New Republic* by his wits. "I think I can do this, but I never get anything I apply for. I seem to be permanently side-tracked from activity, and not quite able to make my private side-tracked career."

Randolph appraised his relations with the *New Republic* more severely than others might have. A colleague recalled that Bourne frequently visited the office and conversed at length with Croly and Lippmann on politics and with Francis Hackett on literature. The colleague assumed he had considerable influence.[14B] The implication is that (if the estimate is correct) no one on the *New Republic* was out to get him.

And Francis Hackett recalled that, "Bourne was treated with extreme consideration on the N.R. I gave him Dreiser to review, to give one example, when I should have done him myself. He had the freedom of the office, often came to lunch, and . . . we got on well. But Bourne was *exigent.* Had we starred him, we'd have had to pamper him." [15]

What frightened Randolph was that—aside from publishing occasionally in *Atlantic*—he did not have "a show anywhere else." "There is a new wizard down here named Merz," he told a friend, "who can do anything from writing advertisements, running the business department, editing the magazine to doing articles far cleverer than any of us can do. However, he has no bashfulness in him, and we tremble for our futures. I become more and more negligible, and if I attempted to advertise myself would only succeed in being foolish. All this is very fainthearted of me, I know, but I feel more or less caught in a trap and do not yet see my way out." [16]

Discontent about his lot with the *New Republic* was due in part to the agony of writing *The Gary Schools.* The work was promised to Houghton Mifflin Company, but Bourne then found his writing had gone stale. The result seemed disastrous. Whereas he felt his Gary articles in the *New Republic* had been a "mere impressionistic survey,"[17] Randolph found himself floundering in a surf of loosely connected notes and background material.

Once more he miscalculated his ability, but nevertheless when the book went to press in January 1916 he declared himself distressed by its "banality." He wrote Alyse that he longed "to redeem it now by some slashing work, but have a miserable *Peace Symposium* to prepare for my old friends of the International Conciliation. The *New Republic* keeps me busy, either eating my stuff or rejecting it, so that I have an impression of working most of the time for them. Then the business of qualifying as an education expert keeps me at the libraries. And the *Atlantic* would take some articles if I could only get around to the business of writing them, 24 hours a day and the strength of ten wouldn't achieve the work I want to do. And I spend my time drinking tea, talking about my woes, or psychologizing privately about my domestic complications. I have given this matter enough analytic attention to make a Henry James novel. If I am finally cast, I shall certainly take my revenge by writing it."[18]

The pitfalls of book writing and the failure to realize through the *New Republic* his professional aspirations were only peripheral sources of problems. This trouble was women and sex. The two had created havoc with him for years, and no one knew this better than he. In 1913 Randolph met Beulah Amidom, an 18-year-old Barnard student from North Dakota whom he described as "so glowing and earthy and passionately intelligent, one of the most beautiful persons I have ever looked upon."[19]

A firm friendship grew before he went abroad and they often talked all night. "My mind seemed full of exciting things when I was with him," she later wrote, adding that he had written her: "When I drop a stone in your pool, I always get a ripple."[20] Beulah knew Dorothy Teall, also a Barnard girl, a friend of Randolph from New Jersey, and a member of a family which was close to the Bourne family. After he returned from Europe, the trio often went out together, and soon Randolph—always in love with love anyway—became deeply involved.

Apparently he at times convinced himself that Beulah somehow would be won. After an April day in the country, he wrote Dorothy (with whom he long had had a father-confidant relationship), that:

"The day was so much more glorious than I dared to expect. You could hardly feel all the innumerable little touches by which [Beulah] soothed and delighted my soul. There were those moments under the trees—Do you remember how she laughed when I threw acorns at her? How she hugged the brown ground? There were unpropitious moments in that unlucky corner where we halted and saw the lovers, but things flowed again when we started to walk, and even the nightmare of the trolley ride could not dissipate the high mood of the afternoon.

"And then the after-dinner conversation! . . . How she dramatized her whole generation, and how hotly distressed she was as she gazed into her future, so passionate and yet so intellectual! Ah, a great mood, and a great day. You were lovely to share her with me; I'm afraid I monopolized her too much, and bored her with my quantity. I wonder if she liked me any better after it. I think she did like me for stretches that day. I wish I had not caused any lapses from her radiance, as I did when I probed her so deeply on the bank [of the stream].

"She seemed all the more daringly lovely because I had that week a letter of really excoriating savagery, ending in a page of sentimental slang. I still marvel. It could not be the same [Beulah], it seemed. She was so much bigger and lovelier than that letter, though that did have a fine prophetic ring." [21]

Beulah was to graduate in two months and Randolph slowly realized what he was up against. In mock jocularity he asked Dorothy if she did not think it would be old-fashioned for him to marry Beulah. "Why don't you get *her* to marry *me?* That would be truly delightful, and it would save me so much spiritual trepidation." The rest of the spring was a succession of aborted efforts to arrange outings and theater and tea dates with Beulah. But he saw the inevitable. In June, in writing Dorothy to thank her for a nice gesture, he remarked that "it came at a time after the Beulah shipwreck when I had begun to feel that I was no more than an incident in anybody's life and to wonder if I could stand that sort of thing for the rest of my days. Nobody does feel more than I at times this hunger, this *besoin d'etre aimé,* and I annoy my friends, I think, by asking so much."

Beulah Amidon dropped out of his romantic life, although he occasionally saw her. Her passing he described as a "sore mutilation of my best life." She began a writing career which started with the *Survey,* a magazine for social workers, and then became engaged. By the time her fiance temporarily was listed as missing in action, she may have come to know what Bourne meant—if she already did not—when he said that, "Being in love is so much more fierce and brutal a thing than B. herself seems to even care to imagine, that every one should be warned against it. I don't find that it corresponds to anything that is said about it in books. I am surprised to find that so much is written and said about it when it is scarcely a subject that as things go to-day, can be mentioned in polite society. I am a complete Shavian on the subject."

New York City is not ideal for being miserable in. Randolph was always wavering between loving and despising Manhattan, and occasionally he fled. Part of July 1915 was spent with Carl Zigrosser at the Ulster Park, New York, farm of Zigrosser's parents where he had happily passed the summer of 1912. Then he decided on Dublin, New Hampshire, predominantly an artists' colony tucked in the far southwestern corner of the state just northeast of Monadnock Mountain. Dublin had been suggested by a newly acquired friend, Elizabeth Shepley Sergeant, whose writing on French culture was appearing increasingly in the *New Republic*. Her judgment proved unerring.

In early August he arrived with a friend he called Fergus who never has been called anything but that. This really was Edward Murray, a Columbia musician friend. Murray at this time seemed mainly interested in the art of living, according to Bourne's piece "Fergus—A Portrait" in the May 22, 1915, *New Republic*. Murray's career had not yet jelled, although he had tried violin lessons and composing songs.

The pair were pleased that the "mere shack" they had expected had electricity and sufficient furnishings, and although life was otherwise rustic, they stayed out of each other's way. After a shaky beginning (checked by a prudent switch to canned food), Edward's cooking began to result in meals. Their cabin was in a broad lakeside meadow bursting with goldenrod, dotted with pines. The shelter was private, but near the road.

Randolph often spent his days at a nearby dock writing *The Gary Schools* or stretched on a hillside absorbed in summer afternoon dreams. When Edward returned to New York City several weeks later, a 74-year-old Bohemian New Englander, a painter named Eastman Chase replaced him. From artist in his studio in MacDougal Alley, Chase easily made the transition to cook in Bourne's cabin.

Hour after hour they talked poets, artists, and painting, a diet enriched by Chase's once having had a gallery in Boston and appearing to know everybody and everything. And there was plenty of company despite the rural setting. The painter George de Forest Brush had his studio in a barn on the same property, and the Abbot Thayer family lived nearby in a compound of rough studios and rooms. Thayer was 66, the peak of his artistic career long past. He was a distinguished naturalist and a domineering and eccentric man whose strange dress, ways, and social relations would have appeared ludicrous and pathetic had it not been for his great mental and moral dignity. His saintliness and intellect were reminiscent of the Thoreau and Emerson whom he revered.[22]

Randolph probably was flattered to be included in Thayer's fastidious choice of friends, for Thayer was a Boston blue blood who associated with the wealthy Brahmins at Dublin. But if the Thayers had rejected him, Bourne would not have perished. A New York poet, Ridgely Torrence, came over one day from MacDowell Colony near Peterborough and took his awed friend back with him to MacDowell Colony, site of the composer's grave and cabin. Also, there was Mrs. E. H. James, a highlight of Bourne's life in Paris. Apparently Mr. James—who, when he was not busy libelling King George, spent most of his time setting up red republics—was not in Dublin. Nevertheless, Randolph gave Mrs. James a party at which she probably launched into one of her typical recitations of poetry and drama. Another couple were the American geologist Raphael Pumpelly and his wife.

The Dublin visit was the most serene period of Randolph's life; yet it was equally varied and exciting. "A society that is rich and also cultivated is a very demoralizing thing," he said facetiously.

"I have never come across this kind of people. Perhaps they don't exist outside of New England. But the people here get things off with such taste and simplicity, and pose so little that one is fairly seduced to such an aristocracy. There are a few nouveau from St. Louis and Baltimore, just to furnish the dark background, but the general atmosphere is most charming. Look around you as you will, you will not find a false or ugly note in the place, woods, houses, roads, lake.

"The occasional flashy houses are hidden in the trees. The wood-road winds unspoiled around the lake close to its shore. You may wander through private woods and estates at will. The mountain looms grandly from many points and all my best friends seem to have appropriated the most charming houses and the best views. Autos pick you up on the road, and a friend or two come around and take you out. You get invited to dinners and teas, where you do not feel your lack of clothes, and you don't care whether you make a hit or not.[23]

He adored Abbot Thayer as much as Thayer's family did: two or three times a week he and Edward played for the family and their guests in return for supper. The understanding originated late one afternoon when a gigantic downpour tore across Monadnock. "Everybody stayed and Mr. Thayer showed us all his color diagrams and demonstrations and told a great many stories, and everybody was delightful . . . . After supper they unearthed an antique piano brought over from Germany after 1848, a fiddle, and Fergus and I played Schubert songs for an hour out of an old Liederbuch. Mr. Thayer's appreciation was almost embarrassingly estatic, and he proffered sketches and dinners and thanks if we would come often and do it again. I liked his simple emotional way and his telling us we had 'watered his soul'. . . . He took us down to the road with the quaintest of lanterns, and spoke constantly of the music." [24]

Edward Arlington Robinson and Amy Lowell also were at Dublin and one evening they read poems. The obese Miss Lowell recently had given so provocative a talk in Dublin that it sent Mrs. Thayer home "beside herself with fury," and stirred an unidentified mild Harvard professor to recount Amy's "atrocities" on shipboard. "I went to her house," Randolph reported, "in considerable trepidation expecting to be pummelled and overawed. Instead I spent a wholly delightful evening. She walked right at me as one of the oldest of friends and we had a truly grand gossip. I found her immensely witty and keen, and willing to spread out the contents of her mind before you. Suprisingly fair and a friendly lover of all sorts of queer and little people, whom she touches off inimitably. She has a delightful zest for life, and would be a much greater person without her money and position, which apparently give people these extraordinary reactions and breed unpopularity for her. She seems quite innocent of this, however." [25]

Another warm acquaintance seemed made, but it was short-lived. On a later visit to Amy in Brookline, Massachusetts, he was "attacked" by her giant dogs. No physical harm was done, but the pets made a horrid ruckus with their jumping on him and barking. He was so shaken—and convinced the dogs had viciously attacked him—that he could not rise to any of Amy's sallies during dinner. She decided he was a "weakling" and later insisted to Louis Untermeyer and James Oppenheim that his deformity appeared in his "tortured and twisted mentality." "Everything he writes shows he is a cripple," she announced.[26]

Randolph remained in Dublin into early October, trying to persuade others to stay or writing friends to come up. He had come close to stopping time, good reason for not upsetting things. New Hampshire scenes reminded him of the Roman Campagna from Janiculum—the same valley, same hills, and even Crotched Mountain resembled Mount Socrate. And so—lolling in meadows by the hour, the faint sound of barking foxes playing in and out of his musing—he tried to forget the books he had not read, the thoughts he had not worked out, or the articles unborn.

Since late in his career at Columbia, it had been customary for him to look back in June on his preceding year and denounce it. Now, he felt, there was a chance to start afresh. "Do your varied consciences hound you along like [sic] mine do?" he asked a friend, "so that nothing is ever a real vacation, and nothing ever a real normal drudge of work? My only solution is to get so somehow proud of myself that I cannot bear to have the world deprived of what I could tell them. Unfortunately I am still far from that condition . . . ."[27] What happened, however, was that upon return to New York he soon was deep in a traumatic love which in comparison made the Mon Amie and Beulah incidents appear mere flirtations.

Randolph fell desperately in love with "Diana" (for that was not her name). To one person who knew her she was "very beautiful" and to another she was handsome, but not strikingly beautiful. Randolph met her through Village friends after his return from Dublin, probably early in the fall of 1915. She was a free spirit, and, according to one who knew her, a person of unfilled artistic potential.

He adored her and wanted to marry. Diana at that time did not believe in marriage, which does not mean that she would have accepted if she did. Despite his affliction, Randolph appealed to women because of his charm, conversation, music and companions. But according to a person who knew him well, "he had only to venture an inch over a forbidden line to have them fly from him like shy birds, startled from their leafy bower."[28]

Details of the affair are confused. It is clear that Randolph's first experience was tied to a deep but frustrated romantic love. It was a catastrophe that hurt him profoundly. In May of 1916 (according to his diary in the Columbia archives) they broke, although he occasionally saw Diana after that. As he usually did when a real or imagined disaster befell him, Bourne poured out his heart to friends. In letters written in 1916 he told a bitter, aching story the theme of which was psychological incompatibility.[29]

One reply intentionally hit him hard, but kindly, and possibly revealed more about him than he cared to admit. It said in part: " . . . I wonder if it *is* so much of a wound? Aren't you more or less a pretender to the theme of love unrequitted? Aren't you more or less of a sentimental Tommy—a gentle vivisectionist of that most fascinating thing in the world, love in all its various manifestations? Don't you fall in love just for the experience? I do . . . . Anyhow, your dark devilish (well, she sounded devilish!) Chryod [?] must have been fascinating, and I don't wonder at your losing your heart (you could never make me believe you lost your head at the same time—there is too much wit (i.e. 'wit' in the old time sense) in it . . . . I haven't much faith in your lovelorness. There have been three different ones—*Only Ones*—since I have known you. You will be falling in love with me next." [30]

Tender solicitation may have soothed temporarily, but a letter which suggests that he knew as early as January 1916 how futile it was to pursue Diana indicates his lacerated condition. A year was needed to recover one's poise, he said half-seriously. He was convinced nothing could be accomplished until there was "a stable and satisfactory way of living, with the right golden and protecting person." He realized that his talk sounded parasitic and clinging vine-like. But recently he had felt "very much like being served and cared for and coddled." All one's friends seemed to be living in the most charming apartments, admirably married. "I flit around from one to another, a homeless, helpless waif, eternally passing into the cold from their warm and confident firesides. And I seem to face a long future of such waifness." [31]

Toward Diana resentment mingled with yearning. A friend of Randolph said Diana showed him a letter in which he called her "*une femme perfide*." To another friend he wrote that he had been accused of having sacrificed his gods to his passions long enough. But once resolved to change, it would occur to him that it was impossible to do so because of his temperament. His spirit would be torn, Bourne said, torn until pursuit seemed hopeless. And then he did "not know but what I would let down my perfectionism and snatch at what I can get." If serious women will not marry you, he contemplated, then they cannot quite acquit themselves of the responsibility and sentimentality of your turning into a genuine pursuer of ephemeral loves. It was strange, he commented, how the American spirit could not see anything between the eternality and sentimentality of bourgeois alliance and bourgeois cheapness and vulgarity. Diana, he confided to Alyse, "is the only Pagan and passionate thing that has ever crossed my horizon and she was soon submerged in the general unreality, efficiency and cheapness managing to do their deadly work upon her idealism. I pray that some time I shall meet people who have some kind of high seriousness about personal relations which is not metallic and which fuses the senuous with it. [Diana] was a hyphenate. Then I pray that something will get me to the continent. Or perhaps it's all just as impossible there too. I'm all at sea. The poignant thing is to have glimmered it and lost it. Something really has been taken out of me. I have lost faith." [32]

Problems that winter of 1915-16 were compounded by a rupture with Carl Zigrosser who had been one of his dearest friends. They got on famously when they took an apartment, but each naturally went his way, Carl building a career in art, and Randolph with his writing. Romance intruded when Zigrosser became engaged to Florence King, a suffrage worker.

Apparently Randolph resented Florence even before the engagement because she tried to dominate his life. He also was bitter because he felt Florence had betrayed a confidence. He wrote harshly of her, yet he was more hurt than angry. "My affairs are a hopeless tangle. I must move in a few days," Bourne told a friend.[33]

There was a painful confrontation between the friends on Christmas Eve 1916, and later an unhappy encounter at a party given by Gladys Thayer, daughter of Randolph's painter friend, Abbot Thayer. The break dramatizes his fierce commitment to people and how seriously he took personal relationships. But he apparently was not blameless. Years later, Carl recalled [34] that several factors made a break inevitable, and included was the violation of confidence by Randolph and mutual acquaintances. Moreover, Diana violated a confidence about him by telling it to Randolph who then used it to break Carl's relations with two other persons. What is clear about the falling out is that in Randolph's basic unhappiness and insecurity, a person like Florence King "threatened" the few toeholds Randolph felt he had.[35]

Randolph was cautioned that perhaps he was "taking an unnecessarily tragic and solemn viewpoint in withdrawing from all those who happen to be associated with you at the time [of breaking with Carl]. Aren't you?" [36] He disagreed but even if he had not, he realized that a turning point in his personal life had been reached. Having led the experimental life once so vigoriously advocated, he frankly was tired of it. The experimental life had proved its worth; now Bourne knew what he wanted, even if it was as far away as ever. "Love, fame, joy in work, would bring, perhaps, the resources for the freedom I want to move about and yet have a center and a hearth. All my problems are interwoven; if I had one solved, it seems to me that the key to all of them is love, and the deprivation the one impediment to blossoming."[37]

Moreover, Randolph in the summer of 1916 realized that he was making a conscious break with old friends. When a college friend sailed for Russia, Bourne believed the departure marked "the cutting of the last bond with an interwoven group that has proven not quite free and fair."

Acquiring a new circle was prophetic of how his writing would become concerned with new subjects; how it would be more refined but also more forceful, less idiomatic and more tasteful. Once he had said that he loved "people with quick, roving intelligence, who carry their learning lightly, and use it as weapons to fight with, as handles to grasp new ideas and situations, and as fuel to warm them into a sympathy with all sorts and conditions of men."[38] His circle was now composed of such figures, persons absorbed in the restlessness of pre-war America.

There was Floyd Dell, a shy midwesterner who had succeeded Francis Hackett as literary editor of the Chicago *Evening Post*. Then Dell went to New York where he became an editor of the *Masses*. Later he would write best-selling books. And as Elizabeth Shepley Sergeant and Paul Rosenfeld appeared more frequently in the *New Republic*, they became closer friends with him, especially Rosenfeld, although Randolph also spoke freely with Elizabeth. Paul was a sensitive, robust 26-year-old Yale graduate who had lived a varied but undirected life. A pianist, he was on his way to becoming one of the nation's most distinguished, widely read, and controversial music critics. Elizabeth Sergeant's writing career would stretch far beyond the penetrating pieces she filed from Europe during the war.

After the *Seven Arts* began publishing in November 1916 Randolph became acquainted with its editor, the poet James Oppenheim, 34, a short, beautiful man with the softness characteristic of people from the ghetto—people who do not and cannot exercise, people always in a tailor's chair or at a workbench. He had a sad, sweet quality about him which attracted Bourne. Oppenheim was a disciple of Whitman, deeply devoted to America, but pathetic in that he thought his own poetry much greater than it was.

In Waldo Frank, a fiery 27-year-old-editor of the *Seven Arts*, Randolph found a kindred soul whose distaste for phoneyness perhaps even surpassed his own. Together they often played Bach sonatas at Frank's apartment on East 30th Street. Alvin Johnson, economics writer for the *New Republic*; the poet Ridgely Torrence, 41; the journalist and writer Herbert J. Seligman; Dr. Beatrice Hinkle, a famous psychiatrist and disciple of Jung; Elsie Clews Parsons, an ethnologist and widely published essayist; Alyse Gregory, an ardent suffragist who had known Randolph since before he went to Europe, who became managing editor of the *Dial,* who later married the English writer Llewelyn Powys, and in whom he frequently confided—these persons were among those who became his life as much as his work was.

But his closest male friend was lean, intense, 30-year-old Van Wyck Brooks, whose long career in criticism and literary history was beginning to level off on the plain of maturity and wider acceptance. Brooks was a native of Plainfield, New Jersey, and from a middle-class background similar to Bourne's. The pair had rebelled against many of the same things. Concerning Brooks, Randolph said, "I feel we are the product of the same civilization, but he is finer, better integrated, much more smoothly running . . . . I have the pleasing sense of new friendships. This last year has meant a sloughing off of much that wasn't congenial, but which I hung onto from sheer gregariousness."[39] Brooks remembered that, "I really knew him scarcely more than a year and a half, and during that time we were more or less constantly together."[40]

It was with a trio of women that Randolph was perhaps most frequently seen. One night in the winter of 1915 he met two young women at a party. One was Esther Cornell, an aspiring actress who had been graduated from Bryn Mawr. The other was Agnes de Lima, a Vassar girl involved in social work and educational reform.[41] Both were about 28, two years younger than he. A third member of the group was Frances Anderson, a staffer on the *New Republic* and then the *Masses.* Esther and Agnes shared a Village apartment. So excited about life, ideas, and people were they that low salaries and long hours were secondary. The group was frequently together for meals, picnics, parties, concerts, and the theater. Although Frances dropped out in June 1917 when her engineer groom took her to the interior of Brazil, Esther, Agnes and Randolph remained unfaltering friends.

The girls knew of the catastrophe with Diana and realized in June 1916 that he had not recovered. After unsuccessful efforts to find a summer retreat, the girls stumbled on a place belonging to an acquaintance of Frances. He was John Rae, a widely-known commercial artist. His Caldwell, New Jersey, residence, 16 miles west of the city, was perfect. It was an artist's home with an enormous living room and tiny bedrooms added, it seemed, as an afterthought. Randolph moved in with the girls and stayed the summer except for occasional trips into the city.[42]

Although he had low moments in Caldwell the summer there renewed him. After breakfast he set to writing on the porch and resumed after lunch. The extensive yard was not too great a distraction, for it was enclosed by handsome cedars, thereby destroying, Bourne complained, what might have been a good view of nearby hills where he often walked. Frances and Agnes commuted to New York and, although Esther usually was at the house and they spent much of the time talking, Randolph still managed to get his manuscripts off.

The Caldwell summer with its frivolity, its seriousness, good talk, and good company saved him from deep-seated melancholy. The girls called him "Little Randolph" after the brother in Henry James's *Daisy Miller*. To the Southern mammy who was inherited from the owner and who cooked and kept house he was "Mastah." This delighted him and to Lawrence K. Frank, a college friend, he "obviously was 'king of the castle'."[43]

After dinner most evenings he played Beethoven, Brahms, Chopin, Schubert, Debussy, beginning and ending with Brahms preludes. One evening, however, a bore drove him to the Chickering baby grand piano at which he pounded harder and louder than the girls had ever heard him: he was trying to drive the man away![44]

On weekends friends of Randolph and beaux and friends of the girls visited Caldwell. One night Van Wyck Brooks might be there talking avidly of writing and New England; another night Walter Lippmann and Alvin Johnson. As Johnson revealed his plans for a new kind of education which later became his New School for Social Research, Bourne played with the ideas, questioned, and suggested.

His personal life from the autumn of 1915 through 1916 and into 1917 was often unhappy and his work consequently suffered. But he certainly did not collapse. Fear of poverty, if nothing else, always would have kept him trying something. "Poverty is a hideous thing," Randolph observed. "Not to have enough to command the resources of mere getting around, of having what you need is appalling. And still worse is to have the slender minimum resources that you have, so uncertain. One takes a certain satisfaction, I suppose, in the discovery that one's problems are hopeless. When one has decided that, they become interesting problems . . . ."[45]

At the same time, he never was so disgusted that he could not step back and inspect himself. His ambition, what he called his will-to-power, and his conviction that despite everything one must be creative, presented a realistic impression of what his career needed, although he was unsure what direction it should now take. "I wish," he said, "I was artist enough to use my experience without tangling myself up too much again in my imagination. The reformer got such a terrific start in my youth over the artist that I'm afraid the latter is handicapped for life. The reformer with an *amour-propre* is a temperament pretty quenching for any upflow of art in one, isn't it?"[46]

That certain elements of his public thought more of his work than he did at even the most confident of moments was demonstrated by the speaking engagements in Chicago, Milwaukee and Madison, Wisconsin, and in Boston. In Boston he found he did not shrink from *New Republic* colleagues "who terrify me when I see them in New York but who make me wholly buoyant here. Felix Frankfurter, for instance, who teaches law at Harvard, and Harold Laski, an Oxford Jew, now teaching at Harvard, an incredibly brilliant specimen of the young English radical school. These two, with Walter Lippmann, made up a Jewish trinity which is the wonder of the world, or at least my world."[47]

At one point Randolph had considered going West. Alvin Johnson tried unsuccessfully to get an appointment for him at Stanford when he was there as a visiting professor. But now Bourne felt his career and personal life were brightening. A year before he was tickled that his writing had elicited so many denunciatory letters to the editor of the *New Republic,*[48] and he still relished a fight. A new career soon would open on the *Dial* and in April 1917 the *Seven Arts* would begin to publish his work.

When he wrote of Laski, Frankfurter, and Lippmann, Randolph was visiting Boston and Harvard where he spoke before a Jewish society about the role of the Jew in American civilization. An article of his, "Trans-National America," in the July 1916 *Atlantic* was reworked for the Harvard presentation, and published a month later in the December 1916 *Menorah Journal* as "The Jew and Trans-National America." His Cambridge address was one tile in a mosaic concerning American culture and civilization which Bourne had slowly been working out.

To him and other contemporary iconoclasts, America was culturally and artistically coming of age, and they wanted a hand in the outcome. They heard America singing.

"Let us admit that the appreciations of the Brahmins marvellously coincide with what Matthew Arnold has stamped as right. But perhaps for most of us there has not been the environment to produce that happy coincidence. Our education has forced us all to be self-made men in artistic appreciation. Our tastes suffer from hiatuses and crotchinesses and color-blindnesses because no effort has been made to integrate our sincere likes and dislikes and focus and sharpen our reactions. Until the present ideal is overthrown, we have no chance of getting a sincere and general public taste. We can have only the mechanics of an art education. I do not mean that America has been unique in this. We have only been a little worse than other countries because we have been more conscientious." —Bourne, *New Republic,* 1-15-16.

VI

AMERICA! AMERICA!

His own generation, Randolph Bourne said when he reviewed Lytton Strachey's *Eminent Victorians,* would prefer to have sprung from a society it could revere: it was much easier and pleasanter to love your parents than to dislike them. Unfortunately, he contended, the Victorian age deserved much of the reproach it received for creating a generation of rebels and malcontents.

Reiterating the assertion that the age had encased middle class Americans and Britons in tastes and values discordant with 20th century life, he claimed good naturedly that "contempt, disdain, irreverence, flightiness, bumptiousness, and rebellion" were the result. The fashion for malcontents had been to roll their various resentments into a blanket indictment of the Victorian age, a maneuver which to him in 1918 seemed to have been possibly too successful.[1]

Perhaps Randolph knew he was summing up—in the lull between war's end and the new paths American cultural life would take in the 1920's—a clash that had been going on most of the century. On one side were the holdovers, heirs, and advocates of the genteel tradition. On the other side was a growing body of iconoclastic artists who—while maybe cherishing most of the things dear to their predecessors—lived, saw, and interpreted life in new ways.

At bottom, the Generation of 1915, as Van Wyck Brooks later named it, sought what at the time was widely called a "usable past." The very fact of their hunting for a worthy tradition testified to their deep commitment to America—often expressed in severe criticism—and to the fact they were convinced their country was entering a period of rich cultural creativity and, therefore, maturity.

The promise of American civilization had long concerned reflective Americans. During and briefly after the War of Independence there had been an ill-tempered reaction to British culture. And as early as 1837 Emerson had called on America to strike out on its own. In his "The American Scholar" address before the Phi Beta Kappa society at Harvard, he told his audience that each age must write its own books. If there was a period in which one would desire to be born, he said, it was an age of revolution when old glories are tested by rich new possibilities. "We have listened too long to the courtly muses of Europe," Emerson announced.

But seven years later it was clear to him that where culture was concerned Americans had not spoken with their own minds. For he noted: "It is remarkable that our people have their intellectual culture from one country [Britain] and their duties from another." Nevertheless, America to Emerson was the country of the future, and clearly it must have kings and nobles; but "only let us have the real instead of the titular." "I call upon you, young men, to obey your heart and be the nobility of this land."

Emerson's plea, occasionally repeated, went unheeded, or at least American culture produced little which turned the heads of the rest of the world. In 1881 Josiah Royce in his *Fugitive Essays* intoned in a different context: "Send us a thinker that can show us just what makes men's destiny more than poor and comic, just what is the ideal that we ought to serve . . . ." It was a sentiment which foreshadowed the sentiments of Bourne and his radical contemporaries.

True, there had been, as George Santayana said, a mid-19th century Indian summer of the mind, brilliant in its russet and yellow season. But it was all a harvest of leaves. Expressing a then widely-held view, Santayana in his *Character and Opinion in the United States* wrote that "These cultivated [19th century] writers lacked native roots and fresh sap because the American intellect itself lacked them. Their culture was half a pious survival, half an intentional acquirement; it was not the inevitable flowering of fresh experience."

Bourne and like-thinking contemporaries agreed with Santayana, but what distinguished them from earlier enthusiasts was not only their working to achieve a usable past, but their belief the new day was at hand. In 1909 in *The Wine of the Puritans,* Brooks began a harsh consideration of the Puritan heritage which would continue into the 1920's. And in 1913 the rebel literary critic John Macy was declaring in *The Spirit of American Literature* that "The whole country is crying out for those who will record it, satirize it, chant it."

Pre-war America—as Brooks would write in *America's Coming of Age* (1915)—was like a vast Sargasso Sea, choked with unconscious life, and swept by "ground-swells of half-conscious emotion." One reason for this was what Brooks called a traditional divorce between highbrow and lowbrow culture, each working against the other. Now, with untold social forces and social issues rising to the surface, American culture was entering a new awareness.

The informed public at this time was vaguely aware of what was happening in America, what with a nude zigzagging down the staircase at the 69th Street Armory art show in New York City, and the *avant-garde* indulging in a revelry of nose-thumbing.[2] The public also was vaguely unsure of a world in which Isadora Duncan always was dancing, "that world of which John Reed was the Byronic Hero, Mabel Dodge the hostess, Randolph Bourne the martyr, Van Wyck Brooks the oracle."[3]

The rebellious aspect of the age superficially appeared to the uninitiated as frivolous and sulky. To those trying to mold a great national culture the task had sacred overtones. To the poet Ezra Pound, changing America was not merely on the point of what many persons termed it, a Renaissance, that is, a *Risorgimento,* or rebirth. It was to be a *Risvegliamento*, an awakening; and that implied "a whole volley of liberations; liberations from ideas, from stupidities, from conventions and from tyrannies of wealth or of army."[4] Enthusiastically he wrote to Harriet Monroe, founder and editor of *Poetry* magazine, that the "awakening will make the Italian Renaissance look like a tempest in a teapot!"[5]

In his autobiography, *Intellectual Vagabondage,* Floyd Dell, a Bourne friend, recalled that the 1915 generation embraced the modern world, believing it was good, yet simulaneously desiring to know why it was good. The previous century provided no answers; Carlyle and Ruskin were only bewildering. "We wanted," Dell said, "though we did not realize it, a literature of our own—books produced by, for and out of the age in which we lived. But there was quite literally no such books."

To the poet James Oppenheim the issue was clear. Art not only was an expression of national life, but a means of its enhancement. "We have no tradition to continue; we have no school of style to build up."[6] "We stand," he wrote in the *Seven Arts* for April 1917, "at the faint beginnings, the trembling dawn of our second great epoch."

Bourne was deeply involved in the cultural aspect of the emergence from American innocence, in what Alfred Kazin called the "joyous season." Yet it is extravagant to say that the "best significance of Randolph Bourne lies in the joining, through his work, of the political and the cultural currents of advance,"[7] or that he "now seems a seismograph on which were recorded the greatest hopes and fiercest despairs of his time."[8] Such evaluations do indicate the source and magnitude of his contributions.

His commitment to the coming golden day was derived perhaps as much from frustration as from dedication and optimism. He and his contemporaries seem to have been frustrated by what was and what could be in America. They felt their land fitted Turgenev's description of Russia: *grande et riche, mais desordonee,* huge, rich, but disorderly and disheveled; that—as Harold J. Laski later remarked—the idea upon which the spirit of America was founded ran perhaps 30 to 40 years behind the facts of social and economic life.

Randolph agreed with Brooks that inherited American culture had failed to meet present needs and therefore to fertilize the roots of national culture. This distressed him because he believed with Pound that letters were a country's foreign ministry and that only through the arts do nations understand and respect one another. But American culture was in a state of arrested development, it seemed to him. He probably had pondered the problem since student days, so that upon return from Europe his writing on the matter was more of an elaboration of ideas than the acquiring of new insights.

Emerson complained years before that, "We are full of vanity, of which the most signal proof is our sensitiveness to foreign and especially English culture." It may be true as Max Lerner wrote[9] that after Emerson a fusion of national and universal elements was "transformed into a national egoism that hardened itself against all foreign importations." But by the time Randolph was a young man, sentiment had swung back again, particularly to adoration of British culture. He considered such a posture as a distasteful cultural humility.

To Matthew Arnold and legions of followers, culture was, as he put it in *Literature and Dogma,* "To know the best that had been thought and said in the world . . ." and to make that knowledge current everywhere. Bourne recognized the peculiar force this idea had for Americans. It seemed a democratic ideal and apparently every one with energy and perseverance could reasonably expect to acquire what Arnold called culture. After all, he said, the Arnold ideal was a quantitative one and culture was a matter of acquisition. One added little by little to his hoard until he reached a radiant limit.[10]

He also recognized that the Arnold dogma coincided with the post-Civil War economic boom of the American middle class, people sufficiently alert to feel their limitations and aware of broader life overseas. In the British mind, Randolph believed, the Dickens land-of-liberty American had been replaced by the American who measured his greatness by his orientation to Europe. Indeed, it almost was a test of respectibility whether one had gone abroad at least once. Yet such cultural humility always had astonished Europeans. The situation disgusted Bourne. In fact, "To a genuinely patriotic American this cultural humility of ours is somewhat humiliating. In response to this eager inexhaustible interest in Europe, where is Europe's interest in us? Europe is to us the land of history, of mellow tradition and the graces of life, of the best that has been said and thought in the world. To Europe we are the land of crude racial chaos, of skyscrapers and bluff, of millionaires and 'bosses'."

A French philosopher might come to the United States, Randolph commented—probably meaning Henri Bergson who lectured at Columbia in 1911—and Americans learned from him the trends in foreign cultural life. But he does not ask about American thought. American cultural humility prevented one's forcing on the visitor's attention the nation's developments. Advertising genius, powerful where soap was concerned, wilted before the task of revealing the American mind. The result was that the country's culture was unjustly taken at its face value.

When it came to culture, Americans were either ignored or considered parasitic, he argued, and justly so because their goal and ideal of culture made them so. But the Arnold notion of culture had emanated from the very barbarism from which Arnold had recoiled in horror. A sensitive taste cannot be acquired "by torturing appreciations into conformity with the judgments of others, no matter how 'authoritative' those judgments may be. Such a method means a hypnotization of judgment, not a true development of soul."

Fundamental to Arnold's notion, Bourne wrote, was the implication that if one learns to appreciate the best, he will discriminate generally. This, he contended, was the reverse of the psychological process, because a true appreciation of the magnificent was obtained when the judgment had learned to discriminate accurately and tastefully between the good and bad, sincere and false, of the familiar and contemporaneous art and writing of every day. To set up an alien standard of the classics was merely to give lazy taste a respite and to prevent genuine culture.

The principle of authority had been ousted from religion and politics, only to take refuge in culture. A consequence was the growth of the "tyranny of the 'best' " to which the people had been disciplined. This tyranny joined with cultural humility to prevent the United States from producing a true indigenous culture. America of course needed to be fertilized by other civilizations, but the situation was so out of hand that native genius was strangled wherever it appeared. The artist was compelled to win foreign approval before he could feel he had accomplished anything. Much of the source of the trouble was America's inability or unwillingness to judge him.

As a remedy he suggested a new kind of nationalism which would result in a keen introspection of the beauty in America and produced by America. Cultural chauvinism, Randolph maintained, was the most harmless of patriotisms; in fact, it was absolutely necessary for the growth of civilization. Exhibitions like the recent Amory art show would not be welcomed in another country because of the way it inspired "groveling humility." Such imitation was unjustified. Neither contemporary American genius nor that of the last half of the 19th century was so barren as some claimed. One would have to go far, according to Bourne, to find men of greater talents than those of Whitman as a poet, William James as a philosopher, Emerson and Thoreau as essayists, MacDowell as a composer of music, Saint-Gaudens as a sculptor. In any other nation such men would be honored. Interest would center on them as symbols of a national spirit around which judgments and tastes would revolve.[11]

In the accomplishments of such men Bourne saw a justifiable and practical way of focusing attention on the genius and individuality which America would recognize if it but looked.

"To come to an intense self-consciousness of these qualities, to feel them in the work of these masters and to search for them everywhere among the lesser artists and thinkers who are trying to express the soul of this hot chaos of America—this will be the attainment of culture for us. Not to look on ravished while our marvelous millionaires fill our museums with 'old masters,' armor, and porcelains, but to turn our eyes upon our own genius, and cultivate with an intense and partial pride what we have already achieved against the obstacles of our cultural humility. Only thus shall we conserve the American spirit and saturate the next generation with those qualities which are our strength.

Only thus can we take our rightful place among the cultures of the world to which we are entitled if we would but recognize it.

"We shall never be able to perpetrate our ideals except in the form of art and literature; the world will never understand our spirit except in terms of art. When shall we learn that 'culture,' like the kingdom of heaven, lies within us, in the heart of our national soul, and not in foreign galleries and books? When shall we learn to be proud? For only pride is creative." [12]

Preoccupation with the tyranny of the best was continual, and he naturally returned to the question when he became involved with education. At the time of the essay on cultural humility in 1914 the highly self-centered culture he had loved in France was fresh in memory, and Randolph was charged with enthusiasm about the potential of national culture. Later it occurred to him that American education was intimately connected with what he now called the "cult of the best."

In an essay occasioned by a request of the American Federation of Arts that the Carnegie Foundation investigate the teaching of art in the United States, he remarked that little had been thought about the implications of the extensive expansion of libraries, museums, and publishing. Using art training as a particular example, he said America must clarify what a genuine education in art means and then learn whether current method produced it.[13]

Characteristic of a Deweyite viewpoint, he asserted that artistic appreciation had come to mean a familiarity with the "good" works of art, that is, an historical approach, rather than the cultivating of spontaneous taste. Again he insisted that art now meant acquisition of accepted ideas or of art objects themselves. "Culture," he complained, "has come to mean the jacking-up of one's appreciations a notch at a time until they have reached a certain standard level. To be cultured has meant to like masterpieces."

This orthodoxy had produced a formidable canon which was actually a branch of moral education: a striving after righteousness had been identified with art. Reverence of classics had replaced criticism. The historical and the encyclopedic had crowded out the utilitarian and the aesthetic. The dogma was "unpleasantly undemocratic." Randolph never denied "the superlative beauty of what has come to be officially labelled 'the best that has been thought and done [sic: Arnold wrote "said"] in the world.' " But he objected to making that the universal norm, "for if you educate people in this way," he stressed, "you only really educate those whose tastes run to the classics. You leave the rest of the world floundering in a fog of cant, largely unconscious perhaps, trying sincerely to squeeze their appreciations through the needle's eye. You get as a result hypocrites or 'lowbrows,' with culture reserved only for a few. All the rest of us are left without guides, without encouragement, and tainted with original sin."

Education was valueless, Bourne asserted, if it did not devote itself to clarifying and integrating natural taste. The emphasis must always be on what one likes, not on what one "ought" to like. Education never had developed a test, he remarked, of whether bad taste was a positive thing or merely a lack of artistic consciousness. This was largely because of the Arnold dogma which thwarted the development in America of distinctive style and an indigenous spirit in art. If one is trained to like the "best" then one is unprepared to discriminate between the significant and the irrelevant which every day experience produces.

The Arnold approach was injurious, he maintained, because it forced and predetermined one's emotions about art. Civilized life was one aesthetic challenge after another and no training was worth anything unless one could react to forms and settings. "To have learned to appreciate a Mantegna and a Japanese print, and Dante and Debussy, and not to have learned nausea at Main Street, means an art education which is not merely worthless but destructive." Bourne argued that the mere callousness with which Americans confronted ragbag city streets proved the futility of the Arnold ideal.

It was no longer valid to state that American art had had to fight so hard to accomplish what it already had. Culture had been bogged down too long by preoccupation with what one ought to like. The Arnold cult had attracted those whose taste coincided with the canons, but it "perverted a much larger host who have tried to pretend that their taste coincided. And it has left untouched the joyous masses who might easily, as in other countries, have evolved folk culture if they had not been outlawed by this ideal."

One would not harp, he said, except that the ideal still prevailed and was responsible for filling America with ugliness and for choking off much creativeness. Understandably, Randolph protested because the social aspect of art had suffered: art to most meant painting instead of decoration, design, and social setting all of which are significant to daily life. "Our moral sense has made us mad for artistic 'rightness.' What we have got out of it is something worse than imitation. It is worship."

He granted that arbiters of art, if they worked outside the Arnold ethic, might well come to agree with Arnold as to what was best. That would be the result of discovering their own tastes, instead of taste's being imposed from above. Imposition was wrong because the approach closed off corridors which led in newer and perhaps rewarding directions. Yet while Bourne frequently touched on this idea it never was made clear just how taste would develop spontaneously. Presumably if one took the raw man, he would develop tastes and modes to suit himself as had the caveman painter.

This attack could not change the fact that there was a body of art to which intelligent, educated men attributed timeless merits. Bourne always had believed that to make something out of the world and of the world one must deal with it as it is, not as one would have it. A fact of life, as Arnold put it, was that life is short, art is long, and poor information is abundant; the critic must do a great deal of sifting for other people. Arnold did not conclusively show the merit of his "best" notion. But it was not discredited by Randolph, although he made a good case against it on practical grounds. It should be re-emphasized that he did not denounce the great work Arnold identified as culture. Rather, the assertion was that the cult of the best had a pernicious effect on contemporary culture because it closed the minds of the public and stymied the artist. The way this contention is most significant is in an historical context, for it was part of the rebellion against the genteel tradition.

Bourne was too close to events to see their full implications. He was right that the Arnold canon coincided with an age which had more buying power than ever. But he did not recognize—as could later observers—that Arnold's popularity in America stemmed from a deep-seated discontent over the lack of a critical center. Moreover, intimacy with Britain was not mere slavishness. There was an ineradicable kinship of language, culture, and interest. He and his contemporaries sent Arnold into a temporary eclipse whose effect was good for encouraging American culture. After World War I Arnold re-emerged in academic and non-academic circles as a hero. He had been, as Lafcadio Hearn said, a classical spirit in the middle of the romantic movement, a living point of departure to whom men turned for leadership.[14]

In this connection one might conclude that Randolph sold Arnold short, instead of using him to best advantage. For Arnold in his time —like Bourne later— reacted against what he felt was the bastardization of culture. In fact a reading of Arnold's *Culture and Anarchy*

(1869) shows how strikingly close the two were. Of two forces which Arnold identified in history, Hebraism (strictness of conscience), and Hellenism (spontaneity of consciousness), Arnold embraced the latter. Moreover, he rejected the notion of culture reaching down to the level of inferior classes. "It seeks to do away with classes," he declared.

Bourne rebelled against the Arnold ethic not solely because of the conscious break his era was making from the genteel tradition. It also was because those ideas were indelibly connected with notions of God and universal moral verities. It was the same kind of reaction Bourne had to John A. Ryan's *Distributive Justice* (1915), a work which expressed Randolph's own sentiments concerning economic and social justice and reform better than he ever did. But Father Ryan's work, praised widely by radicals, was posited on natural law, and that was anathema to Bourne.

On one thing, certainly, he and Arnold would not have quarreled: the role of the teacher as guide of artistic sensitivity among youth. Randolph's teacher was expected to battle the established order. Cultural education which was comprised of marching around museums in high school years was misdirected, he believed. Just as he had lauded Caroline Pratt's Play School (later the City and Country School in New York City) for setting pupils to difficult but not unreasonable tasks during the elementary years, so he thought it was in these years that artistic expression and selection should be the basis of art education. "It is a question of emphasis," he believed, "of making the teacher see that the constant challenge to taste is one of the most important functions of the school."[15]

If the student grew up without even hints as to what was "good" or "bad" he could—over a period of sampling and comparing—develop discrimination. The teacher would have to throw out the older processes which demanded a sureness on the student's part in guessing what the teacher wanted. A result would be that expression and criticism would "play into each other's hand," that is, the pupil would learn to react intelligently to the stimuli around him.

Even if one granted that the canons were right, he said, one would need hosts of teachers who were atuned to the "best" themselves. Yet that was unrealistic. Experience showed that there never would be enough Matthew Arnolds to go around. Moreover, most teachers repeated what someone told them was the best. The teacher need not be mentor. He could be a guide, a provocateur. Instead of the ability to impart judgments to students, the teacher needed the sensitivity to react to and direct the pupil's inclinations, always asking what he liked, why, and how it compared with something else he liked.

The teacher, Bourne maintained, need only provide the paraphernalia of art, the materials and processes, for the student to do his own work. If the teacher was of sound taste he could criticize and aid the student. But if he were not, he at least would be prevented from hypocrisising the student's taste. "If this attitude became general in our aesthetic education," he said, "it would not be long before the results became noticeable. We should get a variety of tastes—some of them traditional, some of them strange and new, but most of them at least spontaneous, indigenous. At present we have no way of knowing whether any particular manifestation of public taste is conventional, fashion-induced, imitative, or sincerely felt. Much spontaneous taste might turn out to be traditional. The majority of children trained in discrimination might prove to be incipient Brahmins. On the other hand we might get strange and vigorous expressions like the contemporary architecture and sculpture of Germany . . . . Out of an education in taste will grow creative art as a flower from rich soil."

Bourne was not exclusively or even predominantly preoccupied with the academic aspect of evolving American culture. His interest centered on practical applications of ideas to society. Architecture was one example of that interest. After inspecting model building projects Bourne had written from London, "Architecture, commercial art, landscape gardening . . . I am almost ready to believe . . . the king of the arts because of [their]completely social nature . . . ."[16]

So much of America was ugly to him because it was impractical and ill-conceived. He had been impressed in Germany and elsewhere by the way Europeans built towns, streets, and squares rather than the careless collection of houses, shops, and churches which gave so many American communities a frowsy appearance. The old world antithesis of America's "chaotic savagery" had implications of meaningful social life and activity and expressed the attitudes of spirit of the people. But, "To say that the American city in its design and style represented our spiritual capacity would be almost to say that we were a nation of madmen."[17]

In Europe, he wrote, town-planning had gone hand-in hand with the alleviation of social ills, but that had not happened here. The result was ugliness and economic and human waste. Of all nations, the United States had not yet realized that well-planned cities meant financial benefits. Her cities were so bankrupt, Bourne claimed, that any scheme to reverse the situation might seem like wild utopianism.

The obstacles were depressing. With rare exceptions architects were indifferent and insensitive to America's needs.[18] And private interests were unlikely to understand the need for town-planning until they realized that "stagnant pools of obsolescent buildings" created moribund land values, and resulted in more costly future means of correcting wrongs. Private interests had to understand that a city was organic; that it was a matter of right relations between its parts and its functions; that ugliness and disharmony of purpose and buildings were a cause of depreciation.[19]

City planning, or rather its failure, he felt, was a specific example of how earlier individualism needed to be junked, and the power of the state used. "The time will perhaps come when the common sense of the community and the courts will consider standards of beauty worthy to rank with those of safety, health and morals, in whose interest the police power is at present exercised." Who knows? Randolph asked, eventually ugliness and dilapidation may seem as much a violation of social well-being and decency as offenses now outlawed.[20]

Even before returning from Europe he published a study championing continental efforts at intelligent city design, using as a prime example Hemstead Garden Suburb, near London. He called it the "practical application of private socialism" and described how designers clustered living quarters together, thereby allowing generous green areas for recreation, beauty, rest, and reducing the number of space-wasting streets. The idea has since been heartily accepted, if not so heartily implemented, but Randolph was ahead of his time—not its needs, only its sentiments. If he was not heeded it was not for want of an understanding of the crux of the matter: "We cannot afford, in this twentieth century, to let men inflict their own depraved artistic taste upon the community, any more than we can afford to let them give expression to their debased moral sense."[21]

If the relatively small body of commentary on architecture and city planning did not stir his contemporaries, his literary criticism did. Indeed, one history of American literature declares that while John Macy with his *The Spirit of American Literature* (1913) signalized the demand for a new link between literary and social criticism, it was Bourne "who became to rebellious youth, the clear-minded leader and critic, then after his death the canonized saint."[22]

One of the earliest signs of a maturing literature is the appearance of literary critics in force, and Bourne was representative of that trend. Literature to him was another vehicle of liberation from the past, as well as a way to examine man's soul and heart. As later explained in detail,[23] he had become a cultural revolutionist upon discovering that fashionable literature was oblivious to modern society and problems. Previously literature and art in America had shamefacedly disguised passion and emotion. Sex-taboo was really art taboo, and "a bare-legged dancer, jumping into the America of 1900 would have caused a moral panic. Our growing up was in an atmosphere that was afraid of personal and esthetic expressiveness unless it was carefully justified and decently clothed. We scarcely realize how vividly the interests of to-day record the immense loosening-up of that stiff old America which so long had the manners of a maiden aunt.[24]

What Randolph and the generation of 1915 shared was protest against their elders—particularly humanism as represented by Paul Elmer More, Stuart Sherman, Irving Babbitt, and Paul Shorey—rather than a common aesthetic philosophy. How wide was the breach is demonstrated by what Ellery Sedgwick, editor of *Atlantic,* told him in 1917: "I will look up Van Wyck Brooks, of whom you speak. I am sorry to say I do not know him nor his work."[25]

The age—as Sinclair Lewis later recalled in his Nobel Prize acceptance speech—was determined "to give to the America that has mountains and endless prairies, enormous cities and lost far cabins, billions of money and tons of faith, to an America that is as strange as Russia and as complex as China, a literature worthy of her vastness." To Randolph this commitment involved maintaining a conscious hostile attitude toward what he called the "dessert theory" of culture,[26] and a constant examination of the social implications of literature. In these years two important critical positions were evolving. One was the aesthetic viewpoint which stressed art and whose early stalwarts were Pound and T. S. Eliot. The other was the social criticism of Brooks and Bourne.[27] Bourne shared the conviction of the radicals that literary criticism was impelled to become social criticism because the future of American literature depended on the reconstruction of social life. In fact, he even expounded a theory of sociological fiction.

In reviewing Upton Sinclair's *King Coal,* he contended that one must judge the sociological novelist by standards of sociological pertinency rather than literary art. In sociological fiction, went the argument, one never looks for the subleties of personal life or for the living and breathing persons the good novelist portrays. The difference was that the sociological writer uses people only as bricks in his institutional edifice. "It is," he remarked, "the family, church, industry, that the story is really about. It is the institution that is the hero or the villain, and the institution either in process of reformation or in shrieking need of it. Where the literary artist would let the institution and its 'message' play insistently out of the palpitating life of the individuals, caught in the struggle with it and busy with a thousand personal desires and adjustments, the sociological novelist sharply isolates institutional consciousness and denies his people thoughts and feelings that do not contribute directly to the missionary effect he wants to produce." [28]

But he by no means denigrated craftsmanship: Zola's work, for example, still lived not just because of a meticulous handling of institutions, but because of a great feeling for personal life. Americans, Randolph said, were not so gifted and as many a novel was ground out according to a formula, one could only ask whether its sociology was sound and true and its message urgent. Such stories "should not pretend to be more than a movie transcription of life. It is sociological observation 'filmed.' There is no claim to artistic value, and we do not ask for any. All we say is, Does the novel make visible conditions as they are and as they ought to be speedily altered?" [29]

It is not surprising, then, that there was praise for Theodore Dreiser, who, it was admitted, was a clumsy writer. The point was that Dreiser more than any other American writer had felt the "subterranean current" of life in America, and had done more than any other writer to smash taboos, and bring problems out in the open. The chaos in the souls of Dreiser's characters, Bourne implied, represented the chaos in America's soul, not to mention in Dreiser's own soul.[30] Dreiser moved Randolph because he found in him a groping effort to express the America that was growing, although the former's unhappy flaw was to have the artist's vision without the sureness of the artist's technique.[31]

Although esteem for several foreign writers—among them realists like Gorky and Dostoevski—exceeded admiration for current American writers, he nevertheless praised much of the work of Willa Cather, Vachel Lindsay, even some of holdovers from an earlier day like George Washington Cable and Hamlin Garland. Occasionally a travesty made him cranky. Of one unfortunate effort he stated that the author "fills her pages with so much vulgarity that I may perhaps be permitted the vulgarity of saying that at this perfectly obvious trickery I felt exactly as if my pursuit of the sincere and convincing in American fiction had been met by an unusually impudent thumbing of the nose. Her glaring deficiencies of taste spoil one book after another." [32]

While Bourne was far more sanguine about the future of American literature than the above passage suggests, he nevertheless saw major blocks to its maturing. In an essay written in 1918 he chided Mencken, whose work he disliked, for what was called the naive discovery that the artist in America had to struggle with the mob. Mencken made literary art sound like vulgarity and Mencken deserved the strictures by Stuart Sherman about him. Assailing philistine and puritan elements in American society was becoming overdone, he suggested. "Let us look for the enemy of the literary artist in America today," Bourne advised, "not among the animal obsessed novelists or the dainty professors who make Mr. Mencken profane. The real enemy is still the genteel tradition which tends to smother the timid experiments of a younger generation that is not satisfied with the husks." [33]

The American writer, moreover, was in danger because the public, always taking on the trappings of gentility, tended to be too hospitable. The public tended to be a confusing force, undiscriminating in approval and eager to have the new without the disturbing. The vogue of the little theatres and magazines demonstrated the public's almost pathetic receptiveness to anything pretending to literary art. But where was the criticism, he asked, to distinguish the fresh, sincere, and creative from the merely stagy and blatantly rebellious? A new criticism had to be created to meet not only the work of new artists, but also what he said he feared was the threat of a new orthodoxy, that is, a new way of paralyzing creativity.

The task was to get intelligent, pertinent, and contemporaneous criticism which would be both encouraging and severe; which would protect young prophets from seduction by glamor and social patronage. He said he personally was acquiring an almost Stendhalian horror of contemporary middle class correctness. Society, whether the mob or the cultivated dinner-party set, was the deadly enemy of the writer. The potential for treachery was doubly worse because "timidity is still the reigning vice of the American intellect, and the terrorism of 'good taste' is yet more deadly to the creation of literary art than is sheer barbarism. The literary artist needs protection from the liberal audience that will accept him though he shock them, but that will subtly tame him even while they appreciate. If this literary promise does not fulfill itself, it will be because our younger writers have pleased a public too easy to please. As we look around at those who have ideas, our proper mood is not pleasure that their work is so good, but discontent that it is not better." [34]

It is possible that if Randolph had lived, his attention would have turned predominantly to literary criticism and perhaps even to fiction writing on his own. It cannot be known what critical approach would have been taken, although it may be that there would have been a discouragingly small audience in the 1920's for a sociological approach to literature. That this is by no means sure is pointed up by a long essay written in 1930 by the distinguished editor of the *Bookman.* In attacking him and other anti-humanists like Brooks, Seward Collins observed that "while Mencken's kind of criticism is dying as the force of his own writing and the audience for it diminish, the work of Randolph Bourne and Van Wyck Brooks still seems able to attract new disciples, and their views might be said to be in the ascendency in this country just now." [35]

Had Bourne continued as a literary critic, he may have confronted and perhaps solved some of the conflicts which both a sympathetic and an unfriendly observer could see in his outlook. In his essay "The History of a Literary Radical" and often elsewhere he declared that an American had to strive to interpret and portray the life he knew, a safe enough assertion. Then in an apparently clear remark he declared the American could not be international in the sense that anything but the life in which he is saturated, with its questions and its colors, could be material for his art.

Here and frequently elsewhere—in his reaction to the Arnold dogma and in his enthusiasm for American culture—Bourne was straining. He may have approached the growth of American culture from the wrong side: it is questionable whether a nation produces great art by being intentionally nationalistic. As Morris Cohen asked in his *American Thought: A Critical Sketch,* Why must American art be fundamentally different from other art so that the presumption would arise that nothing European could respond to American needs? Can there not be elements, Cohen wondered, which are as universal in appeal as the elements of science? Bach, Mozart, Beethoven did not try to be German, nor Rossini or Verdi Italian. They regarded their work as quite independent of non-artistic considerations. Bourne probably would have replied that the viewpoint of Bach and other masters was no longer possible or desirable in the 20th century.

Eventually Randolph would have been obligated to face the issue of the validity of his sociological criticism—particularly when it became clear what the Soviets and Nazis did to art. The artist, of course, is concerned with the perfection of his work, with the object of his work. But Bourne would have conceded that the artist is a man before he is an artist. In college he had assailed the notion of the then widely known critic Joel Spingarn, a Columbia professor,[36] that art was merely expression, and expression was art. This notion, it was asserted, was wrong because it allowed for all kinds of monstrosities, destroyed barriers between the excellent and poor, and, worst of all, made man, not beauty, the center of art. In other words, Bourne was more orthodox than not in what he thought art was, but untraditional in what he believed should be the subject matter of art.

His sociological approach arose of course in reaction to the 19th century excess of the theory of art for art's sake. It also stemmed from evils attributed to the Puritan heritage. At this remove Puritanism does not seem so awesome. Mid-century Americans see the Puritan limitations which he saw, but they also see Puritanism's lingering into the 20th century as testimony of the dignity of the individual and his duty to achieve both spiritual and material prosperity.[37]

Later Randolph may have become equally dissatisfied with putting social values first in art. For, as Jacques Maritain has written,[38] to do so converts the social impact of a work into an aesthetic value. The good becomes not that of the work—an artistic good—but of human life, an equally, indeed, greater goal, but not strictly the mission of art. That is, the artist comes to feel that his product must be ruled and shaped and created not in regard to creative intuition or ability, but with regard to some social requirement. The result is that judgment is not on artistic grounds, but on the emotions, purposes, or interests of a moral or social order. These are the implications of Bourne's notion. Whether they would have been pursued and whether or how they would have been resolved remains in the realm of conjecture.

If Malcolm Cowley is right when he states in *After the Genteel Tradition* that the real war against the traditional in letters was fought in the decade before 1920, then Bourne must be credited with much of whatever gain the generation of 1915 made.

The young never lost his favor. Indeed, he persisted to his death in considering himself part of youth. He probably was well aware that although his conception of the role of youth happily coincided with wide felt sentiment of the day, it easily could be overdone. Although the European war strengthened a concern with the youth movement—that is, the general revolt in Western nations of those in their teens, twenties, and thirties against the established order—it was not until 1916 that there was a return to the theme. The ideas were incorporated in a program adopted from William James.

In his essay, "A Moral Equivalent for Universal Military Service," youth was warned that it would have to be more creative than it had been if it were to defeat the militaristic trend represented by widespread discussion of preparedness. Americans were experiencing a genuine craving for service, but the drive needed orientation. As youth clearly was keyed up, but as the nation was not at war, its energy was being wasted. What Randolph proposed compares with the Civil Conservation Corps and the Peace Corps. He suggested an army of youth warring against nature, not against men, "finding in drudgery and toil and danger the values that war and preparation for war had given." [40]

When James proposed the idea in 1910, he said it was considered too utopian. In 1916, however, universal service no longer was only preparation for war; it was recognized as a form of education. Therefore the logical step was to construct universal service on a strict educational foundation. Such a system would not need a colossal national oganization to effect it, for one already existed in the form of the school system. Americans demanded fruitful returns from their education and this was a chance for all to benefit. Whereas military service used only the physically best men, the moral equivalent would employ almost all men and women. Suppose the state said, Bourne theorized, that "All children should remain in school till the age of sixteen years. Between the ages of sixteen and twenty-one they shall spend two years in national service. This service shall be organized and administered by the state educational administrations, but supervised and subsidized by the national government. The service would be performed as national service, but its work would be constructive and communal in its purposes and not military. Special military training could be given as a branch of this service to those who were best fitted for it. But defense would be but an incident in our constructive life, and not the sinew of our effort."

He envisioned an army of youth doing work like the Peace Corps both in town and country—helping to erase uglines in America, to check waste of human and physical resources, and, as it moved about in its work, learning America. But, "if our service is to be universal, it cannot be mere unskilled labor in mines and farms and forests . . . . What we need is a service which shall not so much do the old work of the world as create new demands and satisfy them. This national service could do the things which need to be done, but which are now being done. It could have for its aim the improvement of the quality of our living. Our appalling slovenliness, the ignorance of great masses in city and country as to the elementary technique of daily life—this should be the enemy of the army of youth."

This was a greater heroism and self-sacrifice than valor in battle, Randolph implied. America must prevent the energies of its youth from being squandered in defense and drudgery. The need was to learn to live, not die; to be teachers and creators, not destroyers; inventors and pioneers. The need was to inspire in youth what Bourne had once called the "divine madness" [41] of the peasants who dragged the stones used in the cathedral at Chartres.

Implicitly, too, the moral equivalent was aimed at what he recently had termed the smugness and easiness of middle class radicalism. The middle class radical somehow got the notion he was living dangerously. The fact was that he had hardly soiled the hands or taxed the brain. "The young radical today is not asked to be a martyr, but he is asked to be a thinker, an intellectual leader. So far as the official radicals deprecate such an enterprise they make their movement sterile." [42]

The moral equivalent was meant as a solution to what he considered the turgid condition of the middle class radical. But the idea did not catch on and was dropped. Perhaps the plan did not confront the preparedness enthusiasm in time; perhaps what it called for the federal government to do was too far ahead of the times.

The America across which Bourne would have sent an army of youth; for which he wanted an indigenous, pertinent literature; the America whose architecture and communities could be magnificent; the land whose citizens could be trained and inspired to discover ways other than the traditional for artistic enjoyment and expression, that nation was in danger, he contended in 1916, of destroying whatever harmony existed among the peoples who had come to its shores.

At the time that he expressed his moral equivalent, he was noting that the country's reaction to the European war had shown the failure of the melting pot theory. Indeed, much of the nation was shocked to find diverse nationalistic feelings among the inhabitants who were born abroad. Paradoxically, he observed, the more immigrants became established, the more they cultivated the traditions of their homelands. [43]

To face the fact was neither to admit that Americanization had failed, nor that democracy had failed. What it meant was to re-examine what Americanism may rightly mean. Moreover, it meant asking whether the ideal had been too narrow and whether it was time to assert an ideal higher than the melting pot. The United States had acted as if Americanization were to take place without the consent of the governed, but it inevitably had to be what the immigrant would have a hand in making it. An ignorant recent arrival was not to have the role of a long-established New Englander, but he was raw material for the future.

One would realize on reflection, Randolph contended, that perhaps no group has had as fierce an allegiance to the homeland as the Anglo-Saxon stock. But because the ruling class created the copious and scornful epithets, there had been no designation of English-American. The Anglo-Saxon needed to ask himself where he would be had the nationalities not come to America. Would he prefer to be as the "superior" South was, little touched by immigrants, or like the great "alien" states of Wisconsin and Minnesota?

The truth, it was argued, was that foreign cultures had not been melted down. They remained distinct but cooperating. What the nation emphatically should not want was that distinctive qualities should wash into tasteless, colorless uniformity. The United States already had too much such "insipidity," he felt: masses who are cultural half-breeds, neither assimilated Anglo-Saxons nor nationals of another culture.

"Just so surely," he warned, "as we tend to disintegrate these nuclei of nationalistic culture do we tend to create hordes of men and women without a spiritual country, cultural outlaws, without taste, without standards but those of the mob. We sentence them to live on the most rudimentary planes of American life. And just because the foreign-born retains this expressiveness is he likely to be a better citizen of the American community. The influences at the fringe, however, are centrifugal, anarchical. They make for detached fragments of peoples. Those who do not find liberty achieve only license. They become the flotsam and jetsam of American life, the downward undertow of our civilization with its leering cheapness and falseness of taste and spiritual outlook, the absence of mind and sincere feeling which we see in our slovenly towns, our vapid moving pictures, our popular novels, and the vacuous faces of the crowds on the city street. This is the cultural wreckage of our time, and it is from the fringes of the Anglo-Saxon as well as the other stocks that it falls."

America, Bourne said, was a unique sociological fabric. It was poverty of imagination not to be thrilled at the incalculable potentialities of so novel a union of men. Old nationalisms would breed the poison the world was witnessing in Europe, he predicted. Except perhaps for the South and New England—both of which were passing—there was no distinct national culture. The country's destiny was to be a federation of cultures. It was for America's ethnic colonies, deriving power from European culture and living in mutual toleration, free from ancient tangles of race, creed, and dynasties, to work out the federated land. Europe transplanted to America should be inextricably mingled, but not homogeneous; merged but not fused.

As long as the nation thought of Americanism in terms of the melting pot, its cultural tradition lay in the past, Randolph wrote. But if the melting pot had failed, the democratic experiment was by no means ended: it barely had begun. Tradition lay in the future. Cosmopolitan ideals would replace the thinly disguised panic which called itself patriotism. "In a world which has dreamed of internationalism, we find that we have all unawares been building up the first international nation . . . . America is already the world-federation in miniature, the continent where for the first time in history has been achieved that miracle of hope, the peaceful living side by side, with character substantially preserved, of the most heterogeneous peoples under the sun."

The United States was coming to be not a nationality, but a trans-nationality.[44] America should not begrudge dual spiritual and legal citizenship to its foreign-born. This was especially so because the war had shown America could not remain aloof and irresponsible. It had to work out a position of its own without being embroiled in the European world.

As a trans-nationality of all countries, it was spiritually impossible for the nation to pass into the orbit of any one nation, Randolph asserted. And it would be folly to hurry into a premature and sentimental nationalism, or to play carelessly with forces which can be inflamed easily, and drag one into war. America ran a good chance of becoming not "the modern cosmopolitan grouping that we desire, but a queer conglomeration of the prejudices of past generations, miraculously preserved here, after they have mercifully perished at home."[45]

The Anglo-Saxon effort to fuse nationalities would only create enmity and distrust. "The crusade against the 'hyphenates' will only inflame the partial patriotism of trans-nationals, and cause them to assert their European traditions in strident and unwholesome ways. But the attempt to weave a wholly novel international nation out of our chaotic America will liberate and harmonize the creative power of all these peoples and give them a new spiritual citizenship, as so many individuals have already been given, of a world."[46]

What Bourne would witness was not a building of the Beloved Community on a trans-national scale. Even before President Wilson asked for a declaration of war on the night of April 2, 1917, nativist prejudices against hyphenates were beginning to spill over, and the situation would get worse. The general progressive sentiment which his article had challenged in 1916 would culminate in the tight immigration laws of 1921 and 1924. Had he lived, he by then perhaps would have surrendered his aspirations for a trans-national America. The war swept away so many hopes which the generation of 1915 held for the future of American civilization. If Randolph could not agree entirely with the remark made by a depressed Gertrude Stein about the plans the war ruined—"The future is not important any more."—he was increasingly dubious about the future. Before war ended he would stand almost alone in articulate, wrathful denunciation of America's participation in the war. He would feel the desolation a man knows who judges himself sane, but thinks that almost all other men are both wrong and mad.[47]

"The intellectuals . . . have identified themselves with the least democratic forces in American life. They have assumed the leadership for war of those very classes whom the American democracy has been immemorially fighting. Only in a world where irony was dead could an intellectual class enter war at the head of such illiberal cohorts in the avowed cause of world-liberalism and world-democracy. No one is left to point out the undemocratic nature of this war-liberalism. In a time of faith, skepticism is the most intolerable of all insults." —Bourne, "The War and the Intellectuals," June '17

VIII

WAR: MENTAL UNPREPAREDNESS

In that crazy spring of 1917, wrote John Dos Passos in *Nineteen Nineteen,* Randolph Bourne "began to get unpopular where his bread was buttered at the *New Republic.*" The description is more colorful than accurate, but it is fittingly pungent. For the entry of the United States into World War I was for Bourne the beginning of his winter of discontent. April 1917 was the harbinger of a dark night of the soul. Later, those who sympathized with his position during the conflict would agree with Dos Passos that he "put a pebble in his sling and hit Goliath square in the forehead with it."

Given the feeling of the times, Randolph's position was a precarious one: neither pro-Entente, nor pro-German. He declined to believe Germany was the embodiment of Satan or that the war was one of right and wrong. To him it was a distant clash of cultures. Prior to American involvement much of his writing dealt with what the United States could do to keep its sanity. Then when the country entered the conflict, he believed it a duty to prevent the war from passing into mythology as a holy war.

If in April 1917 Bourne believed he saw events clearly, he was one of the few who did. Developments were confused. Since the resumption of submarine warfare by Germany on February 1, events had moved with what in retrospect seems a methodic certainty. Destruction of American shipping and the apparent futility of merely arming American vessels convinced President Woodrow Wilson that America's benevolent neutrality should be replaced by war with Germany. It was an agonizing ordeal. The nation obviously wanted peace, and Wilson clearly was willing to lose face personally; and, through restraint, risk the nation's losing prestige. As the historian Ernest R. May has written[1] "The struggle for peace ended in war. Reviewing its history, one has a sense that it could not have ended otherwise . . . . There was no way out. Triumph for the immoderates was only a matter of time."

The country since 1914 had been subjected to a barrage of sophisticated British propaganda (and generally inept German publicity), but the nation did not want war, despite the fact that in April 1917 sentiment favored Britain. The electric atmosphere in Congress favoring war the night of April 2 did not correspond to the general public feeling. There at first was no widespread enthusiasm for fighting, for any reason: only resignation.[2]

By mid fall 1917 whatever lethargy toward the conflict had existed the previous spring had been mostly converted to chauvinism. Whether Walter Millis is right when he says the progressive reformers at first were the most militant[3] or whether Henry F. May is correct when he writes that the earliest and most consistent supporters of the Allies were the beleaguered defenders of 19th century tradition[4] is not so important as the fact that the war spirit became feverish.

Americans had followed the President in neutrality because he seemed to protect their honor while keeping them out of war. When technical neutrality ended, the public was resigned to war because it believed Wilson had tried all decent alternatives. Generally, they felt intervention was a moral act and would result in good.[5]

Because belief in progress was so strong, it generally had been held by Americans that war among civilized nations was an anachronism.[6] This was why the people were attracted to a President who seemed to be a crusader for righteousness. Understandably, the war was justified in progressive rhetoric and in progressive terms.[7] To make the world safe for democracy and to achieve a peace without victory were fitting unselfish aims.

Such romanticizing and dramatizing of themselves by Americans took "unconsciously the form of a morality play." [8] As the New York *Globe* proclaimed: "If war comes it will be a holy and righteous one—a war on war, a war for peace, a war for a better world." [9] It was the story of a hero provoked to mortal combat. In the process the conscripted progressive, reform, and liberal spirit was badly mangled at war's end. War, many would be truly surprised to learn, was ugly.

As Harold Lasswell explained later,[10] war was a magnet which drew man's highest aspirations as well as his meanest frustrations and inclinations. Guilt and satanism were attributed to the enemy, while righteousness was monopolized by the allies. Wilson—superb propagandist—balanced an idealism which struck home to the hearts of well-meaning countrymen with a militancy geared to the reality of modern warfare.

In the spring of 1917 most Americans were too close to events to realize that the nation was rehearsing—incited especially by allegations of German atrocities—for a hate bath. Noncombatants often would be treated with barbarism, perhaps not surprising in that under the conditions of the time very few persons in the belligerent country were noncombatant.[11] As Ralph Barton Perry wrote in 1918, "You cannot expect to incite people to the emotional level at which they willingly give their lives or the lives of their sons, and at the same time have them view with cool magnanimity the indifference or obstructiveness of their neighbors." [12]

Perry, of course, was trying to explain, not excuse, the madness of 100% Americanism. Americans generally knew and understood the propaganda of political parties, but the expression of European rivalries was strange to them. British propaganda did not lure the United States into war, but it did stoke low-banked fires which later raged undisciplined. Issues were divided conveniently into black and white; when a person even remotely was identified with the forces of darkness, he suffered recriminations, as Randolph Bourne did, from the self-appointed forces of wisdom. It was this maelstrom which intruded on his life, tossing him, pounding him, sobering him, and finally spewing him out with war's wreckage, his career thwarted at least temporarily, and the future uncertain.

The sling shot is a lethal weapon, the more so when one attributes to it qualities and powers it does not have, as was done in World War I where Bourne and other dissenters were concerned. The most masterful book could not convincingly reproduce the war passion in the United States, 1917-18. Surely the mid-century American believes stories about the era are exaggerated and over dramatized—particularly by contemporary and later liberals sympathetic with conscientious objectors and with persons prosecuted under the Espionage and Sedition acts. Assertions made about the domestic war mood and behavior in the United States become credible when one turns to newspapers.

Compared to the treatment of news in World War I by even the best newspapers, the handling in mid-century by even mediocre newspapers of news concerning communism and the Soviet bloc resembles a model of fairness and truth seeking. Why and how furiously the war spirit consumed the United States (and what were the consequences) concerned Randolph Bourne personally, for he was grouped with those whom the *Wall Street Journal* meant when it warned, "We are now at war, and the militant pacifists are earnestly reminded that there is no shortage of hemp or lampposts." [13]

The war in 1914 surprised and depressed Randolph and his generation, but it did not immediately evoke the frenetic resistance found in his later writing. In the flood tide of neutrality, and reacting to the preparedness campaign, he told a friend, "I am still a determined pacifist, and look upon Roosevelt and the other preparednessers as madmen." [14] But while he would declare participation in the war to be evil, it shall be seen that he had a conception of pacifism which to him was unique, clear, logical, and practical.

Americans, he wrote early in 1915, in trying to learn who started the war, ignored the deeper factors. Governments can start wars, but must have behind them an intense animus like what he believed was the collective consciousness of each European nationality. The reason sentiment was so heavily pro-British was that the English did not talk in terms of national feeling but in terms of morality, a language easily grasped. Compared to Britain's propaganda approach, German discussion of *Kultur* seemed grotesque and fantastic.[15]

The truth, he asserted, was that all the warring nations really interpreted themselves just as the Germans did: national culture rather than morality. In not understanding this, the United States was exchanging its opportunity to judge the directing animus of the war for an easy, superficial explanation in terms of personal wickedness. "We have succumbed to the temptation of feeling holy," he wrote. "We have put our appreciation outside of certain deep currents of the destiny of western civilization. We are staggered at the emotional running-amuck of the German professors [in publicly supporting their government's war through statements and like means]; but what are we to say of our professors who exhibit an emotional shallowness and defective social psychology which are even less defensible?" [16]

What had happened was that interweaving and complex national cultures had grown up side by side in Europe, each land with its distinct national quality. The growth of education—plus unification and industrialism—had spread these national values more widely among classes than ever. As nations were brought by industrialism into sharp competition, he said, they realized the need to assert themselves. It had been assumed that improved communications of all kinds would break down national differences. Instead contact with different ways heightened each culture's realization and appreciation of itself and sharpened animosity toward alien culture.

Consequently—although business, machinery, technical methods, and dress became uniform in Europe—artistic styles, literary values, moral attitudes, thought habits, and even manners remained stubbornly national. "The objective, mechanical, impersonal side of civilization has been tending to uniformity. The subjective, spiritual, stylistic, valuational side has remained intensely diverse," Bourne wrote.

These clashing tendencies promised not doom but a more superb Europe, a kind of mutual society of national cultures, each possessing self-consciousness and a strongly-marked personality, but tolerating the others. The war from that viewpoint, Bourne argued, could be a vast liberating movement, clearing the way for a more conscious, intenser world. The 19th century had been a long travail, a groping toward self-consciousness.

"Old, long forgotten cultures like the Irish and the Bohemian," he observed, "have had a reawakening, and are insisting on asserting themselves. The war has thrown all these national cultures into the furnace. Each looks eagerly towards emerging magnified in the eyes of the world. The little cultures look forward, too, to their place in the sun. A great wave of consciousness seems to be sweeping the European world. . . .

"The argument is that this national feeling has not only provided the real animus of the war, but is also neither illusory nor deplorable. The Continental peoples are not deluded, but have hold of a reality. The tendencies which they are working out are exactly those which hold the brightest promise for a twentieth century Western civilization."

In German culture Randolph found values from which there was much to be learned, and which would help explain how the war occurred. A people can be warlike, autocratic, ruthless, and still be in the vanguard of socialized civilization, he remarked, meaning in particular Germany's advanced welfare legislation. Instead of blind hostility toward things in German life which were unacceptable to Americans, there should be a questioning whether and how Germany's militarism could be separated from its accomplishments, particularly in science.[17]

One had to remember that the Germany which produced militarists, also produced Goethe and Hauptmann. One had to try to imagine the discipline, self-cultivation, and self-expression which ressurrected Germany after the Napoleonic defeat. A people once so romantic, pietistic, and mystically ineffective had learned to love struggle; Germans believed only the "fit" survived; and when a people succeeded in the way the Germans had, one should not be surprised at the jealous reaction of enemies.

Germans had accepted the militaristic, rigid hierarchial organization of their life, based on unquestioning obedience: so saturated were they with its spirit that they did not feel oppressed, Bourne said. Trained to harness, the German moved easily because he fully understood the unwritten rules. Absence of freedom of speech in Germany did not seem worse to him than the way he said American society prevented critics of its ruling classes from protesting, that is, by hypocritically demanding that order be preserved.

To understand Germany, he maintained, one had to realize that the German did not revere personal freedom—or freedom *from*—the way Americans did. But although Germans were more closely tied to the state, they did not feel oppressed, nor were they necessarily less free. Graft and muckraking were not constant as in the United States where so many public officials were politically appointed instead of professional and serious. Yet for all the rules in German life, Germans did not seem meek or void of individuality. Out of a harsh, autocratic state had come major humanitarian benefits. Someday men would call on German civilization for an example of how science and art could be applied to man's problems.

"Personally," he declared "I love with a passionate love the ideals of social welfare, community sense, civic art, and applied science upon which it is founded itself. But I detest the crass bravado of militarism, its ruthless waste in international swagger of the energy and elan that should be used for internal discipline . . . But I detest still more the shabby and sordid aspect of American civilization—its frowsy towns, its unkept countryside, its waste of life and resources, its stodgy pools of poverty. And I want my country to prove to me that it can get all the good things of this German Kultur, its soaring art, its glory of science, and its communal sense without forcing upon itself a discipline and a set of delusions such as have caused the present tragedy."

Then in September 1915 in an essay of similar approach, the German's artistic and intellectual accomplishments were stressed instead of his social and technological progress. Randolph complained that the Anglo-Saxon world had slighted itself in not being more receptive to Germany's ways. Rejection so often was mere reflex action, he protested. Anglo-Saxon life may have been right in repudiating German ideals and accomplishments, it was admitted, but one should know what it meant when rejection occurred; renunciation could mean accepting the inferior.[18]

To denounce German civilization implied America's setting up ideals more worthy than Germany's. But little ideological help would come from Britain and France, both fighting to conserve rather than create. America's role should be to take over the German craft and direct it along efficacious currents. "Whatever the German has that is life-enhancing—and a nation that lives so habitually at a maximum of energy must have more than we—that we must have, but it must come as the fruit of our intense desire and our intelligence in adapting means to ends, not as an imposed historic value."

It is uncertain whether many of Bourne's readers were open to a dispassionate investigation of allegations made about German life and ideals or to consideration of what should be borrowed from German civilization. What is clear is that the European war greatly unsettled intellectuals of all postures—including Bourne—and many of them were either building anew or throwing up breastworks about their ideological domains. The contribution for most intellectuals to make, he suggested early in the war, was to understand war's human and social significance. "We want an analysis of the social and psychological influences that have produced the contrasting civilizations that now purport to be fighting each other."[19]

This remedy perhaps soon seemed pallid and ineffective. For by late summer 1915 the issue had been thought through to a broader assessment of why intellectuals had not meaningfully probed what the war meant to American life and values. The reason was that for all their sophistication, intellectuals were mentally unprepared. Now, a year after the initial shock, the younger generation was asking not how the world could be returned to its pre-war state, but what its outcome would do to their world, he said.[20]

It had been generally accepted, Randolph commented, that the 19th century had been looked on as predominantly benevolent in its progress, an age wherein inventors overshadowed statesmen, an age when industrial progress made for the advancement of social and political democracy. The trouble was that the drama was not resolved as predicted because the forces which had been considered the motivating factors were actually weaker than the traditional ones. An optimistic cosmopolitanism had encouraged one to forget that European states represented tight, integrated cultures with diverse history, group-wills and philosophies. One had gaily washed the colors out of maps, leaving only boundaries.

Moreover, an Anglo-Saxon standard for all had naively been postulated, partly on the presumption that social control would follow democracy. This viewpoint was greatly reinforced by confidence in international socialism; when war began one learned quickly that there were socialisms not Socialism. Even nationalism had been taken exclusively as a positive factor. No unpleasant consequences were seen in the unification of Germany and Italy. In short, one's background or what one thought was his background looked very different after a year of war, and the question was what to do about it.

"While the world is breathless," Bourne wrote, "we can try resolutely to reconstruct our shattered background, find out what kind of a world we live in. We should make the time one of education, and not of prophecy or objuration or bewailing. No one knows what will come. Certainly merely getting the war over will not bring back the old ideals. If we desire that new world where all can live, we must first thoroughly understand how all want to live."

A month later Randolph was both favorably impressed and worried by what seemed a shaking off of the calm moral grandeur revelled in a year before. On the surface it appeared to be a change for the better, but much of the "strange restlessness and discontent"—which Bourne felt had replaced lack of inspiration—expressed itself in a desire to be part of the war and in extolling military virtues. Already it was being asserted in America that warlessness was tame and ignoble; that war, not peace, was the reality.[21]

War, he replied, was real only in its caricature. It widely exaggerated passions and become a form of organized liberatinism or collective anarchy. Drilled, regimented, and obedient, a whole nation runs amuck. Its carnival of instinct was the apotheosis of small-boyism: one smashed towns instead of windows. The question always was what do with the peace. Randolph claimed that thus far the fortunes of war had favored Germany because of how superbly she had ordered her life during peace and for peace. German organization for war therefore became incomparably efficient. What the United States had done with its peace, he suggested, was as shallow as what he said Britain did with hers. But, "Our American unpreparedness for peace is the really sinister peril. The best preparation for war would be the most relentless attention to putting American industry, agriculture, education, politics upon the soundest and the most prosperous footing possible. If the war has taught us anything, it is that every movement that makes for the physical vigor of the people, for the education of children up to their capacities, for the cooperation of labor in industry, for the socialization of public utilities, for the conservation of country life, makes directly for preparedness for war. If we continue . . . to shudder at the foreign specter instead of making our peace life the realest thing in the world, we shall deserve all that is predicted by our professional prophets of disaster."

After April 1917, Bourne's *New Republic* commentary on the war was restricted to his book reviews. Whether or not he had continued writing major pieces on the war, it seems certain that he would have parted with Weyl, Croly, and Lippmann. Instead of calling the development a rupture or saying, as some have asserted, that he was locked out at the *New Republic,* the end of him after April 1917 as a major contributor should be considered as an agreement to disagree.

It is not that Randolph and the *New Republic* trio explicitly acknowledged the change as such. But although he in the future would be long on disagreement with the *New Republic* and on denunciation of its policies, there is no evidence that a personal animosity was the basis for the ideological antagonism. In other words, the notion the *New Republic*—for which he continued to write reviews until his death—somehow persecuted him is unsound.

The break is not complicated. Although the background is not pertinent here, it may be summed up by noting that *New Republic* editors had come to believe that war against Germany was imperative to protect not only America's present and future economic rights and needs, but those of the Atlantic community with which the United States had immense trade—trade which might be destroyed or hurt should Germany prevail. The *New Republic* editors believed that the country should follow a policy of "differential neutrality," which meant being sympathetic and favoring Britain, but with the intention of holding her accountable after the war.

Moreover, they generally came to feel that intellectuals and reformers were obligated to do what they could to see their ideals implemented. Lastly, Lippmann, Croly, and Weyl cherished the British political and cultural tradition and feared for its future.[22]

Confronting this viewpoint, as a *New Republic* editor later said, was an "intransigent" Bourne, and the result was a break, although the editor did not know why.[23] That an insoluble disagreement was near became evident in February 1917. Full page advertisements in the issues of February 10, 17, and March 3 and 31—signed usually by Randolph, Amos Pinchot, Max Eastman, and by a liberal figure of the day, Winthrop D. Lane—implored the public to pressure Congress to stay out of war. The advertisements were sponsored by the American Union Against Militarism, which later became under Roger Baldwin the National Civil Liberties Union. A full page ad also appeared in the New York *Times* and in other newspapers.

In addition to citing historical precedents for staying out of war, encouraging a postcard campaign, begging contributions, and declaring that the people had a right to vote in a referendum before going to war, the advertisements also cited contemporary factors which allegedly were pushing the nation toward the precipice. Wall Street, it was asserted, for example, had sold "2½ thousand million dollars" of war supplies to the Allies; because the Allies now made most of their own supplies, Wall Street needed a new market. Polls, the advertisements said, showed that the public wanted no war. Germany, it was correctly asserted, did not fear the United States militarily, and even if the nation never clashed in battle with Germany, a declaration of war could be disastrous economically.

The only thing Germany feared, the advertisements remarked, was losing America's friendship. War would mean losing the potential influence a neutral power had. War meant the people not only would pay for the war, but fight it. War would not vindicate the national honor, and should not necessarily result from diplomatic rupture, the appeals declared. Whether Randolph accepted all the assertions, his name was signed to them. Many of the points were ones the *New Republic* editors did not and could not support. The editors were tolerant of disagreement but did not believe the magazine obligated to devote precious editorial space to arguments which seemed clearly wrong—his or anyone else's.

At the same time the advertisements of the American Union Against Militarism were running in the *New Republic,* publicity also appeared there for the *Seven Arts,* which began publishing the previous November. The 5,000 buyers [24] of the *Seven Arts* were treated to one of the most exciting journals of the age. The list of its contributors reads today like a who's who of established and dawning major artists. In addition to the contributions of its editors—James Oppenheim, Waldo Frank, and Van Wyck Brooks—other writing appeared by Dos Passos; O'Neill; John Reed; Mencken; D. H. Lawrence; Paul Rosenfeld; Sherwood Anderson; Ernest Bloch; Marsden Hartley; Kahlil Gibran; Louis Untermeyer; Frost; Romain Rolland; Amy Lowell; Dewey; Bertrand Russell; Carl Van Vechten, and Floyd Dell.

Oppenheim had raised $50,000 to start the review[25] by convincing a bored woman of means, Annette K. Rankin, of the potential of a magazine dedicated mainly to encouraging national culture. Mrs. Rankin sold her collection of Whistlers and promised the editorial department that it would take no orders from the business office.

Mrs. Rankin—a neurotic, very tweedy woman of medium height with mousy hair—wore good English suits, walked in a straightforward way and "was not good looking, but obviously very gentle."[26] She was being treated by the psychiatrist Beatrice Hinkle and later, as shall be seen, would have second thoughts about not interfering with policy. Shortly after the magazine folded, she drowned herself.

Meantime, the *Seven Arts* was already established when in the spring of 1917, Randolph sat in its office on lower Madison Avenue talking with James Oppenheim. "I shall never forget," Oppenheim wrote, "how I had first to overcome my repugnance when I saw that child's body, the humped back, the longish, almost medieval face, with a sewed up mouth, and an ear gone awry. But he wore a cape, carried himself with an air, and then you listened to marvelous speech, often brilliant, holding you spellbound, and looked into blue eyes as young as a Spring dawn. His coming was the greatest thing that happened to the *Seven Arts*. . . ."[27]

Bourne, Oppenheim declared, was the "real leader, I take it, of what brains and creativeness we had at the time." He recalled that Randolph once told James that writing for the *New Republic* had been "institutionalized" and the *Seven Arts* had ungagged him. After chatting, Oppenheim asked him to write for *Seven Arts*. Bourne smiled and said: "You wouldn't allow me to say what I want." Replied James: "Try us."

Now Bourne had the opportunity to expand his personal war against United States participation in World War I. In the opinion of Waldo Frank, he played one of the key roles in the magazine's effort to influence American life. "We felt the war also was a cultural crisis which inevitably had a political dimension. We felt Bourne was our arm in the world of action," he later commented.[28] It was this writing, as shall be seen, which allegedly wrecked the *Seven Arts* in October 1917.

It was appropriate that his first war essay for the magazine was an attack on pro-war intellectuals, in particular the *New Republic* thinkers. "The War and the Intellectuals," which appeared in June 1917 set the tone for the rest of his writing on the war in both the *Seven Arts* and the *Dial*.[29] The mood was that of an enraged man whose contempt for the ideas of his adversaries was camouflaged by a restrained prose style which avoided personal attacks.

The inspiration for his first piece was supplied by "Who Willed American Participation?," an unsigned article in the April 17, 1917, *New Republic* in which it was stated:

"The effective and decisive work on behalf of war has been accomplished by . . . a class which must be comprehensively described as the intellectuals. . . ."

"For the first time in history a wholly independent nation has entered a great and costly war under the influence of ideas rather than immediate interest and without any expectation of gains, except those which can be shared with all liberal and inoffensive nations."

Bourne could hardly believe what he read.

To those who retained an "irreconcilable animus against war," he wrote, it was bitter to see the unanimity which intellectuals demonstrated in supporting war. The intellectuals had competed in riveting a war-mind on 100 million people; then they complacently asserted they willed war, and moved a sluggish people into a battle for high purposes. Irreconcilables wanted "to understand this willingness of the American intellectual to open the sluices and flood us with the sewage of the war spirit."[30]

It seemed to Randolph that the intellectual class did not try to clarify the ideals and aspirations of American democracy: they might have failed, of course, but they did not even try. The whole era, he protested, has been spiritually wasted; its outstanding feature had been not American but an intense colonialism to Britain. America might have been made a meeting ground for the different national attitudes. An intellectual class, cultural colonists of the different European nations, might have threshed out the issues here as they could not be threshed out in Europe. Instead of this, the English colonials in the university and press took command at the start, and we become an intellectual Hungary where thought was subject to an effective process of Magyarization."

Where, it was asked, did one get the idea of America's "moral spotlessness"? Were not the intellectuals fatuous when they said America's war was stainless and thrillingly doing good? Where good could have been done, he believed, was in using the bargaining power the United States had as a great neutral, but this was not done. America's war followed, as did all wars, a monstrous diplomatic failure. The effort for peace was little more than a "polite play."

Bourne was suspicious, as he had been before,[31] of the optimism of many intellectuals for a league of nations which would enforce peace. If the United States had been sincere in thinking her participation in such a league might attain international good, would not the country have made entry into war conditional on a solemn general agreement to respect in the final settlement principles of international order and justice? Could the nation have afforded, if its war was to end war by establishing a league of honor, to risk defeat of its vision and betrayal in the settlement? Yet, America was at war, and no such agreement was made or suggested. "The case of the intellectual seems, therefore, only very speciously rational. They could have used their energy to force a just peace or at least to devise other means than war for carrying through American policy. They could have used their intellectual energy to ensure that our participation in the war meant the international order which they wish. Intellect was not so used. It was used to lead an apathetic nation into an irresponsible war, without guarantees from those belligerents whose cause we were saving. The American intellectual, therefore, has been rational neither in his hindsight nor his foresight." [32]

After analyzing the mind of the pro-war intellectual in what can be called a highly condensed version of Lasswell's later version of the war mentality, Randolph remarked that a realist thought he at least could control events by linking himself to them. Perhaps the realist could, but when it came to controlling war it was difficult to see how the child on the back of an elephant was more effective in stopping the beast than he who tried to halt him from the ground. In other words, American intellectuals manufactured consolations for themselves. Any guiding done by intellectuals would merely be in deciding "whether they shall go over the right-hand or left-hand side of the precipice."

The problem was that if intellectuals obstruct, they would surrender all power for influence. If one responsibly approved the war, one would retain power to guide and would be listened to as a responsible thinker, while those who obstructed would commit intellectual suicide. But criticism would be accepted by the ruling powers only from those intellectuals who sympathized with the general tendencies of the war.

Was there no solution, Bourne wondered, for the intellectual whose ideas were not yet, clear, who was patient, and who was not fatigued? It was an important question, he believed, for intellectuals had forgotten that the real enemy was not Germany but war. There was work to be done. It was imperative "to prevent this war of ours from passing into popular mythology as a holy crusade. What shall we do with leaders who tell us that we go to war in moral spotlessness or who make 'democracy' synonymous with a republican form of government? There is work to be done in still shouting that all the revolutionary by-products will not justify war or make war anything else than the most noxious complex of all the evils that afflict men. There must be some to find no consolation whatever, and some to sneer at those who buy the cheap emotion of sacrifice. There must be some irreconcilables left who will not even accept the war with walrus tears."[33]

"You may remember that you lost your head in 1917, and you are intellectually ashamed; but you take comfort from the assurance that practically every one else did also. Randolph Bourne did not lose his head. He kept detached, he kept alert, he kept bitter when we were a herd, when we seemed drugged, when we were all sweet complacency. What we say now without being either brave or original he said then, not, perhaps, with the maturity of a Bertrand Russell or a Romain Rolland, but at least with fine courage and imagination. It may turn out that the cleanest picture of ourselves when we were not ourselves is here in these . . . pages."
—*Nation,* 4-17-20, review of *Untimely Papers.*

IX

WAR: THE ARTS ARE BUT SIX

Before the summer of 1917 was over, Bourne was saying that the intellectuals had been betrayed even before America had had much impact on the military outcome. In an August 1917 *Seven Arts* essay, "The Collapse of American Strategy," he contended that in getting organized to fight, public opinion had forgotten what had been the basis for participation in the first place.

American democracy, it was noted, had consented to war because it believed certain definite international ideals were at stake. The meeting of aggression was the immediate pretext, but intellectuals had supported the war with the hope that an international order would prevent war ever again. It was almost wholly on that ground that intellectuals justified themselves, Randolph said. Justification and strategy alike were inseparably linked to ideals. "It was implicit in their position," he wrote, "that any alteration in the ideals would affect the strategy and would cast suspicion upon their justification."[1]

The case for United States participation, particularly espoused by Wilson, hung on the continued partnership of ideals, strategy, and morale, Bourne argued. The President's April 2 declaration of war address seemed to have presented an unimpeachable case. American hesitation was overcome by the apparent demonstration that priceless values were at issue. A relapse to previous hesitation could only be checked by the sustained conviction that the Allies were fighting single-mindedly to save cherished ideals. The question now was how much the conviction had been sustained and how accurately United

States strategy had justified its participation. He asserted there was a prevailing apathy to the war in many parts of the nation. Was the apathy caused, he asked, by a weakening of the assurance that America's war was decisive in securing the values for which war was presumably waged?

The original logic of participation rested mostly on renewed submarine warfare, Bourne believed. By that time most liberal opinion had concluded that the sensibility of neutrality had ceased. Isolation was discredited when it appeared urgent for the country to join a covenant of nations which would emerge from the peace settlement. Therefore the nation was bound to contribute resources and good will: its position made it certain that however it acted the United States would be the deciding factor in the war.

Until renewal of the submarine campaign, moreover, benevolent neutrality, however strained, was still endurable, particularly when supplemented by the hope of mediation in the maneuvers for peace without victory and by the principle of Wilson's January 22, 1917, speech to the Senate on terms of peace in Europe. "This attempt", Randolph maintained, "to bring about a negotiated peace, while the United States was still nominally neutral, but able to bring its colossal resources against the side which refused to declare its terms, marked the highwater level of American strategy." Thus the strategy of peace without victory failed because Germany refused to state terms, and the war continued for sheer lack of a common basis to work out a settlement.

Then the submarine threat suddenly forced the issue. The safety of the seas and the whole allied cause seemed in deadly peril and in the emergency benevolent neutrality caved in. Liberal opinion found no recourse except war. But now months later those who advocated armed neutrality seemed to have had a better case. The need had been for immediate guarantees of food and ships to the menaced nations and for the destruction of the attacking submarines.

Armed neutrality suggested a way to deal quickly and effectively with the crisis, he felt. Loans, food, ships, convoys, could have been ordered without a declaration of war, without working up the nation's morale, and without building a vast military machine.

What war had meant, therefore, was an inevitable and perhaps fatal delay. The nation was unready[2] for battle and the only hope of effective aid could have come from concentrating on a ship and food program, supplemented by a naval program. The war, Randolph asserted, could be ended most promptly by convincing Germany that the submarine had no chance of prevailing against the endless American resources which would have raised the siege on Britain and France and have cleared the seas. Instead of centering its energy on destroying the submarine danger and ending the war, the United States dispersed its powers in propaganda, agitation, discussion, dissension, and censorship.

"Five months have passed since the beginning of unrestricted submarine warfare. We have done nothing to overcome the submarine. The food and ship programmes are still unconsolidated. The absorption of Congress and the country in the loan and the conscript army and the censorship has meant just so much less absorption in the vital and urgent technique to provide [*materiél*] which we entered the war.

"The country has been put to work on a vast number of activities which are consonant to the abstract condition of war, but which may have little relation to the particular situation in which this country found itself and to particular strategy required. The immediate task was to prevent German victory in order to restore the outlines of our strategy toward a negotiated peace. War has been impotent in that immediate task.

"Paradoxically, therefore, our very participation was a means of weakening our strategy. We have not overcome the submarine or freed the Atlantic world. Our entrance has apparently made not a dent in the morale of the German people. The effect of our entrance, it was anticipated by the liberals, would be the shortening of the war. Our entrance has rather tended to prolong it.

"Liberals were mistaken about the immediate collapse of the British Commonwealth. It continued to endure the submarine challenge without our material aid. We find ourselves, therefore, saddled with a war-technique which has compromised rather than furthered our strategy."[3]

Events had compromised the country's strategy even more, Bourne felt, because instead of making for a negotiated peace which the United States said it desired, the strategy had had the unexpected result of encouraging the wish of the allies to smash Germany totally. In the President's April 2 speech it was stated that the principles of negotiated peace were unimpaired; now this no longer seemed assured. The Allies had not announced their war aims in such terms as to make the peoples of the Central Powers disgruntled with their regimes.

Furthermore, the government had failed to encourage liberal sentiment in the enemy's lair. Bourne cited the denial of passports to American socialists intent on meeting with Russian and German socialists: a chance was lost to contact the most liberal element in

Germany, and the initiative for peace was lost. The tactic of making the allied governments state their war aims had been an integral part of the original strategy and "the American liberals trusted the President to use American participation as an instrument in liberalizing the war-aims of the Allied governments. In the event, however, it has not been America that has wanted peace sufficiently to be preemptory about it. It has been Russia."

It was argued that the most serious thing—in a note which the United States sent May 26, 1917, to the Russian provisional government—was the implication that Wilson not only had lost to Russia the initiative for negotiated peace, but the absence of even a desire for it. "The day has come," Wilson declared, "when we must conquer or submit."[4] This, Bourne felt, was an unhappy change of pace by a President who had insisted the nation had not altered its principles. To Randolph, peace without victory did not seem reconcilable with conquer or submit. It seemed a conversion to the philosophy of the knockout blow.[5] This, he contended, was the collapse of American strategy.

The collapse was indicated by Wilson's Flag Day address on June 14, 1917. The speech today reads like a battle cry characterized by belligerent language never before so prevalent in Wilson's communications. Wilson pledged a struggle to the death, to an utter crushing of the Central Powers, that is, in effect, the transformation of the United States from a mediator to a steam roller. Woe be to those who stood in the way, Wilson declared.

Liberals had interpreted entry into war as primarily defensive with the intention of restoring conditions in a way that a negotiated peace would be unavoidable. Such a strategy was predicated on the idea that a military decision was either impossible or not worth the colossal sacrifice it would demand. "But," Bourne observed, "it is only as the result of a sweeping military decision that any assured destruction of Mittell-Europa could come. In basing his case on Mittel-Europa, therefore, the President has clearly swung from a strategy of 'peace without victory' to a strategy of war to exhaustion for the sake of a military decision.[6] He implies that a country which came only after hesitation to the defense of the seas and the Atlantic world will contentedly pour out its indefinite blood and treasure for the sake of spoiling the coalition of Mittel-Europa and making readjustments in the map of Europe effective against German influence on the Continent. Such an implication means the 'end of American isolation' with a vengeance. No one can be blamed who sees in the Flag Day Address the almost unlimited countersigning of Allied designs and territorial schemes."[7]

In effect, he summed up, the liberals had been humiliated by the perversion of their strategy. The best hope was for a speedy peace with Germany before she was exhausted and demoralized so that democratic tendencies and leadership could be released. Democracy certainly could not be imposed from without.

Meantime, it had to be recognized that the hopes the liberal intellectuals entertained when they supported the President had been betrayed. The submarine danger was not ended. The power for mediation was lost. Democratic leadership of the Allies had not been retained. The initiative for peace was surrendered. The United States had obliged itself to send massive armies to secure an Entente victory and had prolonged the war. Reactionaries had been encouraged in the Allied nations and democrats discouraged in Germany. By guarding neutrality, Randolph wrote, America might have effected a speedy and democratic peace, but "In the war, we are a rudderless nation, to be exploited as the Allies wish, politically and materially, and towed, to their aggrandizement, in any direction which they may desire."

Bourne was right about the sputtering preparation for war. In the summer of 1917 it could not have been seen how the nation was to have gotten *materiél* program operating by early 1918—a stupendous, unprecedented logistic feat. Severe weather in the fall of 1917 probably made his evaluation of the position the United States was in seem the wiser at the time.

Much of what was asserted amounted to informed, intelligent conjecture which cannot be confuted any more than it can be unerringly posited. Certainly his protest was intimately tied to the times. It dramatized a predicament about which liberals complained during the war and lamented later in post-mortems and memoirs. Also, the very fact he protested the shift from peace without victory to a conquer or submit strategy reflected changes occuring in modern diplomacy and warfare which few recognized at the time.

In September 1917 in his *Seven Arts* contribution, "A War Diary," he again maintained that apathy toward the war was widespread. He brooded about the possible negative affects of the war on the lower and middle classes and theorized that it was highly possible the war would help produce a "semi-military State-socialism" by which was meant—it appears from the mention of government's cooperation with financiers, industrialists, and managers—not a socialized democracy but what later was called fascism.

So long as those "big men" remained loyal, Randolph said, it made no difference how the millions of little human "cogs" reacted. It already was seen, moreover, that technical organization for war had outdistanced popular sentiment. This meant that patriotism had become superfluous; government did not have to ask whether citizens wanted to fight or whether they understood what they were fighting for, but only whether they would tolerate fighting. Acquiescence had become the all-important factor.

Again he attacked the liberals and noted a complaint by the *New Republic* that a league of peace was more remote than eight months before, and that the state department had no policy. "If after all the idealism and creative intelligence that were shed upon America's taking up arms, our State Department has no policy, we are like brave passengers who have set out for the Isles of the Blest only to find that the first mate has gone insane and jumped overboard, the rudder has come loose and dropped to the bottom of the sea, and the captain and pilot are lying dead drunk under the wheel. The stokers and engineers, however, are still merrily forcing the speed up to twenty knots an hour and the passengers are presumably getting the pleasure of the ride."

Bourne foreshadowed a forthcoming attack on Dewey and pragmatism, arguing that choice of alternatives was impossible in wartime for those against war because of the coercion which all governments—democratic and autocratic—use: it was naiveté to be shocked at arbitrariness. Accepting war was to see disappear one by one the justifications for accepting it. Willing war meant willing all the evils bound up with it.

The theme of the dissenter cultivating his own garden and working for national improvement was returned to. An important sector of Americans, particularly the younger generation, opposed war because "of the myraid hurts they knew war would do to the promise of democracy at home." There was a refuge to be found, he felt, in skepticism, a shelter behind which could be constructed a wider consciousness of the personal, social and artistic ideals America needed. This, it was insisted, could be a constructive skepticism.

Such a spiritual reserve would be needed because so many people had dumped their emotional capital into Europe—just the way goods and credits had gone abroad. The war would leave the United States spiritually impoverished because sentiment was drained into the channels of war.[8] To Bourne the task for American malcontents and aloof men and women was clear. If the nation had lost political isolation, it was the more obligated to rescue its spiritual integrity. "The war—or American promise: one must choose. One cannot be interested in both. For the effect of war will be to impoverish American promise. It cannot advance it, however liberals may choose to identify American promise with a league of nations to enforce peace. Americans who desire to cultivate the promises of American life need not lift a finger to obstruct the war, but they cannot conscientiously accept it."[9]

Dissenters might feel intimately part of their country, Randolph observed, but they could not feel themselves part of the war. They could be apathetic with a clear conscience because of other values and ideals for America: the country would not suffer for their lack of support so long as it had the backing of industrialists. Meantime the younger generation held that those who turned their thinking into war-channels had abdicated leadership. "For many of us," he declared, "resentment against the war has meant a vivider consciousness of what we are seeking in American life."

The same month the above lines were published others appeared attacking Dewey, pragmatism, and its practitioners. The vehicles were "Conscience and Intelligence in War" which appeared in the *Dial,* followed by "Twilight of Idols"—a motif obviously borrowed from Nietzsche—which appeared in the October *Seven Arts.* The inspiration was a series of articles by Dewey in the *New Republic.*[10] The pieces deplored the attitude which identified dissent with disloyalty: but they also expressed impatience with allegedly ineffective pacifists.

In "Conscience and Compulsion" which appeared in the July 14 *New Republic,* Dewey defended pacifists, but remarked that "If at a critical juncture the moving force of events is always too much for conscience, the remedy is not to deplore the wickedness of those who manipulate events. Such a conscience is largely self-conceit. The remedy is to connect conscience with the forces that are moving in another direction. Then will conscience itself have compulsive power instead of being forever the martyred and the coerced." Dewey's position angered Bourne who explained what he understood to be the plight of the pacifist.

The mere conscientious objector had received too much attention, Bourne felt. Not all pacifist feeling was so evangelistic as that of the conscientious objector. There was, he insisted, an anti-war sentiment which had tried to be realistic and which did not hope to defeat war merely by sitting on its hands. That element neither welcomed martyrdom nor wished the sentiment attached to it. Dewey, he charged, overlooked the attitude which Bourne was outlining.[11]

As for Dewey's advice about what to do at a critical juncture of events, the philosopher ignored the point that alternatives in war are rigorously limited. "Is not war," Randolph asked, "perhaps the one social absolute, the one situation where the choice of ends ceases to function?" In war everything must be yielded to the one purpose. There may be an illusion of freedom for a while, but soon a pragmatist would see there was only one end: victory.

Peace without victory, he said, became in such a situation a contradiction. Opposition to Wilson's peace gestures had arisen for the reason that war had made Europe a realm of the absolute: conquer or submit. "In wartime there is literally no other end but war, and the objector, therefore, lives no longer with a choice of alternatives."

Dewey was dealing with the one situation in which his philosophy no longer worked, he argued. In American society the forces moving in opposition to the war were stigmatized as subversive. Never has a government in wartime refused to use relentless coercion against forces moving in the other direction. There was of course the alternative of revolution. Did Dewey approve of that? he wondered. Dewey had not stated what wartime social mechanisms were relevant or permissible which did not mean cooperation with the war effort. "One resists or one obeys. If one resists, one is martyred or coerced. If one obeys, the effect is just as if one accepted the war," Randolph maintained.

The locale of the pragmatic conscience in wartime, he said, was a vacuum where there was no leverage. Not only did it blot out choice of ends but also of means. Dewey might have believed that the pacifists should aid the war because of the social reform sure to result; that they would be willing, in effect, to take the bitter with the sweet. But no such reforms had occurred. Labor was no better off, and those profiting financially from the war were not proportionately helping to pay for the war, and education was being impoverished.

Mere conscientious objection in wartime was not so futile and unintelligent as Dewey represented it, it was contended. At base, alternative ends were illusory whereas such was not true of other social situations. It perhaps was not noble, Bourne admitted ironically, to concentrate on one's own integrity, but it was perhaps better than being a hypocrite or a martyr.

Many pragmatists scolded pacifists for lack of organization and for being only obstructive. Actually there were fertile constructive suggestions by pacifists, but "no social machinery existed for harnessing their conscience to action. The referendum would have been a slight democratic clutch. It was hooted out of court. Armed neutrality was foozled. The forces that were irresistably for war had control of the war-making machinery. The pacifists sounded ridiculous and unreasonable, because the drive was the other way. The war suction had begun. Choices were already abolished, and the most realistic and constructive pacifism in the world would have been helpless."

Then in an October *Seven Arts* essay, "Twilight of Idols," was continued the argument that to pragmatists the philosophy of creative intelligence had still seemed to be working—that is, to those who went along with the war—because there was no need to test its applicability. While the essay dealt generally with pragmatism, it was a more severe indictment of Dewey in particular than had been the *Dial* writing. It implied that James would not have been "hoodwinked" the way Dewey was. James would have called for a war gallantly played, but with insistent care for democratic values at home. Dewey's thought, however, was "slackening" and inadequate for the emergency. Dewey's recent articles, the piece said, had seemed "a little off-color." [12]

A philosopher who so little understood sinister forces of war and who was more concerned about excesses of pacifists than those of the military, Randolph said, or was only amused at the idea that any one should try to conscript thought; who believed that the war-technique could be used without dragging along the mob fanaticism, unjustice and hatred indeliby tied to war, was addressing some other element of the younger intelligentsia than that to which he personally belonged.

To talk—as he believed Dewey did—as if there was not emotional and behavioral mob disorderliness such as the unsuccessful attempt by soldiers to lynch Max Eastman was to demonstrate that one's philosophy had never been confronted with the pathless and the inexorable . . . . Only a lack of practice with a world of human nature so raw-nerved, irrational, uncreative, as an America at war was bound to show itself to be, can account for the singular unsatisfactoriness of these latter utterances of Dewey." [13]

Then Bourne turned around and accused himself—in a passage which possibly was among the most difficult for him to ever have written—of miscalculation. Surely he spoke for many of his contemporaries when he stated "what I come to is a sense of suddenly being left in the lurch, of suddenly finding that a philosophy upon which I had relied to carry us through no longer works. I find the contrast between the idea that creative intelligence has free functioning in wartime, and the facts of the inexorable situation, too glaring. The contrast between what liberals ought to be doing and saying if democratic values are to be conserved, and what the real forces are imposing upon them, strikes too sternly on my intellectual sense. I should prefer some philosophy of War as the grim and terrible cleanser to this optimism-haunted mood that continues unweariedly to suggest that all can yet be made to work for good in a mad and half-destroyed world." [14]

The accusations against Dewey were softened by praising the effect of pragmatism on educational thinking and reform, but the compliment was another way of asserting the philosophy was applicable only to peacetime. For Randolph contended that "What concerns us here is the relative ease with which the pragmatist intellectuals, with Professor Dewey at the head, have moved out their philosophy, bag and baggage, from education to war."

Dewey's articles, Bourne complained, held no clues for working out democratic needs either during or after the war. The reason apparently was that Dewey had no program. Consulting war boards and evoking patriotism merely meant concealing intellectual feebleness. If one said the clear formulation of democratic ends must be postponed until war's end, then the argument defeated itself, since allegedly one was supporting the war because it would save and advance democracy. Adopting a "win first" policy was intellectual hara-kiri.

"What is the matter with the philosophy?" Bourne asked. "One has a sense of having come to a sudden short stop at the end of an intellectual era." He answered his query by asserting that the pragmatist "awakeners" lacked poetic vision and a concern for the quality of life. Dewey and his disciples had turned out to have no coherent system of large, transcendent ideas. They had taken pragmatism so fervently as a religion of technique and means that ends had been suffocated. "To those of us who have taken Dewey's philosophy as our American religion, it never occurred that values could be subordinated to technique. We were instrumentalists, but we had our private utopias so clearly before our minds that the means fell always into its place as contributory."

Randolph probably was aware of the difficulties which is position entailed or which critics would say it entailed. As a pragmatist he was in an uncomfortable position when it came to posting absolutes such as freedom of speech and press. For the problem was to win the war, and obviously a very pragmatic nation had chosen to curb basic freedoms. All right, one pragmatist could say, you believe our participation was wrong; my pragmatic choice is for war.

It is clear in examining anti-war and pro-war stances that each side accused the other of being unrealistic. To this day Bourne is accused, as it were, of writing himself resentfully into a corner, thereby ending up needlessly ineffective.[15] Yet it should be noted that again and again in his writing before and during the war he advocated Dewey's pragmatic notion of what should be done at a critical juncture.[16]

Perhaps the classical criticism of his behavior is that by the brilliant Harold Laski, a personal acquaintance who admired and respected him. In an eloquent review of *Untimely Papers,* Laski praised Randolph highly and exclaimed that no one could read him without a thrill. But the position, Laski argued at length, was in the final analysis sterile. "The business of the world is the business of the world. One can not stay at Armageddon to philosophize upon the abstract injustice of war."[17]

But should Bourne be criticized so sternly? One might say that upon deciding pragmatism was useless he should have dropped it and addressed himself to the reality of war and America's being at war. War was the abiding reality, it might be said. It should be remembered, however, that at the basis of the position was the conviction that the United States did not have to be at war—or at least did not have to immediately do more than make sure that food, ships and *materiél* were convoyed to Europe.

There is no reason to believe that Randolph would have felt the same way about the war, if for example, the country had been invaded or its ports blockaded.

What seems to have often happened in discussing him is that he really is criticized for choosing "wrongly" rather than for not choosing at all or for being no longer able to choose. For in effect what he was saying was this: My antagonists believe that one must get with the tide of events and do his best to curb and direct the tide. I have examined both the situation and my conscience, and I see my adversaries to be mad. There are no practical alternatives. Those who say so are fooled. Were there any chance to influence events, I would try to do so in ways other than my present dissenting stance. There is no chance, however. I choose to be irreconcilable.

Was this so wrong? Did not a whole generation of liberals, reformers and progressives find out eventually that they had no significant influence during the war, and none of consequence on the peace settlement? Was not that the reason for wide spread post-war bitterness? If one is to criticize, it should be for what he stressed. Instead of hammering at the foolishness of intellectuals, he should have tried to show not only how he believed they had failed, but also how they could pick up the pieces. Very likely Randolph thought he was accomplishing that by deploring their ways and then stating what the malcontents should and could do.

One might also criticize him for never directly dealing with the question of what a German victory would mean. The issue probably was not commented on because he believed that America could ship to the Entente what it needed to hold out against Germany and perhaps win decisively. But what if everything sent the Entente did not prevail? What then for the United States? There is no reason to believe Bourne would not have supported war with Germany if it meant survival.

It is true that he raged against the war, and correctly indicated its sinister effects. But never was Britain's and France's being at war condemned. He did indeed say war was the one social absolute where choice of ends ceased to function. He insisted that willing war meant willing the grotesqueries accompanying it. He hated war.

But he never explicitly or implicitly asserted that war was an absolute evil. He was not a Roger Baldwin.

There is no reason to believe that the protests would have continued if he had believed his writing could seriously hurt the effort.

A careful reading of Bourne—despite the fact that he was called (and at least once called himself) a pacifist—fails to show any evidence that he would not have supported a war on which depended the preservation of American sovereignty and institutions, however democratically imperfect they were.

The point is that he believed that involvement in a particular war in his time was stupid and needless, although perhaps not for Britain and France who had less choice. He was by no means alone. Many felt the same way: young Harold Stearns, for instance, who was neither a pacifist or a conscientious objector and who was not called; the music critic Paul Rosenfeld, Randolph's friend, who was drafted, who was not a conscientious objector or a pacifist, but who felt the same way.

There is no substantial evidence in letters and writings that later he would not have supported the war against Nazi Germany and her allies, although he probably would have protested internment of Japanese-Americans, application of the Smith Act, the glorification of military virtues which was renewed during World War II, and the widespread blanket indictment of the enemy as satanic.

He hated war. Who did not hate war, who was not perverse and understood what 20th century weaponry could do? Especially hated was what he believed to be America's stupid, needless, animal-like involvement in the First World War. But that he could not ever have believed there was such a thing as a just war cannot be entertained seriously.

Bourne sympathized with the Russian revolution and then with the Reds in the ensuing civil war. He felt the same way about Ireland's insurgency.

It traditionally has been believed that for war to be just there must be four conditions: (1) just cause, (2) lawful authority, (3) right intention, (4) right use of means,[18] and that war is not just unless all four factors apply. Obviously he did not believe the requirements were filled or that America went to war for defensive reasons. But he would have been willing later to fight if he were convinced a defensive war was imperative.

Because Randolph Bourne thought America's participation wrong, he did not bother with distinctions like the difference between physical evil and moral evil, major questions concerning war. He knew that a state which never would wage war under any conditions would be doomed. He knew that a state would collapse if it did not protect the lives, property, and liberty of its citizens. Once he called himself a pacifist. But mostly Bourne called himself an irreconcilable, a malcontent, or a dissenter. If one looks at him only as the "pacifist patriot" there is ground for agreeing with those who say he blindly wrote himself into a corner, and—as Laski said—became "a lonely vagabond whose soul does not dwell in the common haunts of men."[19]

To see Randolph correctly in this case is to see him as he saw himself: an irreconcilable in an ungrateful role who saw events more clearly than most contemporaries, who made an honest, courageous, and unpopular assessment of events, but who clearly was ready to change should circumstances change.

It cannot be emphasized too strongly—because of the myths which have grown up and the sentimentalities written—that his writing about war and United States participation was the product of a deep reflection which was applied to circumstances, to place, and to time. It must be concluded that in other times and other places he would have supported, perhaps embraced war. "It is *this* war," he was saying in effect, "this stupid, senseless war-making by America that I am denouncing, not all war." Bourne, however, never lost faith in dialogue.

It would have been exciting if a direct dialogue had occurred between Dewey and him. As shall be seen in Chapter 11, Dewey was bitter about the attacks, and would have nothing to do with him. But the October 1917 *Seven Arts* in which Randolph's "Twilight of Idols" appeared was the last issue. Trouble had been brewing for some time, much of it caused by his articles. Later, Van Wyck Brooks would assert that the articles "destroyed" *Seven Arts*[20] and Oppenheim declared that Bourne "was the main cause of our shutting down." [21] And Robert Frost also felt the same way, for as he wrote to his friend Louis Untermeyer, November 3, 1917, in a poem he entitled *"The Seven Arts"*:

"In the Dawn of Creation that morning
"I remember I gave you fair warning
"The Arts are but Six!
"You add Politics
"And the Seven will all die a-Bourneing" [22]

In September a well-meaning Amy Lowell had warned Oppenheim: "Steps against all forms of hostile expressions are going to become stronger and stronger as the feelings of the majority wax hotter and hotter. This cannot be escaped, and I feel quite sure that you have a higher mision to perform than that of hostile critics. . . .

"Mr. Bourne could come out and say for what we are fighting is a splendid thing, but if Mr. Bourne covertly regrets the fighting itself, in his article, then I should say his article has a hostile influence and that it was a mistake at this juncture." [23]

Editor Oppenheim disagreed. If the magazine's task, he replied, was to deal with American life and expression, any analysis of tendencies must include the discussion of the consequence of participation in the war. If Bourne wrote about the breakdown of pragmatism and the need for poetic vision in its place, it was necessary to show the moment of the breakdown, namely the application to the war technique.[24]

Randolph was by no means the only bone of contention. Oppenheim had steadily been writing acid anti-war editorials, and John Reed's "This Unpopular War" in the August 1917 issue had caused a stir because of his assertion that the masses had no stake in the war. Waldo Frank later remembered that "Justice Department men came around the office pretending they were poets and writers and trying to see if they could turn up any sedition." But generally the publication was not harassed by George Creel's committee, or by Postmaster General Albert S. Burleson, or by Attorney General Thomas Gregory as were organs like the *Masses* and the New York *Call,* the major socialist daily newspaper.

The real trouble was with Mrs. Rankin, whose family pressured her to close down the *Seven Arts.* "I could see how the wind blew," Brooks recalled, "when she caused the flag to be flown at half-mast in honour of the death of [the highly conservative Republican diplomat and lawyer] Joseph H. Choate."[25] Mrs. Rankin finally told Oppenheim:

"The business agreement we entered into at the forming of The Seven Arts Publishing Co., Inc., stated that you were to have entire control of the editorial policy; I entire control of the Business policy....

"As this agreement would not be generally known I wish to make it so now for the reason that I may say publicly that I do not agree with the war policy of the magazine, and I do not approve of the war articles which have appeared in the last few issues.

"P.S. I wish to state further that I am desirous of withdrawing my support, and severing my connection with the Company as soon as possible."[26]

And so Randolph Bourne allegedly toppled the *Seven Arts.* There is, however, a conflicting version. According to Waldo Frank,[27] another angel for the *Seven Arts* immediately appeared. He was Scofield Thayer, a Harvard classmate of Harold Stearns. Thayer soon would become backer of the revamped *Dial* which Stearns had edited. Stearns—now returned to New York from Chicago where the *Dial* was published—may have set Thayer onto the *Seven Arts.* Stearns had written for it and knew its writers.

A protracted feud among the editors, while not personal, had been hurtful. Brooks did not want any discussion of the war. "I could not see why a magazine of art should destroy itself by opposing the war . . . ."[27A] Meantime—because of the magazine's editorial democracy—the material compiled by each editor was scrutinized by the others. Frank and Brooks disapproved of Oppenheim's war editorials. Oppenheim usually had to re-work each one, sometimes several times, before Brooks and Frank okayed it, often without enthusiasm. That caused friction.

Thayer and the backers he had marshaled were willing to preserve the *Seven Arts,* but they wanted a collective editorial board, instead of the existing situation in which Oppenheim was chief. Brooks and Frank approved this and wanted Bourne as a fourth. But Oppenheim felt, as he wrote later: "Good editing is a one-man job, just like good art."[28] The project collapsed. At the same time, Randolph refused to be editor unless the other three were co-editors. It was, as Brooks remarked, the time for men to go write their books.[29]

Oppenheim felt no bitteness toward Bourne, or if he did he lost it. For he later said: "That we should have thought that the arts and the criticisms could rule business appears so ludicrous now as to be beyond laughter; and that we should have tried to stop war (and I don't think it was the intellectuals who started it) was a *beau geste* simply because of Randolph Bourne."[30]

That there still would have been a future for him with the magazine—his restraint and the government willing—if it had not folded, seems certain. Letters in the Bourne Papers indicate he was reaching an audience of sympathetic irreconcilables as well as those who disagreed. And on the anti-war issue he had the respect if not the sympathy of his contemporary writers. To Oppenheim he was "a flaming rebel against our crippled life."[31] And Harold Stearns spoke for many when he said his "were about the only intelligent comments I heard during those horrible weeks of relapse to barbarism."[33] He was, Stearns, added, "about the only one of the younger American writers and essayists who did not let himself be beguiled by the hypocrisies and shiboleths of the war."[33]

The demise of the *Seven Arts,* however, marked the end of Randolph's major published writing on the war. In October when Columbia University denounced Professors Charles Beard, J. McKeen Cattell, and Henry Wadsworth Longfellow Dana as subversive and forced them off the faculty, there was a brief return to the topic by attacking what he felt was Columbia's perversion of American traditions and university ideals.[34]

From then on Bourne's discussion of war was as asides to his book reviews in the *Dial* and the *New Republic.* The matter of course constantly preoccupied him. In a review published in early 1918 he approvingly quoted the opening of Bertrand Russell's *Political Ideals*: "We see that the things we had thought evil are really evil, and we know more definitely than we ever did before the direction in which men must move if a better world is to arise on the ruins of the one which is now hurling itself to destruction."[35]

And by late spring Bourne may have come to feel that since America was so deep into the war there was no halting of it. If he was an irreconcilable, he seems nevertheless to have wanted the reaper hurried quickly to the end of the row. The longer war went on, it seemed, the more acute became the spiritual dilemma. If one regarded it as a war to end war, must not every mind carry into peace "the coming lesson that this horror can never be allowed to break loose again?" Anything, then, he contended, "which mitigated the ghastly reality of war would by so much relax our vigilance against its recurrence. But on the other hand, events require that we gird our loins and pursue the war to the end without faltering; in order to keep the national mind taut for the unfaltering prosecution of the war military operations ought to seem not only palatable but even exhilerating. Hence the universal preoccupation with 'morale.' Faith and delight in war as an effective means must be maintained in order that war may be slain forever as the vilest human scourge and pestilence." [36]

If Bourne could not know what his post-war career would be, he was definitely committed to the United States. In a pique he had written that young men and women were "wondering what neutral country they can scrape enough money together to live in after the war." [37] But he did not include himself in that group. Concluding "Twilight of Idols," he had announced that malcontents who used to go to Europe or starved submissively at home were "too much entangled emotionally with the possibilities of American life to leave it." While he complained in a long letter to Van Wyck Brooks, so well constructed that it really was an essay, that the war had "run into the sand that fine movement for progressive democracy in which so many of us found hope," the message also was packed with violent discontent about the existing situation and about what to do about it, particularly in literature.[38]

At the same time, what readers who did not know him personally could not realize was that Bourne had grasped the most mature insight an artist could take from the war. In an unpublished composition he noted that radicals had concentrated on labor and capital and had overlooked militarists. Sentimentality had prevented one from seeing that while the people were being educated, the emperors were drilling soldiers. "Proletarians, bankers, scientists, poets, business men—the numberless classes that did not want the war—these had the sentiments. The Emperors had the guns." [39]

It had been clearly demonstrated, moreover, that there was no such thing as automatic progress. Sentiment could not do the work of organization or of completion of any project. "If good causes and movements are ever to triumph they must be hard, stern, unyielding. Militarism should have been attacked directly by political means. All the feeble well-wishing of the masses did not hurt it. All the sentiment of the Socialists, millions strong, did not insulate them against that electric thrill of panic and patriotism, which the military cast, with its superior initiative, was able to send through them. Not the least of our disillusionments and chagrins is the realization of how thoroughly worsted in the attack upon militarism we have been. Discarded must be the theories and methods of that failure, if never the ideals."

As shall be seen in Chapter 11, there were reasons for Bourne to be happy during the last years of his life. But, as also shall be noted, he often was disconsolate. To a childhood friend who was in France, he confided that "I feel very much secluded from the world, very much out of touch with my time, except perhaps with the Bolsheviki. The magazines I write for die violent deaths, and all my thoughts seem unprintable. If I start to write on public matters I discover that my ideas are seditious, and if I start to write a novel I discover that my outlook is immoral if not obscene. What then is a literary man to do if he has to make his life by his pen?" [40]

And at about the same time from Virginia where he was visiting his sister he wrote another friend that "All the talk here is most pessimistic about food and the cost of living. I seem to disagree on the war with every rational and benevolent person I meet." [41]

Out of this counterpoint of elation and melancholy came the buoyant first chapter of his autobiographical novel and his sullen unfinished work, "The State." It was in that latter work, to which we now turn, that he wrote again and again the phrase which inspired John Dos Passos to write in *Nineteen Nineteen* with both flair and exaggeration:

"If any man has a ghost
"Bourne has a ghost,
"a tiny twisted unscared ghost in a black cloak
"hopping along the grimy old brick and brownstone streets still left
"in downtown New York.
"crying out in a shrill soundless giggle:
"*War is the health of the state.*"

"Once the State has begun to function, and a large class finds its interest and its expression of power in maintaining the State, this ruling class may compel obedience from any uninterested minority. The State becomes an instrument by which the power of the whole herd is welded for the benefit of a class. The rulers soon learn to capitalize the reverence which the State produces in the majority, and turn it into a general resistance towards a lessening of their privileges. The sanctity of the State becomes identified with the sanctity of the ruling class and the latter are permitted to remain in power under the impression that in obeying and serving, we are obeying and serving society, the nation, the collectivity of all of us."

—Bourne, "The State"

X

LEVIATHAN, AMERICAN STYLE

In the mid 1920's Floyd Dell looked over his shoulder at the previous decade and chuckled. He and his contemporaries, he wrote, had been determinists, with a style that amounted to fatalism. "Capitalism *must* produce Socialism," he wrote in his autobiography, *Intellectual Vagabondage*. "We had seen the elaborate syllogism which proved it. We congratulated each other upon our superior knowledge of the trend of events, and sat about as though we were waiting for the denouement, when we would say, 'I told you so!' "

It is not clear precisely when Dell sobered up from the heady ideological brew to which he had been accustomed, but it very likely was—as with Bourne—when the United States entered World War I. On the proverbial morning after, Dell raised the window shade: "But we were not living in the age of Bakunin, and we could not really believe in the possibility of overthrowing the State by force. To begin with, the State had all the force." Those lines easily might have been written by an ironical Randolph Bourne looking back from the 1920's at a decade when for a while some believed the world might behave the way intelligent men told it and showed it to behave.

The core of Bourne's thought on the State is found in the posthumously published "Unfinished Fragment of 'The State'," a 90-page composition which stops in an uncompleted sentence. It was written sometime after August 1917.[1] "The State" is essentially an effort to show what the war spirit did to American society and institutions.

Crucial to an understanding of this essay is some comprehension of what Bourne meant by (1) Country or Nation, (2) Government, and (3) State.

The status of Country or Nation is that to which man is most accustomed, Bourne wrote. It is not necessarily normal in the sense of its being the most constant or frequent condition, but in its being the standard against which things are measured. "In our quieter moments," he said, "the Nation or Country forms the basic idea of society. We think vaguely of a loose population spreading over a certain geographical portion of the earth's surface, speaking a common language, and living in a homogeneous civilization."

The idea of Country concerned itself with the non-political aspects of a people—ways of living, personal traits, literature, art, and the attitude toward life. By Country was in effect meant community or society.

For Bourne, Government is simply the means to the end of the nation organized as the State. But although he says that Government is synonymous with neither State nor Country, he contends that Government carries out the States' function: "Government is a framework of the administration of laws, and the carrying out of the public force. Government is the idea of the State put into practical operation in the hands of definite, concrete, fallible men. It is the visible sign of the invisible grace. It is the word made flesh. And it has necessarily the limitations inherent in all practicality. Government is the only form in which we can envisage the State, but it is by no means identical with it. That the State is a mystical conception is something that must never be forgotten. Its glamor and significance linger behind the framework of Government and direct its activities."

The State always is latent in society, but it is wartime which brings it out fully. In peacetime—when the feeling for Country is essentially non-competitive—the sense of the State slackens, especially in a Nation that is not militarized. "For war is essentially the health of the State." That is, war invigorates a republic, changing it from Country to State. The State politically becomes—like the Church in the realm of the spiritual—the medium of political salvation. War's distinguishing trait is that it creates a need for universality, and in doing so makes the State the relentless arbiter of man's affairs, opinions, and attitudes. The State, "is the organization of the herd to act offensively or defensively against another herd similarly organized. The more terrifying the occasion for defense, the closer will become the organization and the more coercive the influence upon each member of the herd. War sends the current of purpose and activity flowing down to the lowest level of the herd, and to its most remote branches. All the activities of the society are linked together as fast as possible to this central purpose of making a military offensive or a military defense. . . ."

In peacetime, Randolph wrote, the State fades vaguely into the background. The foreground is dominated by the action of Government which—amid general indifference and contempt on the part of the public—exists in a kind of ongoing Manichaean state of political roughhousing of the "Ins" and the "Outs," each appropriately identifies the other as the force of evil. It is in a republic that almost no trappings exist to appeal to the emotions of the common man.

With the shock of war, the State again comes into its own. The Government, without mandate from the governed, "gently and irresistibly slides the country into war," after going through the paces of menaces, negotiations, and explanations. It not only collects a bundle of insults alleged to have been made by the prospective adversary, but for the benefit of the liberal elements in society a set of moral purposes is trotted out. Then the ambitious are told that a greater destiny in the world awaits the republic.

The result is that even in those countries where a declaration of war technically is the task of the parliament, no legislature has ever been known to decline the request of the executive, once the initial wave had been built up. Private, secret diplomacy having done its task, war is declared, and the people become convinced that they willed and executed the deed themselves: "They then with the exception of a few malcontents, proceed to allow themselves to be regimented, coerced, deranged in all the environments of their lives, and turned into a solid manufactory of destruction toward whatever other people may have, in the appointed scheme of things, come within the range of the Government's disapprobation."

Whereas Country means peace—and therefore tolerance and living and letting live—State essentially is a concept of power, competition, and aggression. In war's excitement all the distinctions between Nation and State wash into a confusion. There is a kind of frenetic rejuvenescence among the people wherein even the previously most inconsequential person plays a part. There is a role for each citizen in the war effort, from the tasks of minding another person's business and reporting "spies" to those of raising funds and fighting. Pulpit, school, and press are mobilized for war. Where prewar dissenting opinion once was irritating, in the State it becomes outlawry for which punishment far exceeds the alleged crime. Citizens once apathetic to their Government now embrace it. Each citizen feels behind him the power of the collective community.

Of course, the ideal of perfect loyalty is never really attained, Bourne noted. Coercion sometimes stiffens resistance. But there is a general unanimity which could not be produced by anything else than war.

What happens is that the herd runs not only amuck, but together; however, "there is nothing invidious in the use of the term 'herd,' in connection with the State. It is merely an attempt to reduce close to first principles the nature of this institution in the shadow of which we all live, move and have our being." In other words, the basis of society is not the family, but the herd, although from the explanation it is not clear how the herd came into being—except that man shares the gregarious impulse of animals.

Herds are formed for protection, the products of which are confidence and a collective feeling of mass strength. That unity is sufficient in itself, but unfortunately—he does not explain why—the herd impulse also demands like-mindedness and obedience at the expense of human progress, novelty, and non-conformity. Even in the most enlightened modern societies the herd impulse showed no indication of abating. At first connected with economic utilitarianism, herdness (he did not use that word) became as fiercely imbedded in the realm of feeling and opinion.

At length Randolph discussed the psychological foundation of the State's potency in wartime, most of it derived, he believed, from the efficacy of its father image. In the State one found security and protection, a kind of "filial mysticism" in which there is a refuge for the real or imagined inadequacies and dangers which plague the offspring.

Yet there was an exception to the pervasiveness of the State during war. The "working-classes" were "notoriously less affected by the Estate symbolism." They are "less patriotic than the significant classes." They experience neither power nor glory, although they cannot actually regress because "never having acquired social adulthood, they cannot lose it." Drilled and regimented, they go out and docilely fight for the State, but without the filial sense and even without the herd-intellect sense which operates so powerfully among their 'betters.'

"They live habitually in an industrial serfdom, by which though nominally free, they are in practice as a class bound to a system of machine-production the implements of which they do not own, and in the distribution of whose product they have not the slightest voice, except that they can occasionally exert by a veiled intimidation which draws slightly more of the product in their direction.

"From such serfdom, military conscription is not a great change. But into the military enterprise they go, not with those hurrahs of the signficant classes whose instinct war so powerfully feeds, but with the same apathy with which they enter and continue in the industrial enterprise."

War, Bourne commented, "can almost be called an upper-class sport."

It is not unreasonable to ask at this point who in Bourne's opinion the working classes were. Through carelessness or perhaps because the components seemed so evident, he does not enumerate them. Ostensibly, he meant the tens of millions who do physical work. This is particularly pertinent in light of his statement that, "War, which should be the health of the State, unifies all the bourgeois elements and the common people, and outlaws the rest." The revolutionary proletariat shows more resistance to herd unity, and is psychically out of the mainstream. "Its vanguard, as the I.W.W., is remorselessly pursued, in spite of the proof that it is a symptom, not a cause, and its prosecution increases the disaffection of labor and intensifies the friction instead of lessening it."

Presuming one accepts the description of the State and what it becomes in wartime then the element which allegedly becomes outlawed was, as suggested, truly gigantic: literally tens of millions. One wonders whether and how Bourne, an avid reader of newspapers, overlooked the fact that the majority of labor supported the American war effort.

He was on sounder and more eloquent ground when berating witch hunting. It was a subject considered in many of his published writings. Sometimes the theme was a transition to the notion that it was not Nations that made war, but States. Not for centuries, not since "the great barbarian invasions of southern Europe, the invasions of Russia from the East, and perhaps the sweep of Islam through Northern Africa into Europe after Mohammed's death," had nations made war. And those wars were caused by the "restless expansion of migratory tribes or religious fanaticism."

Not only would Nations not have reason to war on each other, Bourne argued, but, aside from marauding, nations were incapable of waging mass warfare. War was the chief function of States—fostered, of course, by military establishments. The two are inseparable.

When Bourne says that war is the function of a State system, even the most sympathetic reader finds difficulties. How did war come about? The assertion was that the State with highly sophisticated methods pushed the Nation into war. But Bourne also said that war is the health of the State—meaning, it seems, that war evokes the State to the full health of its robustness: that is, that the State is prior to Government. Bourne does not say explicity that the State always exists and merely blooms when war comes: he just says the State is latent. Technically, of course, it is Government which declares war. Government, it will be remembered, was defined by him as "the machinery by which the nation, organized as a State, carries out its State functions."

But it is still not clear how the State comes about. Obviously it somehow came out of the Nation, that is, the condition of non-competitive peace. How that could have happened is not clear, although there are dark allusions to the desires of what are called the "significant" classes. Was the Government responsible for creating the State? Perhaps. But the Government "carries out its State functions." Did he mean that Government came out of Nation? That could not have been meant, for the Country is non-political and peaceful, and had no use for government. Could it be that Nation organizes for self-defense, but then when the danger subsides, its militaristic guard is kept up by some maneuver of the "significant" classes? Such an explanation may have been in his mind, but he does not offer it.

Randolph does say that "the State-obsessed group is either able to get control of the machinery of the State or to intimidate those in control, so that it is able through use of the collective force to regiment the other grudging and reluctant classes into a military programme." But that cryptic explanation does not explain how the State came to be. Does one, it may be asked, have to bother showing the origins of something which he appears to be unquestionably asserting exists? Indeed, he must because of the many assertions made about the State.

Frequently stressed in "The State" was what Bourne called the adept befuddling of the people. First they were swept up in war fury and then convinced that the war had been democratically proclaimed. Bourne attacked Wilson, secret diplomacy, and American policy in an argument reminiscent of his "Collapse of American Strategy" and other *Seven Arts* essays. Even if one does not concede certain of the basic assumptions and assertions, there is a compelling common-sensical manner in the bitter account of how the Government tricked the people into going to war. Undoubtedly Bourne carefully followed the events of April 2-6, 1917, and saw there was much tentativeness mixed with the bellicosity.

In the House on April 5, Representative Fred A. Britten injected an eerie short-lived note, wondering aloud why he was voting for a war he opposed; he knew the nation was over-whelmingly anti-war. "There is something in the air, gentlemen," he declared, "and I do not know what it is, whether it be the hand of destiny or some superhuman movement, something stronger than you and I can realize or resist, that seems to be picking us up bodily and literally forcing us to vote for this . . . war when way down in our hearts we are just as opposed to it as are our people back home."[2] This was what Bourne meant. Never in modern history, he remarked, had a people been consulted about going to war.

On the other hand, there is in Bourne's attack on Wilson and diplomacy the presumption that the people somehow should control foreign policy, but he does not indicate how that could be done in a world where popular control of foreign policy was absent. Moreover, the argument implies that diplomacy is a perverse mechanism of Government and State. In effect Bourne was contending that diplomacy has no place in the Nation, for the Country does not negotiate itself hypocritically into war. The thesis caused Max Lerner to raise a similar point about the ultimate logicality of Bourne's viewpoint. Regardless of how the State came about, it is clear from what he said that it was an inevitable and functional aspect of the State system. America was part of that State system, and therefore would have to be part of any war which arose. The question Lerner asked[3] was how Bourne could have justified opposition to participation in the war when—it seemed to Lerner on the basis of what was said in "The State" —he believed war was inevitable. There is a reason for not holding Bourne strictly accountable on this point. There is perhaps more justification for holding him to account for his rendering of history. In trying to explain the State as it was in his time, he sought its English origins. Despite all the change the British monarchy underwent, Bourne maintained it retained the State character, preserved when it was transported across the sea and changed only and insignficantly in form.

"The modern democratic State, in this light, is therefore no bright and rational creation of a new day, the political form under which great peoples are to live healthfully and freely in a modern world, but the last decrepit scion of an ancient and hoary stock, which has become so exhausted that it scarcely recognizes its own ancestor, does, in fact, repudiate him while it clings tenaciously to the archaic and irrelevant spirit that made that ancestor powerful, and resists the new bottles for the new wine that its health as a modern society so desperately needs. In America's case the First World War confirmed Bourne's ideas.

The American republic, his contention ran, was the direct descendent of the "early English State." It was first of all a "medieval absolute monarchy." The notion, if ever widely accepted, today would be harshly attacked. Bourne immediately turned around and discussed the feudal lord, a figure who made—although it was not mentioned—constant inroads into "absolute monarchy" and, when not making inroads, was always a threat.

The modern State—the herd organized to wage war against another State—began when a prince anywhere secured almost undisputed control over homogeneous territory and people, and strove to strengthen and maintain his power and pass it to his heirs. The king provided order and safety. The history of the State was the effort to continue personal prerogatives of power and convert upheaval to order.

The king, of course, needed ministers to carry out his will. The State then grew as a gradual differentiation of the king's absolute power, founded on devotion by subjects and the king's control of fighters who were swift and sure to smite. "Gratitude for protection and fear of the strong arm sufficed to produce the loyalty of the country to the State."

Tracing the development of the early State down through the Tudors, then the Stuarts—and finding in Cromwell a shadowy potential for "a sort of Government of Presbyterian Soviets under the tutelage of a celestial Czar"—he dated the re-establishment of the State from the Restoration. Parliament even during the time of inept monarchs was nothing more than a sop to restiveness caused by the king's autocracy.

Government by personal whim and intrigue rambled to a peak of incompetency under George III. Widespread discontent was sure to erupt, but in Britain it could not muster sufficient force. It "came in America where even the very obviously shadowy pigment of Parliamentary representation was denied the colonists. All that was vital in the political thought of England supported the American colonists in their resistance to the obnoxious government of George III."

What Bourne did with American history was even more intriguing than his treatment of European history. In his judgment, there were hopes that the Revolution might result in a "genuine break with the State ideal." The Declaration of Independence not only announced doctrines incompatible with the "Century-old conception of the Divine Right of Kings, but also with the Divine Right of the State." His implicit assumption—possibly defensible—was that because the Declaration stated expressly that government derived it rights from the governed, 18th century thinkers did not believe that the people in turn received their power from God.

Confusing government of the people—that is, arising with their consent and authorization—with government by the people, he declared that the Revolution had in it "the makings of a very daring modern experiment—the founding of a free nation which should use the State to effect its vast purposes of subduing a continent just as the colonists' armies had used arms to detach their society from the irresponsible rule of an overseas king and his frivolous ministers. The history of the State might have ended in 1776 as far as the American colonists were concerned, and the modern nation which is still striving to materialize itself have been born."

For a while during the Confederation it seemed almost as if the State were dead. But the unhappy domestic and external difficulties "all combined to put the responsible classes of the new States into the mood for a regression to the State ideal." This did not have to happen, "provided the inter-state jealousy and rivalry could have been destroyed." But there were no champions of what he called "anti-State nationalism."

The consequence was that the words of the Declaration remained only sentiments. Meantime "the ambitious leaders of the financial classes" convened, ostensibly to repair the Articles of Confederation, and then, "by one of the most successful *coups d'état* in history, turned their assembly into the manufacture of a new government on the strongest lines of the old State ideal."

Bourne at length deplored the way the new constitution was secretly drafted and ratified by means of an undemocratic voting system. His central point was that while democracy and universal suffrage had a chance for a time during the Confederation, "popular elements" saw the fruits of their revolt slip from them. If only the liberated colonies had the advantage of the lesson of the French Revolution behind them, the new constitution would "undoubtedly have been followed by a new revolution, as very nearly happened later against Washington and the Federalists." But, "the ironical ineptitude of Fate put the machinery of the new Federalist constitutional government in operation at just the moment that the French Revolution began, and by the time those great waves of Jacobin feeling reached North America, the new Federalist State was firmly enough on its course to weather the gale and the turmoil."

Americans were saddled with a document whose preamble was a "pious hope rather than actuality." The Constitution was the testament of the "shockingly undemocratic origins of the American State." In completely glossing over the undemocratic basis of the Constitution, American historians had perpetrated an explanation of the document which resulted in Constitution worship. Some modern historians, however, had looked under the carpet. Scholarship had shown that the delegates not only had an unconscious economic interest in the outcome, but a frank political interest in a State which should protect the propertied from the people's hostility.

Historians also had shown how the new government became almost a device for overcoming repudiation of debts, for setting in their place the farmer and small tradesmen (whom the unsettled conditions of reconstruction had threatened to liberate, for re-establishing on the securest basis of the sanctity of property and the State a class supremacy endangered by a democracy that had been inspired and encouraged by the Revolution. None of this was comprehended by the popular mind because the truth disturbed the aura of reverence about the State, and therefore was ignored. "No one suggests," he wrote, "that the anxiety of the leaders of the heretofore unquestioned ruling classes desired the revision of the Articles and labored so weightily over a new instrument not because the nation was failing under the Articles but because it was succeeding only too well. Without intervention from the leaders, reconstruction threatened in time to turn the new nation into an agrarian and proletarian democracy."

It was impossible, of course, to predict what would have been worked out eventually, Bourne observed, but it was clear that at a time when political progress was towards agrarian and proletarian democracy, a force hostile to it gripped the nation and imposed a powerful form of government against which the embryo agrarian and proletarian democracy could only struggle blindly. The propertied thereafter never lost their position.

There was a change, of course, when the Federalists lost the election of 1800, but "Jeffersonian democracy never meant in practice any more than the substitution of the rule of the country gentleman for the rule of the town capitalist." The true hostility between the two factions was minute, compared to that of both of them toward the common man, who, Bourne insisted, was contemptuous of his government.

Both factions were swept away "by the eruption of the Western democracy under Andrew Jackson" and the rule of the common man. But in the long run the reign of the "ancient classes" was not challenged seriously because the anti-Jacksonians banded together. Regardless of the section, the capitalist realized the advantage of supporting the needs of his fellow capitalists, even if those interests—such as the tariff—were incidentally disagreeable. Bad generalship by the coalition allowed a Western free soil minority President to win office. The Civil War ensued. The slave power was smashed. But Northern capital reigned supreme.

From the Civil War to the death of Mark Hanna, the essay continued, "propertied industrial classes ran a triumphal career in possession of the State." There were occasional popular rumblings as in the 1896 presidential contest, but generally "aggressive expansionist capitalism" had some 40 years in which to direct the republic as a private preserve, or laboratory, "experimenting, developing, wasting, subjugating, to its heart's content, in the midst of a vast somnolence of complacency such as has never been seen and contrasts strangely with the spiritual dissent and constructive revolutionary thought which went on at the same time in England and the Continent."

That such rule could linger for so long did not surprise Bourne, for "once the State has begun to function, and a large class finds its interest and its expression of power in maintaining the State, this ruling class may compel obedience from any uninterested minority. The State thus becomes an instrument by which the power of the whole herd is wielded for the benefit of a class."

The era ended in 1904 when a whole people awoke in a modern age, realizing that it had overslept. There was a restless period of doubt and self-criticism led by a President who used the Ten Commandments for political purposes. Theodore Roosevelt made up in dogmatism what he lacked in philosophy, belaboring the wicked, and casting a shadow over the prestige of the captains of industry.

Meanwhile, the ruling classes—annoyed, bewildered, harassed—pretended they were losing control of the State. Their apologists warned against political innovation and the rejecting of the tried and true. Actually, Randolph said, those classes had little to fear from a political system so deeply rooted in property. Moreover, a legal system propped up both property and the party setup. And when war came, business skills were badly needed, thus allowing business to make an alliance with Government.

At the same time, the middle class which previously had been worried and riddled by the campaign against American failings gladly retreated to a glorification of the American State, a convenient way to drive off "all the foul old doubts and dismays."

The Revolution little affected the way America was run, it was asserted. The same class which had tricked the country with the Constitution had remained dominant. Some tinkering was done, but it meant little. The American President was an elected king. Kings often have been chosen by election in European history, and frequent elections merely meant that the notables could closely watch their man in Washington.

The growth of political parties also had little effect on how the country was run because the notables always controlled the parties. The electorate really was just called on to choose between two or perhaps from among a handful of errand boys of the notable. After the system was organized into a hierarchy extending from national to county politics, it became safe to broaden the electorate. No matter who won, the property classes could not lose. The people were merely ratifiers of upper-class slates. Frontal attack on Government was impossible.

"The party system succeeded, of course, beyond the wildest dreams of its creators. It relegated the founders of the Constitution to the role of doctrinaire theorists, political amateurs. Just because it grew up so slowly to meet the needs of ambitious politicians and was not imposed by ruling-class fiat, as was the Constitution, did it have a chance to become assimilated, worked into the political intelligence and instinct of the people, and be adopted gladly and universally as a genuine political form, expressive both of popular need and ruling-class demand. It satisfied the popular need for democracy."

A significant result, Randolph commented, was a superficial judgment by the people that they had a hand in their government. A mood of political complacency was created which lasted unbothered into the 20th century: the truth was that the party system was the means of removing political grievances without surrendering control, and nothing more. The party system "became the unofficial but real government, the instrument which used the Constitution as its instrument." The two major threats to the party system—Jackson and Lincoln—were but short-lived, because each was captured by the old guard.

And campaigns such as Bryan's where one of the parties was captured by the faction seeking transfer of power from "the significant to the less significant classes," split the party. Sporadic third-party attacks merely threw the election to one of the big parties, or, if dangerous enough, produced a virtual coalition against them. Other than Bryan's, Bourne did not say which campaigns and coalitions he had in mind, nor what—granting for a moment the case—there was wrong about the party system being a means to alleviate political grievances.

Many readers of "The State" must have wondered what the writer had in mind in his many debatable contentions. For it is clear that one competent in any of several disciplines could write a damning critique of "The State." One obvious approach would be to show it as a product of the times.

It is known both from his works and reading lists that he was interested in the sociological and psychological writing of his era, as well as the socialist, socialist-inspired, and socialist-tending political literature. Randolph had read Gustave Le Bon's *The Crowd, A Study of the Popular Mind,* first published in 1896, and Wilfred Trotter's *Instincts of the Herd in Peace and War* (1917), "books that absorbed us all in those days," Van Wyck Brooks later recalled.[4]

As early as 1915 Bourne read *The State: Its History and Development Viewed Sociologically* (1914), the translation of Franz Oppenheimer's *Der Staat* (1908), one of the most exciting works of the era. Distinctions had not come about, Oppenheimer contended, because ability naturally and inevitably rose to the top, but through force used by some against others. Unemployment existed, Oppenheimer believed, not because there was not enough work or resources, but because the usable land—far more than the entire world's population needed to live in dignity—was not all worked. It is clear, too, that Bourne had read *An Economic Interpretation of the Constitution* (1913) by Charles Beard, whom he admired immensely. And if he did not read J. Allen Smith's *The Spirit of American Government* (1907), which called the Constitution a tool to thwart democracy, he surely knew the book's thesis. In the light of a vast quantity of scholarship done since on late 18th and early 19th century America as well as what is known about the progressive era, Bourne's approach (and thereby his failings) seem elemental. Although he had warned others of similar pitfalls, he himself was guilty of projecting 20th century democratic liberalism back to the age of the Founding Fathers, an unworkable device.

Merrill Jensen has argued in his *The New Nation: A History of the United States During the Confederation Period, 1781-1789* (1950) that the Confederation was by no means as bumbling as it later was asserted to have been: or at least its evils accompanied its good points. But it certainly was not the embryo democratic bastion Randolph seemed to think it was. The Confederation suffered from very real financial chaos and from a debilitating lack of executive unity neither of which a forceful pen could argue away.

The presumption appears to be that the theme of American history always was the conflict of human rights against property rights. Clearly implicit in the essay on the State is the subtle assertion that men dedicated to property rights were not, therefore, devoted to human rights. Even though the Articles of Confederation had no Bill of Rights, Bourne preferred it to the Constitution. To him the Constitution was neither an effort by wise men to meet the needs of their time by reason instead of violence and force, nor was it the middle position between anarchic localism and centralized tyranny. As a 20th century liberal and radical, he found a lot of money in the possession of the delegates and decided they were venal.

In some ways "The State" is painfully clumsy. Absence of any allusion to the *Federalist Papers*—even to Madison's discussion of democracy and conflicting property interests suggests that the author did not know these essays well or at all. There is every reason to believe he never read any of the Convention's journals, which began appearing in 1911. Had he, he probably would have seen how unrepresentative were many of Beard's quotes.

Randolph was too ready with weak generalizations. In many cases, for example, those who according to his notions should be for and against ratification of the Constitution do not so believe: in New York the owners of the great estates opposed approval, as did the farmers along the Connecticut River in New Hampshire. And in Georgia, where there was representation of each class, approval was almost unanimous in the hope of protection against the Creek Indians.

Bourne charged the Constitution cramped democracy. As a matter of fact, it went farther on that score than the Articles did. The Constitution was adopted by as democratic a process as any of the time. The writer criticized the lessening of democratic control by the states after the Articles were gone. Actually the states themselves, not the Constitution, played a major role in that development. Nowhere, for example, were state constitutions submitted to the people; they were merely proclaimed. And apparently it was forgotten that the power to determine the qualifications for voting had been left by the Constitution to the states.

Even if the above points could not be indicated, it would be evident that the essay tacitly made the false assertion that the idea of mass participation in government was prevalent or at least widespread at the time. The Convention was no more aristocratic than the average political gathering of the time. Furthermore, there is no reason why the Convention should have been necessarily any more plebian than it was. The same general kind of men who drafted the Constitution also drew up the Articles and signed the Declaration of Independence; the Constitution was as liberal as any of those in the home states of the delegates.

Since Bourne's time various scholarly works—including Charles Snydor's *Gentlemen Freeholders: Political Practices in Washington's Virginia* (1952) and Robert E. Brown's *Middle-Class Democracy and the Revolution in Massachusetts, 1691-1780* (1955)—have demonstrated how widespread was the franchise in at least two significant areas. And Brown's *Charles Beard and the Constitution* (1950) and Forrest MacDonald's *We the People: The Economic Origins of the Constitution* (1958) have revealed deficiencies in Beard's use of Convention documents.

Although Randolph could not of course have had the benefit of later studies, his homework was poorly done. In his time the records of the Convention had become available, and many of the writings of the Fathers also were available. But no effort was made to find out what they themselves said. Bourne, it will be remembered, admitted his dislike of scholarship.

One almost gets the impression that he wanted a Constitution written only for farmers and debtors. To him, the Fathers were not the liberals and moderates of their time, but conservative and even reactionary. Therefore, it was easy to see in the electoral college a conspiracy rather than a compromise which may have saved the Convention from failure. It was easy to see dark implications in the secretiveness of the Convention rather than a practical way to get men to speak openly and without fear for their reputations and careers. It also seems that it did not occur to the author that the delegates could have sat for months, even years without ironing out their disagreements and producing a completely clear document.

"The State," suffers from a punishing vagueness. It is never clear just who the oppressors were, although Bourne usually called them the "significant" classes. He often had said the ongoing conflict was with an oppressive older generation. At other times the forces of imposition are identified as industrialists, financiers, the upperclass, militarists, and capitalists—groups which sometimes are opposed. Contradictions and difficulties already have been mentioned, but another major stumbling block may be noted: the notion of peaceful Nation seems to wreck havoc with the Nietzschean will to power concept—that is, the drive of each individual to acquire a sense of control over his environment and those around him.

But the thorniest issue is the consideration of property. First, it should be noted there is no evidence that Bourne was against property. Obviously he thought it efficacious. He wanted it redistributed in some unclear way to those who had been "squeezed down into the small end of the horn." This implies a conviction that man needed property for his own well-being.

It is surprising how little Randolph understood the idea of property before the Age of Jackson. Until the late 18th century, property and liberty were inseparable: It was the only foundation yet conceived for liberty. It was at issue in the fight with Britain. As Edmund S. Morgan has said, "The Americans fought England because Parliament threatened the security of property. They established state constitutions with property qualifications for voting and office-holding in order to protect the security of property. And when the state governments seemed inadequate to the task, they set up the Federal government for the same purpose. The economic motive was present in all these actions, but it was present as the friend of universal liberty. Devotion to security of property was not the attitude of a privileged few but the fundamental principle of the many, inseparable from everything that went by the name of freedom and people so intimately."[5]

If it is clear in "The State" that there was a distaste for property as it was attached to the "significant" classes, it still is not clear *why* its author felt that way. The question not approached is, What is wrong with property and its role in governing, in any century? A search in other writings does not reveal the answer. It is relatively easy to hang a Marxist tag on him, so easy, in fact, that one should not be surprised to find no reward in that direction.

Bourne's work also is distressing because after the State was unveiled, he seemed totally at a loss as to what should be done with it. There was not a single positive suggestion of importance in the work. This may have been because he never policed the area intellectually before bringing up his armor. There are two things which one may demand to know when discussing politics and political theory, especially when a particular government is being discussed. First one pragmatically wants to know how well it is constituted. Randolph did not try to show American government functioning at an unreasonably low level.

A second question is the obvious distinction between the relative best—the best for the governed, considering circumstances, traditions, and the stage of development—and the absolute best, the best for an enlightened and mature people in almost ideal situations. Bourne had warned that democracy could not be imposed on Germany. Yet it appears clear that he thought some kind of agrarian and proletarian democracy workable at the very begining of the repubic. Finally, it is assumed that domestic society (the family) and political society (the state) are somehow identical instead of closely related. That assumption is debatable.

It was asserted that a scholar could easily write a critique as long or longer than "The State." Why then should the work ever be taken seriously? The answer is that however open to attack, it is nevertheless the remarkable creation of a brilliant mind. In an important way "The State" was very much a product of the times. It is a commendable example of how an incisive mind can take ideas and run with them in a challenging, fresh manner. And the discussion of the herd and the modern state's power is applicable in large degree to totalitarian government.[6]

There is abundant evidence that "The State" greatly impressed many when it was published, probably because it summed up many antagonisms. Fourteen years after Bourne's death, John Chamberlain—who was nobody's fool—said that "The State" was "grand political theory."[7] And as many as 21 years after publication Max Lerner called it a "brilliant beginning," and "one of the notable American attempts at a theory of the state."[8]

It has been remarked that Harold Laski had an ultimately harsh view of Bourne's position and "The State." It also should be noted that Laski's evaluation came out of a store of profound admiration:

"[The *Untimely Papers* essays] are turned from protest into positive statement by a long and unfinished essay on the State, in which Mr. Bourne was clearly searching to vindicate the ultimate rights of personality against the demands of authority outside. His liberalism, at bottom, is akin to the protest of William Godwin against the encroachment of political power.

"It had obviously been deeply influenced by the attractive anarchism of Tolstoy and Kropotkin. Even more, I think, it is an un-conscious revolt against that impotence to which the vast machine of war reduced the individual. Bourne seems to have felt engulfed by a moral cataclysm; and his answer to its annihilating effort was the assertion of uncompromising defiance. He hated war; the state was an engine of war; therefore he hated the state.

"Bourne exhausts the vocabulary of rhetorical vituperation to record his conviction that political authority must be made impotent before the demand of conscience. He views the state as a great Moloch devouring its victims, and without the virtue of thinking in terms of their pain. The whole essay is a superb cry of anger against a tyranny he felt to be grinding."[9]

One will have noticed by now that the work has been identified here as "The State" instead of as *The State*. It generally has been considered that it was the unfinished fragment of a contemplated longer major effort. The contrary is closer to the truth. The essay by no means may be dismissed as the inferior creation of a mind which usually turned out better work. But neither may "The State" be taken seriously. It may not be considered as necessarily reflecting Bourne's thought. That it may have done so is possible, but that is something which cannot be known.

The reason "The State" may not be taken unquestionably as part of his work is that the author threw away the manuscript.[10] After his death, it was found in a trash basket, along with "Autobiographic Chapter," by Agnes de Lima, one of the friends who nursed him in the last days. Does this necessarily mean anything? It could. It is very possible that he was not pleased with the piece and that by December 1918 no longer agreed with most or much of what it said; or he may have concluded that the arguments needed better foundations.

It is possible that Randolph may have thrown away the manuscript of "The State" because he was depressed and discouraged—yet without having altered the views expressed in the work. For, after all, he underestimated the caliber of the first chapter of the novel, which also was thrown away. The manuscript may have been discarded accidentally. It is possible he planned to rewrite without reference to the first draft. These alternatives are possible, but unlikely.

What is more likely is that when he began a job he never finished—unpacking at his new lodgings—he found the manuscript of "The State," knew he did not like it anymore, and chucked it. The work contains ideas which in some form had been expressed in *Seven Arts* esasys. Perhaps it was felt they already had been better expressed in *Seven Arts*.

Internal evidence suggests that "The State" was written not as the beginning of a book but for *Seven Arts* or some other review. The essay contains references which are unclear now but which relate to current developments. Obviously the author felt the writing would be clear to any immediate reader. Bourne was too professional to make timely remarks in a composition intended as a book which might not see the light for many months.

Moreover, as the essay ended, the writer returned to a summary of what was said at the beginning and what followed. The recapitulation tried to put the effort in perspective, tying the ends and smoothing the knot. Perhaps "The State" was the first of several essays to have composed a book of the same title. But the so very current comments weigh against such a conclusion.

It is because of these very real uncertainties that one may not hold Bourne strictly accountable. The work is of historical interest on its merits because of its impact on his contemporaries, and because it reflects the thinking of the times. It should be remembered that as published it was not known to have received the approval of its creator, a man who was without question a craftsman and whose standards "The State" does not meet.

"The State" apparently was written sometime after August 1917, very probably projected for what would have been the November 1917 issue of *Seven Arts*, but abandoned when the magazine died. It would have been a logical effort after the earlier essays for that publication. For in the earlier issues one finds as a major theme that which Louis Hartz would call in his *The Liberal Tradition in America* (1955), Lockean unanimity—that is, the tyranny of majority opinion in a democracy.

Louis Filler has written reasonably (and incorrectly), that "it slowly dawned upon Bourne how utterly he had been defeated."[11] One finds no such evidence. "The State" may have come out of gloom and melancholy, but as shall be seen bitterness at war's end was balanced by hope and enthusiasm. A new and significant job with the *Dial* was at hand, and he expected to marry the woman he loved.

Let us turn, then, and course down the last months of Randolph Bourne's career to that raw weekend in December 1918 when America lost a son who loved her as much as any who had been in the trenches.

That which was crooked
Straightened.
That which was defeated
Joined
With that which was
Victorious.
And that which was beautiful
Blended
With that which was ill-planned.
To be separated
And made crooked
Or Straight
Again. —Theodore Dreiser, 1933

XI

CASUALTY OF HIS TIME

After the closing of the *Seven Arts*, Bourne's life was as unsettled as ever, perhaps more so now that he could not look regularly to that magazine as an outlet for serious writing. According to Joseph Ward Swain,[1] a college acquaintance who knew only of Randolph's unhappy side, his intimate friends disliked seeing him because of his bitterness regarding the war.

Almost unavoidably the war separated him from many acquaintances. It took Elizabeth Shepley Sargeant off to France, dispersed some of the *New Republic* writers, and drafted Paul Rosenfeld. Some took civilian jobs in Washington, D.C. "I have been very angry with the world today because I am not living in the country," he wrote Dorothy Teall. "My friends who might go away with me are being drafted, and the others are too poor or busy."[2]

Randolph wanted a chance to defy the draft. One day he confided to Floyd Dell as they sat talking in Dell's apartment in the Village that if called he would become a conscientious objector. This only embarrassed and distressed Dell, who knew there was no chance of that ever happening.[3] "He lived," Dell said in his book *Homecoming,* "within some kind of protective illusion in that respect; no one would have been so cruel as to remind him of what he had succeeded in ignoring."

Apparently what bothered Dell was eventually made clear to Bourne who facetiously wrote home: "I have been classified as totally and permanently, mentally and physically unfit for military service, and when this friend [perhaps meaning Rosenfeld] returns, it will mean that practically everyone of my friends is exempted from the service in some form or another, either as criminals out on bail, or married men, or psychopaths or weaklings."[4]

A significant factor in the chagrin was the momentary stalemate which the career with the *Dial* had reached. At one time he was under the impression he was going to be at the top of the review's staff, but when he died he had no editorial responsibilities. Although his lengthy articles were printed the role with the *Dial* had turned out to be disappointing.

It is not known how he joined the *Dial,* but beginning in December 1916 he was a steady contributor. For several months after July 1918 when the magazine moved from Chicago to New York and was converted from a predominantly book review organ to a format similar to that of the *New Republic* and the *Nation,* his name appeared on the masthead as an associate editor. Among the eight editors and associates were Dewey, Harold Stearns, and Thorstein Veblen.

The *Dial* had planned to convert from a biweekly to a weekly in its effort to influence American thinking about post-war reconstruction. Adequate support was supplied by rich Scofield Thayer, age 30, but a newsprint shortage delayed the expansion until after the war. The problem where Randolph was concerned was not space shortage, but a clash with John Dewey.

The *Seven Arts* essays had already been published when the *Dial* moved to New York. In the *New Republic* for May 4, 1918, Bourne strongly critized *Man's Supreme Inheritance,* a book by Matthias Alexander, for which Dewey had written an approving introduction. Alexander's work had asserted that the body could and should erase habitual ways of incorrectly doing things—working positions, for instance—which had carried into the 20th century. New muscular patterns, postures, and movements needed to be developed.

Randolph indirectly made the review a slap at Dewey, commenting, "Philosophy is a dangerous quicksand. Professor Dewey's instrumentalism has held out to Mr. Alexander a helping hand, but has scarcely saved him from getting at times beyond his depth." Dewey's reply the next week in a letter to the editor was equally shattering as Bourne's article. Wrote Dewey: " R.B.'s' review of Mr. Alexander's *Man's Supreme Inheritance* exhibits such ingenuity in evading perception of its significant points that it seems worth while to make a statement for the protection of readers who might otherwise be misled."

Whatever the immediate cause, it is clear that there was a split between the two, unfortunate in that on most things they agreed. Alvin Johnson, a *New Republic* editor, later told a friend of Bourne that Dewey had been offended by the assault an Alexander and refused to be on the *Dial* editorial board if he were. Dewey later told the person with whom Johnson had spoken that there never was any difficulty between them.[5]

Others at the time also were aware of the clash. Harold Stearns years after recalled that Dewey and Bourne often talked in the office of the *Dial*, the latter with "covert irony."[6] And the writer Robert Morse Lovett who later became an editor of the *New Republic* recalled that as editor of the *Dial* he was supposed to have healed the wound, but that Randolph died before Lovett could get them together.[7]

The recollections of Johnson, Stearns and Lovett are reinforced by one who perhaps was closer to happenings than any of that trio, Merrill Rogers. Rogers was a Harvard man ('14) who had followed the suggestion of his friend John Reed and become business manager of the *Masses* from mid 1916 to the end of 1917.[8] Although the editors of the *Masses* had discussed adding Bourne to the editorial board, Rogers did not know him very well until after the *Masses* officials were indicted in April 1918 under the Sedition Act.

In December 1917 Rogers had married a suffrage worker, Joy Young, who had been a friend of Randolph from days in the American Union Against Militarism. It probably was in March 1918 that Martyn Johnson, publisher of the *Dial,* hired Rogers as business manager; if the *Dial* was to to go big time as a journal of opinion it would need money. Rogers approached his friend Scofield Thayer, class of '13 at Harvard where the two had co-edited the *Harvard Monthly*.

Thayer was worried about the draft and he thought that as an editor of an established publication he might be able to claim exemption. Moreover, Thayer admired Bourne greatly, although he had not met him. Merrill and Joy Rogers invited the men to dinner, and the evening was so successful that Thayer soon put up $30,000 on the understanding that Randolph would be on the editorial board. No editor-in-chief had been determined yet, although Harold Stearns as managing editor was doing much of the work. "As a piece of editorial window dressing," Rogers recalled, "Johnson conceived the idea of asking John Dewey and Thorstein Veblen to serve also. Veblen accepted, but Dewey, learning that Randolph was to be an editor, reacted violently:

he would have nothing to do with a publication with which Randolph was connected."

As Johnson thought Dewey's name was very important to the magazine's sucess, he consented and promised to withdraw Randolph's name. Thayer was angry, but agreed. As a sop to conscience Johnson decided that he should be given book reviews—on non-war topics. Rogers recalled that this did not thwart Bourne completely. He remembered his delivering a review to the office one day, and—instead of taking it up to the editorial office—handed it to Rogers with a quizzical, apologetic look, and said: "I've done it again. They're not going to like it up there."

He meant he had worked some aspect of the war into even the most innocent subject. An examination of *Dial* articles generally supports Rogers' memory. That a review sometimes dealt with what Randolph liked to call "a most poisonous book"[9] is clear. He himself was philosophical about the outcome. As he wrote home, "I have been relieved of my editorial duties on the *Dial,* but I am to be paid my salary just the same and continue to write. I prefer it this way, as it leaves me much freer. . . . The rich young man who put up the money to back the *Dial* this year is a very good friend of mine, and we are both in the same boat. He has strong tastes and I have strong convictions, and the man who runs the paper is very much afraid of us both, afraid we will have too much to say about the policy."[10]

A month later came a report that there "has been some fuss about my being an editor, owning to my radical views, but I am paid just the same as if I was one, and only have to write two articles a month." In fact, "I seem to be very strong with the young man who is giving most of the money to back the *Dial* this year. He says he gave his $25,000 largely on the strength of my contributions, and he was very angry at their not wanting me as a regular associate editor. So I do not need to worry apparently, as long as the money lasts."[11]

Bourne's absence as a major personality on the *Dial* could not, of course, prevent it from going on to become an excellent monthly in the 1920's, but it might have abvanced more quickly with his help. Harold Stearns, editor-in-chief at one time as well as an associate editor later, valued his work highly. Stearns remarked that the ideas on the war held by his assistant, Clarence Britten—an ex-professor of English from the University of Wisconsin—were delicious but so radical that Stearns had to limit "anti-war contributions to the sly book reviews of Randolph Bourne and to the out-spoken letters of Robert Dell, our Paris correspondent, whose letters came into the office plainly marked,

'Opened By The Military Censor.' "[12] Stearns, of course, used "sly" as a phrase.

Once the war had ended and the postwar Red scare had subsided, Bourne would have played an important part in the *Dial's* success so long as Thayer—who in the 1920's technically was editor as well as publisher with Watson—was connected with it. In fact, the writer Gilbert Seldes told Van Wyck Brooks that just before Randolph's death Thayer planned to make him political editor.[13] *Dial* published "An Autobiographical Chapter" in January 1920, and then in December 1923 a laudatory essay on him by Paul Rosenfeld, both occurences an indication of how much he was esteemed.

Apparently impeccable evidence comes from Dr. J. S. Watson, Jr., Thayer's partner. According to him, the *Dial* was less political in the 1920's only because Bourne had died. "When Thayer first laid plans for the magazine," Watson explained, "it was his intention, in which I concurred, to divide the magazine into two sections, literary and political. As his political editor he selected Randolph Bourne, for whom he felt great admiration. Bourne agreed to take full charge of this department. However Bourne's death . . . put an end to the scheme. Certainly there were other authorities in this field, but none was quite what Thayer wanted. When we finally obtained control of the *Dial* some months later, we agreed to limit ourselves to literary, artistic, and philosophical matters."[14]

Watson's version was affirmed in 1963 when William Wasserstrom published *The Time of the Dial,* a history of the magazine in which he says that Thayer was Bourne's greatest supporter and that he was mainly interested in the review as an organ for his writing. Later, Wasserstrom wrote, Thayer tried to follow Bourne's principles of criticism, especially those expressed in his essay "Traps for the Unwary," which was in the *Dial* for March 1918.

Whatever frustrations Randolph encountered in his professional life were soothed to great extent by his incurable weakness for friends. His closest friends were sensitive to the discouragements career difficulties caused him, and many sympathized with his view of the war. He saw much of Alyse Gregory, a close friend since his return from Europe. Alyse in 1923-25 preceded Marianne Moore as managing editor of the *Dial.* Often he was at Alyse's Village apartment on Patchin Place, and about him she built a salon to which Randolph brought journalists, critics, artists, revolutionaries, professors. On a typical evening, he might be at Alyse's arguing with Walter Lippmann about America's part in the war.[15] "Who of the [Village] crowd," Stearns later said, "can forget those evening meetings in Alyse Gregory's little apartment in Patchin Place?—where some of the wittiest and shrewdest conversations and comment of our day was to be heard almost any time?"[16]

Bourne and Brooks had become firm friends, although they differed on American participation in the war. Of all his friends, Randolph told his mother, "I like and admire him the most, I think. We used to have lunch together here in New York or tea after his work. It is a mutual admiration. He has been tied to a desk in the Century [book publishing] Co., and he looks on me as one who leads the ideal, free, dignified leisurely life of a true man of letters, making my living by my pen with no sordid job to hold down. So, when you think I ought to have a job, remember that I am admired just because I haven't one."[17]

Part of the summer of 1917 was spent with Van Wyck at Brooks' house at Cos Cob, Connecticut. One day the pair began a three-day walking trip along Cape Cod to Provincetown where, as Randolph wrote, the Greenwich Villagers were as thick as mosquitos. Writers like Susan Glaspell and Mary Horton Vorse were there, and they dropped in on Eugene O'Neil who, in a swim suit, sat in a window, trembling from Parkinson's disease.

"I long for a solitary sand dune," Randolph wrote Alyse. "But we had to see Provincetown, and we are romantically settled high up over the water, overlooking the harbor. Brooks is in the next room leading 'la vie littcraire' with many groans. We are both supposed to be writing articles for the *Seven Arts,* but inspiration is very feeble after so many days in the open air. I have a toothache, and life is not very interesting."[18]

Life was interesting enough for both of them to walk most of the way to Boston, where Randolph delighted in the old squares and the red brick houses of Beacon Hill. "The eye is constantly charmed," he told Alyse, "by noble old houses and gracious expanses and wonderful white steeples." For Brooks, this was his own real introduction to a city to which he had been indifferent while a Harvard student.[19]

Randolph also passed some of the summer of 1918 with Brooks and his wife, this time at Sound Beach, Connecticut. It was a pleasant respite from the hot city, where he was living in Paul Rosenfeld's handsome apartment on Irving Place. Paul was then undergoing military training in Virginia.

"I made a tacit bargain to come up and do the typewriting [of the translation Mrs. Brooks had made of a French novel] in exchange for my board," he exlained to Alyse, "but 100,000 words in three weeks taxes my abilities, especially when I am trying to write my autobiographical novel, and satisfy Harold's demands for reviews. Am I missing much in not being around for the debut of the *Dial*? Harold as a dude must be an even more eccentric spectacle than as a Chatterton or Francis Thompson. . . . Your salon is still the center of an intellectual life, evidently. Your weariness? So might any of the great French ladies have spoken between acts.

"I shall be turned out of this little Paradise next week, and Heaven knows where I shall go then. I will have six weeks before the gates of Martyn Johnson close about my soul. . . . Nothing but work under the pleasant conditions that I am working under now, I should want nothing more in life. I wish the Thayers would invite me to Dublin, but I do not see any way to make that any more obvious than it has been made." [20]

This was not only an ironical but a content and perhaps happy Randolph Bourne. If from time to time he had thought seriously of going west, the idea no longer appealed to him.[21] One thing which tied him to New York besides his hopes about the *Dial* was the close relationship with Agnes de Lima and Esther Cornell, two of the three young women with whom he lived much of the summer of 1916 in Caldwell, New Jersey. July 1917 had been spent at the White Plains, New York, home of Esther's mother. Esther was working in Massachusetts on a "war farm," and Agnes was working in New York. "The city," he wrote, "seems in another world, and nothing could be more serene than this rainy hill. . . . Esther's mother and I spend the day together. I sleep somewhat audaciously out on the front porch, and read and write in front of a too smoky wood fire in a fraudulent fireplace. I speculate shall I go to Mrs. James [in Milton, Massachusetts], or shall I stay here? Shall I go away with Van Wyck Brooks in August? Meanwhile I can forget temporarily that I haven't stability in my life. How is the cruel city treating you? Any news of Harold [Stearns]?"[22]

What perhaps most attracted Randolph to Esther and Agnes at first was an absence of the middle class conventionality and "respectability" of which he was contemptuous. Neither the outlandish nor the radically new disturbed Agnes and Esther. To them there was nothing remarkable—except that it was fun—about their walking up the coast of Martha's Vineyard in late summer of 1918.[23]

The walk lasted a jolly two weeks, but at one point they inadvertently disturbed the composure of the Navy. Esther, who had studied modern dance, was prancing and bounding along the rocky shoreline. It was during a submarine scare and Randolph pleaded with an amused

Esther to stop it; it might seem as if they were signalling. At Cos Cob, a gun boat followed them along.

Once arrived at the Vineyard, Agnes had to return to New York immediately, but the other two stayed. A Navy officer stopped them in the street.

"There were three of you when you arrived here," the officer said.

"Yes," Esther replied, "my friend had to go back to her job."

"What are those figures you have in that book you have in your hand?" the officer asked, pointing to a cost record of the journey. "Would you be willing to have all the documents in your possession examined?"

"Documents? What documents?"

"The mail you received this morning, for example."

"Certainly," Esther said breezily.

The officer announced he would go to Boston with them, and sat behind them all the way. In the Boston railroad station Esther turned on her charm. Mightn't they have some lunch? she asked. "I'm starved," she told him, "aren't you?"

Sitting at the station lunch counter, the officer probably felt silly and defeated. He phoned his superior and said, "Just a coupla nuts."

To Randolph he said, "Tell me, how come you get *two* girls to walk with you. I can't even get one!"

The incident apparently amused every one at the time except Randolph, who was frightened and worried that somehow Esther would be in trouble with the authorities. He told the girls that the Justice Department had inquired about him at the *New Republic*.[24] This was not the first indication of nervousness, however. James Oppenheim recalled that Randolph had one fear greater than any other. "That was fear of prison. He could hardly bear the thought of it."[25]

According to another friend of his; he insisted that Dewey had put the Justice Department on his trail—an incredible idea.

"You don't know Dewey," Randolph allegedly said. "He is terribly vain. He was offended by my article and would do anything to injure me."[26]

Bourne may have been further disturbed by the aftermath of a harmless quarrel he had with Alyse Gregory[27] shortly before he went to visit Brooks at Sound Beach in 1918. Afterward, Alyse playfully sent a one-word telegram: "PERFIDE," (French for perfidious, teacherous, false-hearted, or a noun for the same kind of person). Back came a nervous reply with the usual irony: "Your mysterious telegram to Paul [Rosenfeld] and me at Sound Beach will certainly get us all in trouble. The child who does the work here cannot spell. "Perside" [sic, RB showing the misspelling] certainly looks like a code; there is nothing in English that it can mean. It is a mere miracle that Paul was not immediately interned. He has horrendous stories of Paul Strand and others."[28]

Today the matter perhaps would not need attention, except of course that a story has been handed down and repeated for four decades about how—as John Chamberlain put it—Randolph was "hounded" by the Justice Department,[29] and how a trunk of manuscripts and letters lost in the summer of 1918 most probably was taken by the government. It may have been that he was watched by the government and that indeed officials did take the trunk—althought it is not unreasonable to presume it might have been returned, once inspected. The story of how the government at the time checked the mails is of course well know.

On the other hand, it is equally as likely that Randolph himself was the victim of raw wartime nerves. It is significant that a friend remembered his complaining to her that the government did not take him seriously enough to jail him.[30]

It would not necessarily follow that there would be any record of surveillance if he had been watched by the government. But it should be noted that a check by both the writer and Congressman Peter W. Rodino, Jr., with the Justice Department and the National Archives, where some Justice Department materials are kept, did not disclose any records on Bourne.[31]

The story of his alleged hounding by the government remains, therefore, a legend in the medieval meaning of *legendi,* that which is not true or which cannot be verified.

Even if the government had been hot on the trail, the incident at Martha's Vineyard would have been cherished by him because of the way Esther astutely had handled the earnest Navy officer.

For by then Randolph was deeply in love with Esther; this time, the woman also loved Randolph.

In the fall of 1914 he visited a young woman friend in Brookfield, Connecticut. To the same house had been taken another young woman who was dying of cancer, and who had been operated on recently. On his arrival he was sternly warned not to disturb the patient on any account. The next morning, the hostess found him and the patient gone. She stormed angrily outside and found him and the patient—her arm in a sling—sitting by the pump deeply engrossed in a conversation punctuated by the girl's mirthful laughter. Later the patient said: "Randolph would make a good lover. I could love that man."[32]

The same kind of magnetism and tenderness drew Esther to him. Esther was a beautiful creature,[33] with red-gold hair, parted down the middle and turned up on each side of the forehead and about the ears in two soft luxuriant waves. Striking green eyes, separated by a straight, thin nose, stared piercingly and merrily from a background of honey-white skin.

She was the daughter of a Chicago branch of the New York family of Cornell. After first attending finishing school in Chicago, she was graduated from Bryn Mawr. An accomplished pianist, she loved the stage more. A big break came in the fall of 1916 when she toured in the feminine lead role of *The 13th Chair.* Very early in the summer of that year she had gone to Colorado because of poor health, and then after arriving in Caldwell, N.J., learned her lines. However, favoritism —after the troupe arrived in New York from its tryout and was preparing to open—resulted in Esther's losing the lead to another member of the cast, although her pictures were used out front.

Perhaps that was fortunate, for on November 21, the morning after the mystery drama opened, the critic of the New York *Times* wrote that he was bored and that one never doubted who the guilty party was. The play did not run long.

Randolph began to fall in love with Esther in the summer of 1916 when they were at Caldwell.[34] But the courtship was difficult; both were strong-willed. Besides her warmth and her lyric Irish quality, Esther also was jealous, suspicious, and insecure. Moreover, she was consumed with artistic and creative ambition, partly answered by her roles in *Kismet* and a production called *The Silent Voice.* There was reason for Bourne to be jealous also, for Esther was one of the most sought after women in New York City, according to Agnes de Lima and Bourne's college friend, Lawrencse K. Frank. There were tense moments, and they occasionally quarreled.

Spats were the exception. They frequently went out, often with friends, happy and enjoying life. Much of Randolph's courtship was through his piano playing.[35] Esther was uncertain of herself; yet, according to one who knew them both, depended on his adoration.[36] Randolph had no doubts about his love; when they were apart he suffered. "I am wanting to see you very much today," he wrote Esther from Hampton Institute in Virginia where he was visiting his sister and her husband, chaplain of that Negro school.

"I don't know whether to enjoy the full implications of what you told me Sunday. It would be so easy for me to delude myself into thinking that you cared for me more constantly than you do, and really imagined marrying me. When I come to my senses it seems grotesque of me to imagine your being willing.

"You are so radiantly adequate for my future. There is nothing I would not wish for you. But there is also nothing that I would not wish for myself. And I go right on having delusions of grandeur that you could love me and be happy with me."

His whole life, he continued, had alternated between delusions of greatness and a cowering and abject feeling of worthlessness. He turned cold, he said, when thinking that "some day you might find me out and drive me into the latter state again."

What an adventure it would be, he said, "to try to get the most out of life together! We could be very wise, and we are already so very intelligent and so very reasonable. Your reasonableness is divine, there is nothing like seeing it squelch your impulse. And I really get a physical sensation from your intelligence, your arrested glowing inquiring look that makes me feel a flexible, poised instrument within.

"For you do understand—when you will— and that is what counts. I loathe loggy [foggy?] knowledge, but your quality means light and air to me. My own unreasonableness is far less calculable, but my intelligence is good if a little too analytical. Or perhaps you don't really think it is good? I don't wish to be smug."[37]

Love for Esther made him breathless and fretful of losing her. The possibility of boring or disappointing her worried him. "I don't think my spirit is naturally roaming," he wrote her again from Hampton, "but it just has had to be restless because it does so awfully want an abiding place and has not found it. Or if it did it was torn and harried and treated more like a wayfarer taken in for the night than the friend found at last. And until it finds such gay peace with you that I cannot imagine its going unless you expelled it. And don't think I don't realize how immensely it must satisfy you to keep itself free from getting expelled. Because you should have everything the earth has to give you . . . . I wish I was [sic] with you this minute."[38]

Although Randolph naturally wanted her to himself, the few preserved love letters also indicate his hopes for her professional success. When a production she had been in was scheduled to play in Boston, but did not, he consoled and flattered her. "My own career," he remarked, "is strewn with what my egoism insists on seeing as very close shaves when I almost got jobs that I was objectively crying my heart out for. What is your reserved fate? Perhaps the W.S.P. [Washington Square Players] where you could immediately get a bigger reputation than a year in that old melodrama. Perhaps New Mexico. E.S.S. [Elizabeth Shepley Sergeant] has returned and makes Sante Fe so attractive with little hotels along the track, that I do not see what can possibly hold me back once I get out to Chicago. It would seem strange to turn my back on New York and our network of people, and definitely close a chapter in my life, but such things have to be done. I am coming to think of Greenwich Village as a poisonous place which destroys the souls even of the super-villagers like ourselves."[39]

Notions of going west would later seem absurd—strange graspings at straws. For Esther loved him and a union had begun in the autumn of 1917. By the fall of 1918, after many quarrels and much wrestling with the question, she resolved to marry him.[40] She had long since met Randolph's mother and sisters. They hit it off immediately, although Mrs. Bourne for a while opposed the marriage—only because she incorrectly suspected the childhood tuberculosis could be passed on.[41]

Randolph and Esther did not broadcast their plans and possibly for this reason some got the impression that there was only one side to Bourne in those days: a morbid, war-fed bitterness. One winter night in 1918, probably in March, he dined in the Village with Beulah Amidon. To her he seemed tired, worn looking, shabby, and ill-humored. The world, he grumbled, had been at the threshold of great things—mass production, greater education, swifter communication and transportation. "Now comes this irrelevance of war. The monster has slammed the door. It will be a thousand years before it opens again. . . . Men stupid enough to resort to war are too stupid to make peace."[42]

Some time later they met again, and Beulah discussed plans to go to California. Randolph begged her not to go. "All my friends are scattering. All my world is scattered," he said. This, of course, was not long after the closing of the *Seven Arts*, dark winter days, as Oppenheim later wrote, when the two would sit talking and brooding beside the coal fire in Oppenheim's quarters.[45]

But Bourne kept his perspective. Certainly he was not the emotionally shriveled and embittered outcast which legend would have one believe. Not having enthusiasm for war, the bitterness towards its effects took a special path. After Beulah Amidon learned her brother was killed in battle—and almost simultaneously that her fiancé was missing in action (later found alive)—Randolph wrote her, in June 1918. "I know you don't want words of pity or anything I can offer. But I stretch out my hand to you, begging you not to despair. The world is drinking its cup. It passes from none of us. The common lot is easier to bear than the lightening bolt. You do not weep alone."[44]

That some might have thought him in despair is understandable, for a story made the rounds during his life and after that in the last year he was almost destitute. In perhaps June 1918 when he dined in Glen Ridge, New Jersey, with the Tealls, long-time family friends, a dark scene was painted. The *Atlantic* had rejected an article and thus his last support had crumbled. He reckoned how many friends were between him and starvation. There were 11 days' meals to be counted on and he would begin with the Tealls.[45]

This was theatricalism. What was told to the Tealls probably was expressed with an irony that did not come across to his more literal hosts. For while his earnings from January 1-November 2, 1918, amount to only $679.11,[46] he had $827 in the Bloomfield National Bank when he died.[47]

The article reported to have been rejected was "The Uses of Infallibility" a stunning and sympathetic essay on Cardinal Newman, later published in *The History of a Literary Radical* anthology. The rejection of the article always has been an example of how closed were the minds at the time to any disturbing views, and how much Bourne was up against it. The story is that Ellery Sedgwick allegedly refused a completely non-political article because of its author's ideas on the war.

Van Wyck Brooks—who of course knew him well and perhaps got the information directly from him—was among the many who repeated the account: "Ellery Sedgwick wrote to Randolph that he could no longer publish him after the hubbub of the *Seven Arts* articles; he even refused the superb essay on Cardinal Newman."[48]

If such a letter was written, it has not been preserved. The last known preserved communication came shortly after *Seven Arts* folded. It unmistakably but politely took issue. "You socialists are funny people," Sedgwick said. "You evidently got the idea that if you put your back to it, you can move this little world of ours all alone."

Yet the letter was like the others from Sedgwick: fatherly and warm. "As you say, we think differently about things, but on the question of freedom of speech which came up so sharply at Columbia, I am shoulder to shoulder with you."[49] There was no word on the Newman piece, although it very likely had not been submitted yet. Neither is there mention in Sedgwick's autobiography of the alleged rejection.

At times during the last year or so of Randolph's life, as in years before that, an idea would seize him, and momentarily he would be absorbed in it. Once he had facetiously written a friend that, "I crave some pagan monastery, some 'great, good place' where I can go and stay till the war is all over." [50] It was the kind of fantastic idea he liked to play with. He told Agnes de Lima excitedly after talking with Brooks and an industrial engineer who had contributed to the *New Republic*:

"Brooks has gone back after a very rarified two weeks. . . . We met a charming couple called the Ordway Teads who would be perfect for a colony and are keen for it and whom I wish to get for that farm which I go right on believing Esther is going to manage. Brooks and I did a lot of enthusiastic talking about it, and it seems to be our salvation.

"We have a nucleus in the Brooks and Teads. We could probably rent an old house with ten acres of land in Westchester. We could afford an inexpensive cook and perhaps a community auto. Then we could add people in the summer. . . . The possibilities are endless. . . . I should be back in White Plains looking for houses. My imagination takes wing . . . and I am already recovered from my depression."[51]

Alvin Johnson later recalled a similar pipe dream that he once shared with Randolph. Johnson originally had been inspired by a professor of Greek at the University of Nebraska, who introduced him to the Prythaneum at Athens, didicated to Hestia, goddess of the hearth. It was there that distinguished guests stayed. Similar phythanea were in many other Greek cities. An ambitious pipe dream cost no more than a modest one, Johnson decided.

Johnson's idea was a series of prythanea from New York to Miami—each to accomodate perhaps 50 persons—spaced so that the traveler could move easily from one to another.

"Bourne was excited about what he called my chain of monasteries. He took my pipe dream for a confirmation of his monastery. . . . Randolph had no firm distinction between pipe dream and project. If he had lived longer he would have come to an era when great country places were to be had for next to nothing. He might have achieved his monastery. He had faith in his ideas. . . ." [52]

Armistice cheered and inspired Randolph. "Now that the war is over people can speak freely again, and we can dare to think," he wrote his mother. "It's like coming out of a nightmare."[53]

Another nightmare was following in war's wake, however—influenza, probably carried by returning troops. Agnes and Esther had noticed during the fall that he looked badly, and they perhaps correctly ascribed the appearance to intermittent worry about his work.

One sharp evening, as the three walked on 5th Avenue, Bourne observed moodily: "They say the flu gets one in three. You or Esther or me. I think it will be I."[54]

A hack translation job he was hired to do on a French war novel, Larroney's *Vagabonds of the Sea,* later published, had bored Bourne and made him dispirited. Often he worked on the project late into the dark hours. The cold in his apartment at 16 Charles Street made it hard to sleep, let alone work, and a coal shortage did not make the bitter weather more agreeable.

The wife of Merrill Rogers, the *Dial's* business manager, was in Washington. In December Randolph complained that it was so cold in the Charles Street flat that he could not work. Could he work at Merrill's during the day? Merrill gave him a key. Four days later he left a note about moving elsewhere.[55]

Randolph had departed for the apartment Agnes and Esther had taken on the third floor of 18 West 8th Street. The move was prompted by the decision of Esther and Randolph to marry as soon as possible; Agnes agreed to move elsewhere after the marriage. On December 19 a dray delivered him, his trunks, and packages to a not unhandsome red brick building with wide windows. The first two floors were the Play School (later the City and Country School) of the progressive educator Caroline Pratt.

Once settled into new quarters, he made only listless motions at unpacking.[56] A cold had bothered him the past few days. On Friday the 21st, Esther took his hand and noticed it was burning hot. She found Bourne's temperature was 104, and put him to bed. The weather was not so cold as it had been. But although the thermometer reached 48° Friday, it was raw and rainy, a precursor of the weekend's weather. On Friday he dictated a letter to Esther for his sisters which read in part: "It is certainly nice to have two sisters who will invite a lone bachelor to Christmas dinner. If you write mother do not alarm her about my being sick because it isn't important. . . . I haven't been able to get any presents but will do so later." [57]

Friday night was hard. He was still very sick on the next day. Nina Swinerton, a registered nurse who was a friend of the girls and Randolph, arrived. So did Paul Rosenfeld. The four—Nina, Agnes, Esther, and Paul—tended in shifts. They knew what pneumonia did, how it filled the lungs, creating an ugly stifling congestion.

Seven years before Randolph had written in the September 1911 *Atlantic* essay on the handicapped: "Death I do not understand at all. I have seen it in its cruelest, most irrational forms, where there has seemed no excuse, no palliation. I have only known that if we were more careful, and more relentless in fighting evil, if we knew more of medical science, such things would not be. I know that a sound body, intelligent care and training, prolong life, and that the death of a very old person is neither sad nor shocking, but sweet and fitting. I see in death a perpetual warning of how much there is to be known and done in the way of human progress and betterment. And equally, it seems to me, is this true of disease."

He was very afraid of death and it was on his mind Saturday when Alyse Gregory visited. The sickroom was sparsely furnished. Unpacked boxes, and books, and papers lay in disorderly piles about the room. Randolph, propped up by pillows in a single iron bed, spoke with difficulty.

"I don't want to die."[58]

Saturday there was no improvement. He got worse. A specialist that evening said there was nothing more to be done and that the family should be notified. "He has a 50-50 chance," he told Agnes, and departed, replaced for the night by another doctor. When Agnes returned to the room, Randolph said he had overheard. Agnes tried to be casual. "Well, you have a 50 chance," she said.

"No, I've got a 50-50 chance," he replied to emphasize the other 50.

Bourne was discouraged and thought he should go to the hospital. Nina said the epidemic had caused such a crush that one would not get personal treatment. It was best to stay. Randolph agreed.

Saturday night and early Sunday morning were worse than Friday and Saturday had been. His chest was so tiny. It was so hard to breath. Paul tried the oxygen at his mouth, but each time he involuntarily bawked, choking and gasping.[59]

It was raw when Esther went out early Sunday and walked under a leaden sky to the cable office where she wired at 8:14 a.m. to Ruth Bourne in the Jersey suburbs: "RANDOLPH DANGEROUSLY ILL WITH PNEUMONIA. PHONE NEW YORK. SPRING EIGHT SIX FIVE NINE IMMEDIATELY."[60]

At the apartment a short while later, Agnes was on duty as Esther, Paul, and Nina slept exhausted in the next room.

Randolph asked for an eggnog. The doctor consented. Agnes brought it to him. It was whipped to a golden hue. Randolph exclaimed how beautiful it was. Agnes began to make chit-chat. What did he think of a certain popular columnist writing for the *Evening Post*?

"He's a colossal fool!" Randolph said with his old fire.

Agnes helped him sit up farther, craddling him in her arms.

He sipped a few times, and fell back limp.

"Nina! Paul!"

Nina hurried in.

"He's dead," she said.

Esther, sleepless for 24 hours was not disturbed.

Then they wept.

Later in the morning the sirens and whistles of returning troop ships could be heard blaring nearby on the Hudson. Esther wept in impotent challenge to them. The shades were raised and the windows opened as a signal to Randolph's friends.

Word spread quickly. The publisher Benjamin W. Heubsch phoned the news to James Oppenheim, who recounted, "I lifted the sheet from his face in a front room in Eighth Street. He seemed to mean that all had been stopped."[61]

Callers came steadily Sunday. Padraic Colum, the Irish poet and critic, entered, studied the face and said: "He looks the noble warrior."

As the tidings spread out of town, telegrams expressing grief and dumfoundness arrived. Esther and Agnes went to The Woman's Hospital to tell Frances Anderson, the fourth person who had lived with them in Caldwell in the summer of 1916. She was ill with flu and took it badly.[62]

Far away in California, Sarah Bourne continued a vacation, unaware of her son's illness or death. Natalie and Ruth could not bring themselves to break in upon their mother's Christmas sojourn, which also was supposed to be a health trip.[63]

On a rainy Tuesday morning the little Spring Street Presbyterian Church in New York City was crowded to the doors for the service. Norman Thomas, whose first pastorate as a Presbyterian minister had been at Spring Street, stood near a large laurel wreath and spoke on "The Truth Shall Make You Free."[64]

Then the funeral procession skidded and crawled and inched along the slush covered highway that crossed the Jersey meadows to Bloomfield where burial was in Bloomfield Cemetery, a half mile from his birthplace.

Elsewhere, many grieved bitterly. "Randolph Bourne," later wrote Lewis Mumford, who met him only once, at an Intercollegiate Socialist Tea, "was precious to us because of what he was, rather than because of what he had actually written. . . . [He] represented . . .

that passionate resolve and critical inquiry which was part of the very spirit of youth in America in 1914."[65]

In New York that night an exhausted Esther Cornell tossed sleeplessly, obsessed with the vision of her beloved—cold, deep in the mud, and rained upon. Grief stricken, she accused herself of not having cherished him enough.[66]

Many thought life was better because of Bourne and for having known him. Some who read the obituary in the Monday morning New York *Tribune* must have been doubly convinced life was richer because of Bourne. One hardly could have missed the irony of a headline to a story about a Sunday sermon. Directly below the death notice, it read:

Pastor Scores "Reformers"
"Intellectual Itch" Dangerous
Says Rev. Dr. C. A. Easton.

We wind wreaths of holly
For Randolph Bourne,
We hand bitter-sweet for remembrance;
We make a song of wind in pines. . . .

Bitter-sweet, and a northwest wind
To sing his requiem,
Who was
Our age,
And who becomes
An imperishable symbol of our ongoing,
For in himself
He rose above his body and
came among us
Prophetic of the race,
The great hater
Of the dark human deformity
Which is our dying world,
The great lover
Of the spirit of youth
Which is our future's seed. . . .

In forced blooming we saw
Glimpses of awaited Spring.
—James Oppenheim, 1-11-19

XII

LEGACY

A man gets few ideas after he is 25, Randolph Bourne wrote in his 1912 *Atlantic* essay "Youth," and he gets few ideals after he is 20. The spiritual fabric, he said, is woven by then, and subsequent change is a mere broadening and enriching of that basic pattern; nothing essentially new is added thereafter. Two years later in Paris Randolph confided that he felt like a soul "doomed always to struggle towards a salvation which is impossible to be realized by the individual, because it is social."[1] In that piece on "Youth," Bourne at age 25 was peering nervously into the future when he also remarked that, "Nothing is so pathetic as the young man who spends his spiritual force too early, so that when the world of ideals is presented to him, his force being spent, he can only grasp at second-hand ideals and mouldy formulas."

Only one of those notions was applicable when he died. His ideals may have remained essentially the same but the richness of his mind had by then been demonstrated—not so much in original thoughts as in the ability to take the ideas of others and run brilliantly with them. If Bourne was not an impressive original thinker, great ability was shown in what was made *of* ideas rather than in making *up* ideas.

For Randolph in 1918 to have felt as far as ever from the salvation he had in mind in 1914 would not have been extraordinary: he was not the kind of person who could be satisfied or who necessarily wanted to be satisfied where ideas and action were concerned.

Lastly, it certainly may not be said that Bourne had spent himself by the fall of 1918 and that at 32 he would not have had anything significant to say about life, manners, and behavior. Van Wyck Brooks, who knew him well and who felt that he had not yet found himself, predicted that "He, if anyone, in the days to come would have conjured out of our dry soil the green shoots of a beautiful and characteristic literature; he knew that soil so well, and why it was dry, and how it ought to be irrigated." [2]

That of course is an assessment by one who revered Bourne and had great confidence in him. The truth is that while one may indulge in theorizing about what would have happened in the 1920's, in the Depression, and in the following two decades of hot and cold war, nobody knows. There is not even a sound logic which may be applied. If Max Eastman had died in 1918, could one have predicted his later conservative posture? Or that of John Dos Passos?

Someone once astutely remarked that just about everyone had tried somehow to claim Bourne. There are only shaky indications that he would have become some kind of Marxist, but indeed some of that element of the Left have tried to make him their unique embryo intellectual pretty boy. But Ellery Sedgwick in his autobiography said that Randolph would not have ended up a radical and might have become a reactionary, after having seen the failure to obtain so many of the things he strove for.

No one has suggested that he would have swung from his radicalism and liberalism to what some approvingly assert is the American way, the moderate position—a middle-of-the-roadism which deviates little to either side. This is probably because one factor heretofore has been absent in theorizing about his future. What effect would marriage with the woman he loved have had on him? For—presuming the marriage took place and that it succeeded—it is reasonable to believe he would have found that missing emotional security. Happy marriage would have provided the kind of reason for living which as an adult he had missed.

Randolph was not a man for whom ideas and involvement and a sense of accomplishment sufficed. He deeply desired to be loved and he craved even more to love. The latter to him was far more important than the former. It is of course possible he would have become one of the "tired radicals" of whom Walter Weyl wrote.[3] He may have become like the person Floyd Dell described who—once fiercely liberal and radical—later warmed to the idea of a house in the country, steady job, institutionalized marriage, and children. Neither idea was necessarily insipid: Walter Weyl believed there always would be new radicals along to replace the departed, and Dell in discussing the trappings of middle class respectability in his book *Love in Greenwich Village* (1926), was talking about himself.

In 1928 when Paxton Hibben—one of the most remarkable figures in 20th century American history—died, the December 19 *New Republic* commented that the funeral represented the largest gathering of radicals since Bourne's death. Expression of radical sentiment on those two occasions testified to a strain of radicalism running through American civilization—a civilization which generally is thought to be pragmatically adept at stealing the wild thunder of the left and slapping down the short-sighted attitude of the right.

Whether or not there is a clear strain of radicalism in American society—whatever one means in America by "radical"—a lesson derived from the lives of men like Randolph Bourne seems to be how clearly the small radical element has enriched American life. More still, the lives of men like Hibben and Bourne seem to speak of something admirable about American civilization.

America is a nation with an ugly record of physical and intellectual atrocities, ranging from lynching to the disturbing panic of the World War I suppression of freedom of expression. But for the most part the best minds in the nation have not wanted to shut the mouths of men whose ideas they believed contemptuous. Nor have the nation's best minds succumbed to the belief that allegedly abominable ideas could ultimately pull down the American edifice. Perhaps this is because in the imperfect functioning of a free society's agreement to disagree, all the quarrelers seem to feel they are arguing about the same thing. Any sound mind who ever reads Bourne cannot possibly overlook the sophisticated patriotism which exudes from almost everything he wrote, whether the composition is an antagonistic attack on a happening or an institution, or a praising of a novel.

In every society and nation there is a core of citizens who deeply love the fatherland. In not all societies is the malcontent tolerated. In the United States—more often than not—the malcontent usually is free to come out into the clearing with his adversaries, confident that no one will stab him in the back. If the American radical is killed off it is not by treachery but by indifference and by the rapidity of change in society.

Bourne in many ways felt the sense of Hebraic "giveness" about America which Daniel J. Boorstin in his *The Genius of American Politics* (1953) considers a major theme in American life. On the basis of his accomplishment, it does not seem that his radicalism or liberalism would have been destroyed by an inability to change with America. The sense of "giveness" was too sharp for him to have missed the subtleties of a changing society.

How does one explain the aristocrat like Hibben or the man like Randolph Bourne from unremarkable middle class origins who later acquired many aristocratic tastes? How to explain men like them who become profoundly concerned with the imperfections of the United States and who are willing to help clean up after their country fouls its own nest? There is no obvious explanation. But it is clear that such men were willing to risk their personal welfare to try to rectify wrongs. That they ever thought the effort either worthwhile or practical or practicable is a commentary in itself. It demonstrates that America should cherish and encourage its radical strain.

If there is any value to be taken from Bourne's life and career, it is not an examination of "right" or "wrong" in the hundreds of things on which he commented. In addition to the specifics of Bourne's thought—much of which is clearly applicable to our time—we are interested in the worldview from which he operated, and what he thought America needed, was, and could be.

In Bourne there is an ecstatic, but reasonable, view of the potential of American life. In so far as he was a radical, it was not just for the sake of being radical.

There is unfortunately no happy answer to the question where one should put Randolph Bourne. Put him in the essential progressive ethic of personal responsibility and self-sacrifice which the historian Richard Hofstadter has discussed in *The Age of Reform* (1955)? Or with the aberrant and misfit writer Daniel Aaron considers in *Writers on the Left* (1961)? Was Randolph deceived—as Hofstadter says many progressives were—by the elusive goal of trying to institutionalize emotions and sentiments? Was he made bitter by "rejection" so that he came to yearn for absorption into society, to yearn to speak for it, and to celebrate it? This is the kind of artist Aaron depicts in talking generally about the writer who is reared in a society which honors actions rather than contemplation, and distrusts intellectual and physical endeavor which does not show itself "useful." Or was he something else? Again, there are no satisfying explanations.

Even if the idea had appealed, Bourne would not have known where to class himself in the world of ideas. It is known—and it is clear from his work—that he had a clear idea of what he was trying to do: mold opinion. That is a dangerous and thankless task which does not benefit from the relative security and detachment of the occupation which Randolph Bourne professed to dislike, scholarship.

To him, genuine opinion was neither cold, logical judgment nor irrational feeling. It was scientific hypothesis, to be tested and revised as experience demanded. It was a viewpoint based on grounds short of proof or at least of immediate proof. Yet good opinion was not spasmodic, for the mind must cut deeply and range widely. The mind must have cornered predisposing bias and tied it down where it can be watched. The good intellect in forming opinion places the object of its attention firmly in perspective; and meaningfully.

Opinion, an essay of his said, was a provisional conviction held until altered or discredited. Opinion has a definite bias and interpretation, but it continually presses for proof. Opinion does not masquerade as proof; it was to him merely a tool.

Opinion aims, he wrote, "not at mere static comprehension. It does not merely survey the field with serene Olympian gaze. It is a force, and the only force that can be relied upon in the long run to fortify the will and clear the vision. Conviction, gripped after the widest possible survey of the field, is what we must act upon if we are to effect those social changes which most of us desire.

"The world has generally preferred to act from logical consistency or from the high elation of feeling rather than upon daring and clear-sightedness of experiment. The idea of a social and political opinion which, free from moral prejudice, strains towards scientific proof, as the hypotheses of the physicist strain towards the physical laws, is still very new, but it is already playing havoc with the old crusted folkways.

"If such opinion is to be this force of the future, there cannot be too much of its guiding thread. Yet it constantly becomes not easier but harder to form valid opinions. We are stunned by the volume of what there is to know in the human world. We are overwhelmed by the mass of sociological data, and brought to despair even more by the great gaps which must be filled. We have every day set before us infinitely more than we can possibly digest. We run the constant risk of missing completely the relevant and the important. Opinion never had a better chance of being based on substrata of quite meaningless facts. . . . The need for interpreters, for resolute expressers of opinion becomes therefore more urgent."[4]

Bourne is a puzzling and in some ways inexplicable man. But as a person trying—in a lover's quarrel with his country—to make and mold opinion, he stands out clearly as a great influence and inspiration to men of his time. It takes far more than the common man to inspire the kind of evaluation made by Paul Rosenfeld who wrote in *Port of New York* that Randolph "was the great bearer of moral authority while America was at war. He was our bannerman of values in the general collapse."

There always will be evil, but much of what Bourne fought has been ameliorated considerably since his time. That other things are in as hapless and seemingly as hopeless a state as when he protested physical ugliness testifies to his sanity.

Whatever greatness is, it is not appropriate to call him a great American. But it is fitting and reasonable to call him grand, a person whose comprehension of the actuality and potentiality of the United States far out-reached—at least in its expression—that of many of those whom we honor in monuments and statues.

There is considerable truth in Gilberto Freyre's remark—made in praise of Bourne and in attributing to him a terrible night of Saint John—that much of his individualistic revolt was tied to his "bending over his own personality as over a dark pool."[5] But that does not explain much.

What one really wants to know is whether Randolph was in or out of the American mainstream. Even if a definition of mainstream could be agreed upon, no answer would be forthcoming. What he should to great extent be remembered for is for being very significantly the kind of liberal which Lionel Trilling meant when he said in *The Liberal Imagination* that the most needful work of the liberal was not in confirming liberalism in its sense of general rightness, but rather in putting liberal ideas and assumptions under pressure.

Bourne stands out clearly—years after his death—as a devoted son of his country. His power came from a deep capacity to love and yet call upon the "youthful violence" which he said[6] would be needed after the war in picking up the pieces of enlightened reform and change. Strength came in great degree from his ability to evoke a fervent wrath in himself and others. Yet this was no hater. He was clearly, as Waldo Frank once said, "the focus of a mysterious power which profoundly affected everyone who knew him at all well and many who barely knew him."[7] Frank might have added that he was a man capable both of being grandly wrong as only a superior mind can be wrong, and of thrusting home to the very essense of a thing. So far as the United States is concerned, Randolph Bourne was a man who acted meaningfully on a complaint made in his 1912 *Atlantic* essay "The Mystic Turned Radical": "It is the sin of the age that nobody dares to be anything to too great a degree."

REFERENCES

CHAPTER I

1. Randolph Bourne, *A Study of the 'Suburbanizing' of a Town and Its Effects upon Its Social Life* (unpublished master's thesis, Columbia University, 1913), 22.

2. "A Victorian Letter Writer Found Paris a City of Sin," Bloomfield (N.J.) *Independent Press,* April 20, 1961, p. 2.

3. Van Wyck Brooks, *Fenollosa And His Circle—With Other Essays in Biography* (New York, 1962), 259-321.

4. Interview with Bourne's younger sister, Ruth Branstater, 10-16-63. Unless otherwise stated—or unless cited for clarity—material attributed to persons who knew Bourne is derived from the author's interviews and from his correspondence. Interviews and correspondence are listed in the bibliography.

5. Brooks, *Fenollosa, op. cit.,* 260.

6. Interview with Howard Biddulph, 10-23-63.

7. *Ibid.*

8. Interview with Agnes de Lima, 10-18-63.

9. Alyse Gregory, *Randolph Bourne,* unpublished memoir of RB, Yale University, p. 6. Hereafter, "RB" always means Randolph Bourne.

10. Natalie Fenniger to Esther Cornell, 1-7-19 to 2-10-19.

11. Bourne, *Education and Living,* (New York, 1917), 35.

12. Bloomfield (N.J.) *Independent Press,* 4-11-24, p. 7.

13. Unless otherwise indicated, the source of material on the house and life therein is from Bourne's "An Autobiographical Chapter," *Dial,* 48 (January, 1920), 1-21.

14. *Ibid.,* 1-2. 15. Natalie Fenniger to Alyse Gregory, 5-23-48.

16. "Autobiographical Chapter," *op. cit.,* 12. 17. *Ibid.,* 15-16

18. *Ibid.,* 11. 19. *Youth and Life* (Boston, 1913), 343.

20. Natalie to Alyse Gregory, *op. cit.*

21. All references to diary entries are from "Randolph Bourne: Diary for 1901, *Twice a Year,* Double Number 6-7 (Fall-Winter 1940, Spring-Summer 1941), 89-98.

22. 10-16-1900, Bourne Papers.

23. Van Wyck Brooks (ed.), *The History of a Literary Radical and Other Papers by Randolph Bourne* (New York, 1956), 21.

24. *Ibid.,* 22. 25. *Education and Living, op. cit.,* 34.

20. Natalie to Alyse Gregory, *op. cit.*

27. *Youth and Life, op. cit.,* 343-44.

28. Samuel F. Boardman to RB, 6-27-03.

29. De Lima and Branstater interviews, 10-18-63, 10-16-63.

30. De Lima interview, 10-18-63.

31. To Alyse Gregory, 1-19-14. Yale.

32. *Youth and Life, op. cit.,* 346-37. 33. *Ibid.,* 347-48.

34. To Carl Zigrosser, 2-7-12.

35. This material has been based on letters to the writer. One is postmarked 10-28-

63; the other 10-15-63. Mrs. Hummel remembered only a connection with a Ludwig in New York City. The Ludwig we cite is in the directory for those years.

36. First quote from Natalie Fenniger to Esther Cornell, *op. cit.;* last two quotes from Natalie Fenniger to Alyse Gregory, *op. cit.*

37. To Prudence Winterrowd, 2-5-13. PW was a Shelbyville, Indiana, girl who wrote RB after reading one of his articles. They corresponded for two years and finally met.

38. To Alyse Gregory, 7-30-14.

39. *'Suburbanizing' of a Town, op. cit., passim.*

40. Dorothy Teall, "Bourne into Myth," *Bookman,* 65 (October, 1932), 591.

41. To Prudence Winterrowd, *op. cit.*

42. Quoted Mark Harris, *Randolph Bourne: A Study in Immiscibility* (unpublished Ph.D. thesis, University of Minnesota, 1956), p. 28. Harris was quoting in turn another writer. An extensive search in the *Call* did not turn up the story. It could not have been at the time the Paterson *Call* in which the story appeared.

43. 2-24-13.

44. Interview with banker Biddulph, *op. cit.,* and with Howard Dodd, lawyer, 1-22-63. Biddulph commented: "He would ask questions in a scholarly way, but the kind atheists ask . . . He gave the impression of thinking ill of everyone . . . He was constantly having pictures taken of himself . . . He wrote the article just to attract attention . . . It finished him with the people in this town."

45. From Sarah Ward, 2-17-[13].

46. "The Social Order in an American Town." *Atlantic* (February, 1913), 229.

47. Interview, *op. cit.*

48. Material re RB and the Hummels is from Hummel letters, *op. cit.* Another acquaintance of RB said, acknowledging the tricks time plays on memory, that he believed "Randolph . . . attracted the attention of some woman who urged him to go to Columbia and helped him get a scholarship." Joseph Ward Swain to Blanche Messitte, 9-29-37. Swain's copy in writer's possession.

49. *Youth and Life, op. cit.,* 348.

CHAPTER II

1. Frederick Paul Keppel, *Columbia* (New York, 1914), p. 28, quoting an unidentified CU professor.

2. Brander Matthews, *These Many Years: Recollections of a New Yorker* (New York, 1917), 398.

3. Lloyd Morris, *A Threshold in the Sun* (New York, 1943), 79-80. This writer also is indebted to Dr. A. W. Macmahon, a friend of RB and for many years a professor at Columbia. Professor Macmahon in a letter to the writer, 2-18-64, outlined the subleties and shadings of Columbia's growth, and described and put in what he felt was their proper light the outstanding faculty and widely known faculty members of the time, all of whom of course are not mentioned here.

4. *Ibid.* 5. *Youth and Life, op. cit.,* 334.

6. "Randolph Bourne" in *Nineteen Nineteen* (Cambridge, Mass., 1946), 117.

7. Waldo Frank, *In the American Jungle, 1925-1936* (New York, 1937), 60. Other descriptions are in Floyd Dell, *Homecoming, An Autobiography* (New York, 1933),

310-12; Theodore Dreiser, "Appearance and Reality," *The American Spectator,* February 1933, p. 4; Louis Untermeyer, *From Another World: The Autobiography of Louis Untermeyer,* (New York, 1939), 85; Alyse Gregory, *The Day is Gone* (New York, 1948), 115.

8. To Blanche Messitte, 9-7-37. Bourne Papers. Apparently a copy.

9. Interview, 11-4-63. However, a friend of Bourne observed: "Knopf's comments on [Bourne's] arrogance is a nice piece of projection since Knopf was the most arrogant, opinionated person on the campus whom Bourne disliked and openly jeered at." Lawrence K. Frank to writer, 2-3-64.

10. Louis Filler, *Randolph Bourne* (Washington, D. C., 1943), 25.

11. *Youth and Life, op. cit.,* 40-41. Next quotes *ibid.,* 46, 51, 11, 12, 36.

12. *The End of American Innocence: A Study of the First Years of Our Own Time, 1912-1917* (New York, 1959), x-xi. Next two quotes *ibid.,* 9-10, 29.

13. Material on Chase is from A. W. Macmahon to writer, 3-18-64, and interview with Chase 3-25-64.

14. *Youth and Life, op. cit.,* 135.

15. John Erskine, *The Memory of Certain Persons* (New York, 1927) 195.

16. To Zigrosser, 2-7-12. Next quote *ibid.,* 4-19-12.

17. Swain to Messitte, 9-29-37, *op. cit.*

18. To Zigrosser, 2-16-12. 19. *Youth and Life, op. cit.,* 145-56.

20. 9-18-11. 21. Beulah Amidon to Alyse Gregory, 10-4-48.

22. De Lima Interview, 10-18-63. 23. Amidon to Gregory, 10-4-48, *op. cit.*

24. Interview with A. A. Knopf, 11-4-63.

25. "Columbia College," *Columbia Monthly,* 7 (June 1910), 247-48. Next quote *ibid.,* 255-56.

26. Erskine, *Memory, op. cit.,* 194-95. 27. Dana to Alyse Gregory, 6-30-48.

28. "Over the Quardrangle," *Columbia Monthly,* 8 (August 1911), 403.

29. *The Happy Profession* (Boston, 1956), 223. 30. *Randolph Bourne, op. cit.,* 41.

31. Letter from H. H. Nordlinger to writer, 10-22-63. 32. To Zigrosser, 2-23-12.

CHAPTER III

1. David A. Shannon, *The Socialist Party of America: A History* (New York, 1955), 6.

2. *Ibid.,* 5. 3. To Prudence Winterrowd, 11-3-13. Copy.

4. *Youth and Life, op. cit.,* 20. 5. To Prudence Winterrowd, 1-16-13.

6. From Frieda Fligelman, 4-22-13. 7. *Youth and Life, op. cit.,* 350.

8. *Randolph Bourne, op. cit.,* 20.

9. *Youth and Life, op. cit.,* 50. Yet RB resisted coherence when it was rigid and doctrinaire. Next two quotes *ibid.,* 302-303.

10. "Holy Poverty," *New Republic,* 1 (11-14-14) 25.

11. "The Next Revolution," *Columbia Monthly,* 10 (May 1913), 225-26. Next quotes *ibid.,* 226.

12. "A Letter to Mr. John Galsworthy," *Columbia Monthly,* 9 (December 1911),

13. Alvin Johnson to writer, 10-13-63. RB took only one economics course at Columbia University, a survey course during the 1910-11 academic year. He made two "A's" His taking little economics, however, does not necessarily prove anything.

Some students avoid the areas they are strong in or which they particularly like.

14. *Youth and Life, op. cit.*, 80.

15. Stephen Siteman to writer, 11-8-63. S.S. is secretary to Norman Thomas.

16. To Alyse Gregory, 1-5-14.

17. A. W. Macmahon to writer, 2-18-64.

18. To Mary Messer, 12-28-13.

19. To Alyse Gregory, 3-18-14.

20. To Alyse Gregory, 3-13-14.

21. *Youth and Life, op. cit.*, 325.

22. Interview with Lucile Deming, 10-21-63.

23. Gregory, *Randolph Bourne, op. cit.*, 104.

24. See, for example, Heinz L. Ansbacher and Rowena R. Ansbacher (eds.), *The Individualist Psychology of Alfred Adler: A Systematic Presentation in Selections from His Writings* (New York, 1956); J. F. Donceel, S. J., *Philosophical Psychology* (2d ed. rev. New York, 1960), Chap. 21.

25. To Prudence Winterrowd, 3-2-13.

26. Max Lerner, "Randolph Bourne and Two Generations," *Twice a Year* Double Number, 5-6 (Fall-Winter 1940, Spring-Summer 1941), 58.

27. "Chesterton's Orthodoxy," *Columbia Monthly*, 7 (March 1910), 170-72.

28. *Youth and Life, op. cit.*, 192. Next five quotes *ibid.*, 193, 194, 196-97, 108, 200.

29. To Prudence Winterrowd, 1-16-13.

30. To Mary Messer, 12-7-14, a Barnard girl whom RB knew. She was interested in Christian Science, which Bourne detested, and they had a rich correspondence.

31. *Youth and Life, op. cit.*, 352.

32. Amidon to Gregory, *op. cit.*

33. *Youth and Life, op. cit.*, 355.

34. *Ibid.*, 356.

35. To Prudence Winterrowd, 4-10-13.

36. To Prudence Winterrowd, 1-16-13.

37. *Ibid.* This letter is particularly interesting because RB discusses various books he is recommending to P.W., remarking which influenced him and how.

38. To Prudence Winterrowd, 2-5-13. Copy.

39. To Prudence Winterrowd, 5-18-13. Copy.

40. *Youth and Life, op. cit.*, 236-37. Next two quotes *ibid.*, 242-44, 244.

41. This is one of the approaches in Chevalier, Haakon M. *The Ironic Temper: Anatole France and His Time* (New York, 1932).

42. *Youth and Life, op. cit.*, 101-31. Next three paragraphs *ibid.*, 101-102, 107.

43. "Holy Poverty," *op. cit.*

44. *Ibid.*, 120.

45. Ian Watt, *The Ironic Tradition in Augustan Prose, from Swift to Johnson* (Los Angeles, 1956) 42. RB's irony could get out of hand. In a letter to Alyse Gregory (11-12-13, Yale) RB protests about "the dangers of irony again!" He had written a letter from Paris to Columbia *Spectator* concerning fraternities and aristocratic feeling. He said snobbishness is inevitable with American youth. He was quoted in a favorable light, the writer assuming RB approved of snobbery.

46. To Prudence Winterrowd, 2-29-13. Copy.

47. Roderick Seidenberg to writer, 12-15-63.

48. Amidon to Gregory, *op. cit.* One of RB's roommates, however, saw RB in less strained moods. "I didn't have the impression of tortured writing. Rather, sitting at the little Blickensderfer typewriter, a few words, perhaps a sentence clicked off pretty rapidly; then a thoughtful pause, looking at the paper, perhaps off in the room; another phrase or sentence quickly typed; now and then by the sound, some xxs-ing out. Mostly, I would say, decisive writing, conducive to directness and flow." A. W. Macmahon to writer, 2-18-64.

49. The titles of the courses he took are interesting and characteristic. Included

were: Social Evolution: Ethnic and Social Origins under Giddings; Psychological Ethics, and Modern Problems and Social Evolution, both under Dewey; Social History of the Middle Ages under Shotwell; Central Problems of Life and Mind; Modern Life Appraisements under Adler; and Contemporary Philosophy.

50. From Sedgwick, 12-13-11.

51. To Prudence Winterrowd 2-5-13. Copy. RB's income, aside from his scholarship, was, according to a notebook in Box 4 of the Bourne Papers, $570 in 1911; $836 in 1912; and $1,138 in 1913.

52. To Prudence Winterrowd, *op. cit.* Later on March 3, he wrote PW that he was put out with Columbia and felt himself going stale. He said his protest about the scrub women got him in trouble. "I feel pretty certain that I have destroyed my chances of preferment here, and will have to go out and earn an honest living at the end of this college year. This worries me a good deal too, because I do not forget my ineffectual struggles to get a place in the world before I came to college. And if I alienate all my powerful friends by being a radical and a crank, there is nothing for me, I'm afraid, but the 'bread-line.' "

CHAPTER IV

1. "Impressions of a European Tour," Bloomfield (N.J.) *Citizen,* 8-23-13. RB wrote 12 articles in the best tradition of travel literature—charming, rich in character sketches, history, irony, wit, and observation. "I enjoyed writing home about my trip to my local New Jersey paper," he told Alyse Gregory, "because there I could be just as naïve and superficial as I like, without feeling that anybody knew it; but I can't do that with my serious friends, can I? Anyway, nobody would print it." (12-12-13.)

2. Notebook, Box 4. References to other persons are from this notebook or from *ibid.*

3. 8-6-13 and 9-12-13. 4. "Impressions," *op. cit.*

5. To Carl Zigrosser, 7-25-13.

6. This and the next quotations are from "Impressions," *op. cit.,* 8-30-13, 11-29-13, 10-25-13.

7. To Henry W. Elsasser, 9-17-13. 8. *Ibid.*

9. To Carl Zigrosser 9-23-13. RB wrote: "He reminded me of a combination of Uncle Halsey and Prof. Erskine at Columbia (whom I cordially dislike) . . . and all the dominating people who put it over me in the past." (To Mother, 9-12-13.)

10. 9-8-13. 11. To Mother, 9-12-13. 12. 10-11-13.

13. To Mary Messer, 9-13-13. 14. To RB, 1-31-14.

15. To RB, 10-2-13.

16. *History of a Literary Radical, op. cit.,* 82-83. Harold Stearns recounts a very similar reaction in his autobiography, *The Street I Know* (New York, 1935), 110-11.

17. *Ibid.,* 81. 18. To Alyse Gregory, 10-11-13.

19. To Carl Zigrosser, 11-3-13. 20. To Henry W. Elsasser, 11-27-13.

21. To Carl Zigrosser, 11-16-13. 22. To Alyse Gregory, 11-1-13.

23. To Carl Zigrosser, 11-3-13. 24. To Henry W. Elsasser, *op. cit.*

25. To Alyse Gregory, *op. cit.* 26. Swain to Messitte, *op. cit.*

27. Memorandum by Arthur Macmahon for Louis Filler. n.d. Bourne Papers.

28. 5-20-14. 29. *History of a Literary Radical, op. cit.*, 87.
30. To Carl Zigrosser, 2-18-14. 31. Swain to Messitte, *op cit.*
32. *History of a Literary Radical, op. cit.*, 43 32. *Ibid.*, 48.
34. Swain to Messitte, *op. cit.* 35. 4-29-14.
36. Amidon to Gregory, *op. cit.* 37. 4-10-13.
38. To Alyse Gregory, 1-19-14. Bourne Papers. 39. 1-19-14.
40. This and next quotes from letters to Alyse Gregory, 12-1-13; 7-24-15; Friday. (n.d.); Monday. (n.d.); From Stonover Farm, Lenox, Mass., Saturday, (n.d.); 1-3-15.
41. To Prudence Winterrowd, 2-5-13. Copy. 42. 3-2-13. Copy.
43. To Alyse Gregory, 4-10-14.
44. To Dorothy Teall, 10-23-13. Copy. Carl Van Doren in his autobiography, *Three Worlds* (New York, 1936), 86, wrote of his Columbia days that he found that "the graduate study in the Department of English and Comparative Literature at Columbia meant the study of literary history and was almost pure antiquarianism . . ." He did not object or complain, he went on to say, because by coincidence he needed work in classics like Dante and Shakespeare.
44. To Dorothy Teall, 10-23-13. Copy. Carl Van Doren in his autobiography,
45. 3-21-14. 46. 5-3-14. 47. Brooks, *Fenollosa, op. cit.*, 274.
48. See RB's article "Berlin in War Time," *Travel,* November 1914; Notes by Arthur Macmahon in the Bourne Papers; and "Impressions of Europe: 1913-14," in *History of a Literary Radical, op. cit.* All are interesting, particularly the first two. Each emphasizes different things, and in some ways the three sources conflict. "Berlin in War Time" is vivid in description of the Kaiser, war fury, and behavior of the public as war approached.
49. A. W. Macmahon to writer, 2-18-04.
50. This and next quotes from letter to Alyse Gregory, 8-25-14.
51. Brooks, *Emerson and Others, op. cit.*, 131.
52. To Alyse Gregory, *op. cit.* 53. (n.d.) Copy.
54. To Alyse Gregory, *op. cit.* 55. *Ibid.*, 6-14-13.

CHAPTER V

1. Although this is the general version, it should be noted that one historian, Charles Forcey, observes that the term New Nationalism occured only once in Croly's book. Forcey not only argues that Roosevelt probably read little of the book, but also that though Croly and Roosevelt became acquainted, the cause-effect relationship concerning the term did not exist. It was coincidence, Forcey argues. *The Crossroads of Liberalism: Croly, Weyl, Lippmann, and the Progressive Era, 1900-1925* (New York, 1961), 127-30, and elsewhere.
2. To Alyse Gregory, 9-28-14. 3. From Herbert Croly, 8-27-14 and 9-15-14.
4. 9-15-14.
5. Lawrence A. Cremin, *The Transformation of the School: Progressivism in American Education* (New York, 1961), viii.
6. Paul Woodring, *Let's Talk Sense About Our Schools* (New York, 1953), 50, 56.
7. "Our Educational Prospect," *New Republic,* 3 (6-26-15), 210.
8. *The School and Society* (Chicago, 1899), 23-24, *passim.*
9. *Democracy and Education* (New York, 1916), 102.

10. *Ibid.*, 89-90; Cremin, *Transformation, op. cit.*, 122; Woodring, *Let's Talk Sense, op. cit.* 38.

11. Cremin, *Transformation, op. cit.*, 123.

12. *Education and Democracy, op. cit.*, 145.

13. Cremin, *Transformation, op. cit.*, 125; Bourne, *Education and Living, op. cit.*, 225.

14. "Education as Living," *op. cit.*, 11.

15. *Youth and Life, op. cit.*, 18. 16. *Ibid.*, 278

17. "In a Schoolroom," *New Republic*, 1 (11-7-14), 24.

18. "Educating the Educator," *New Republic*, 3 (7-10-15), 263.

19. "The Self-Conscious School," *New Republic*, 4 (4-8-16), 620.

20. "Education as Living," *op. cit.*, 10.

21. *Ibid.*, 11. 22. "Puzzle Education," *New Republic*, 1 (1-2-15), 10-11.

23. "Schools from the Outside,"*New Republic*, 1 (1-30-15), 10-11.

24. *Ibid.* 25. "The Wasted Years," *New Republic*, 2 (6-5-15), 120-22.

26. "John Dewey's Philosophy," *New Republic*, 2 (3-13-15), 155

27. *The Gary Schools* (Boston, 1916), 144.

28. Cremin, an authority on the history of education, says in *Transformation, op. cit.* p. 157: "In the end . . . it was Randolph Bourne's rhapsodic praise in *The New Republic* that made Gary the example par excellence of progressive education." Cremin does not say how he knows this, nor on what he bases the assertion.

29. *The Gary Schools, op. cit.*, 15-16.

30. In Floyd Dell's play, *St. George*, a character says: "What! You've never heard of the Montessori system? Why, my dear, it's simply a lot of things. And you put the baby down among the things—and you never have to bother about it again."

31. "Schools in Gary," *New Republic*, 2 (2-27-15), 199.

32. "Apprentices to the School," *New Republic*, 2 (4-24-15), 303.

33. See, for example: "The Issue in Vocational Education," 3 (6-26-15), 191-92; "The School Situation in New York," 6 (2-5-16), 6-8, "Politics Against the School," 6 (2-12-16), 32-33; "Education for Work," 6 (3-11-16), 145-46; "Organized Labor on Education," 7 (5-6-16), 8-9; "Continuation Schools," 7 (6-10-16), 143-45.

34. "Continuation Schools," *op. cit.*, 7 (6-10-16), 143.

35. Bachman, Frank P. and Ralph Bowman, *The Gary Public Schools: Costs, School Year, 1915-1916* (New York, 1918); Flexner, Abraham and Frank P. Bachman, *The Gary Schools: A General Account* (New York, 1918).

36. *I Remember* (New York, 1940), 254. On 255-56 Flexner wrote that on May 10, 1916, he wrote his wife: "There is something queer about the genus "educator"; the loftiest are not immune. I think the cause must lie in their isolation from the rough and tumble contacts with all manner of men. They lose their sense of reality." William Wirt was a cold and, after he made up his mind about something, an inflexible man. He lacked warmth and charm, and had few close friends. Cremin, *op. cit.*, p. 160, n. 7, observes: "From the tone of Flexner's comments, it may well be that he actually set out to puncture the Gary bubble in the survey."

37. "Main Currents in Progressivist American Education," *History of Education Journal*, 8 (Winter 1957), 48.

38. Carter V. Good, "William Wirt," in Schuler, Robert Livingston (ed.), *Dictionary of American Biography*. Supplement Two. (New York, 1958), 728.

39. [n.a.], *The Public School System of Gary Indiana* by Public Administration Service [n.p.], 5-8.

40. Adolphe E. Meyer, *An Educational History of the American People* (New York,

1957), 328-29. An apparently judicious discussion which uses both philosophy and psychology is Sister Mary Joseph Raby, *A Critical Study of the New Education* (Washington, D. C., 1932).

41. 15,000 circulation in 1915; 24,000 subscribers in 1916; peak of 43,000 circulation in 1920, according to Forcey, *Crossroads of Liberalism, op. cit.*, 191, 253. Circulation and subscribers of course are not the same thing. It is not clear whether Forcey recognizes the distinction.

42. See in the Bourne Papers unidentified clippings of book reviews and *Education,* September 1918, 65.

43. "Randolph Bourne and Two Generations," *op.cit.,* 65.

44. Cremin, *Transformation, op. cit.,* 117.

45. "The Reply," *New Republic,* 10 (2-10-17), 46.

46. As Howard W. Nudd, Director of the Public Education Association, wrote in an introduction in 1916: "Mr. Wirt's contribution has been, not so much in the field of education theory, as in the field of education engineering." William Wirt, *The Official Wirt Reports to the Board of Education of New York City* (New York, 1916), 5. N.Y.P.L. call number STB.

47. *Youth and Life, op. cit.,* 49.

48. In an unpublished four-page MS in the Bourne Papers entitled "The Scientific Manager" it appears that Bourne distrusted one aspect of Taylorism. The efficiency expert operated outside the question of social, economic, and moral forces and issues of his day, it seemed to him.

49. "The Democratic School," *New Republic,* 4 (10-23-14), 298.

CHAPTER VI

1. George Middleton, *These Things Are Mine: The Autobiography of a Journeyman Playwright* (New York, 1947), 110.

2. *Ibid.*

3. Louis Untermeyer, *From Another World: The Autobiography of Louis Untermeyer* (New York, 1939), 42.

4. Albert Parry, *Garretts and Pretenders: A History of Bohemianism in America* (New York, 1933), 269.

5. Floyd Dell, *Homecoming, An Autobiography* (New York, 1933), 247.

6. *Ibid.*, 246. 7. *Ibid.*, 251.

8. Middleton, *These Things Are Mine, op. cit.,* 11.

9. To Alyse Gregory, 12-1-14. Next quote *ibid.*

11. Forcey, *Crossroads of Liberalism, op. cit.,* 184.

12. From Sedgwick, 11-27-14.

13. To Elizabeth Shepley Sergeant, 11-15-15. Copy. In a letter in the Bourne Papers from Dorothy Teall to Agnes de Lima written 6-2-32, there is this remark: "Littell told me that it fell to him to talk to Randolph about a piece he'd turned in that they thought below his standard—he said, 'We think this is not quite up to your form,' and Randolph said, 'You mean the *New Republic's* form.'"

14. This and next quote *ibid.*, 11-15-15. Copy.

14B. Alvin Johnson to writer, 10-13-63.

15. From Francis Hackett to George A. Test, 6-9-60. Duplicate in writer's possession. Dr. Test is on the English faculty at State University College, Oneonta, N.Y.

He did his Ph.D. thesis at Pennsylvania on Literary criticism in the NR (see bibliography), and offered the Hackett material. Hackett continued: "The *Freeman* and the *Seven Arts* and the *Masses* gave aspirants of all kinds a chance to do better what we were doing, yet I think we were not so much above the battle as above the waterline. Mrs. Straight gave us leisure in which to think. That leisure led Alvin Johnson to the New School and the *Ency. Social Science.* It led George Soule to be an economist, Lippmann to be a columnist, and so on. It proved that we were not sappy parasites."

16. To Elizabeth Shepley Sergeant, 8-24-16. Copy. When the United States entered the war, the *New Republic* stationed Charles Merz in Washington, D. C. In later years he had a distinguished career with other magazines and he became an editor of the New York *Times.*

17. *The Gary Schools, op. cit.*, p. viii. 18. 1-21-16.

19. To Elizabeth Shepley Sergeant, 2-25-15. 20. Amidon to Gregory, *op. cit.*

21. This and next four quotes from letters to Dorothy Teall: 4-29-15. Copy; 5-2-15. Copy; *ibid.*; 8-19-15. Copy. Beulah wrote to Alyse Gregory (10-4-48, Bourne Papers) that she was not in love with Randolph nor he with her.

22. For this section on Dublin I have relied, in addition to RB's letters, on *It's Me O Lord: The Autobiography of Rockwell Kent,* (New York, 1955), 99-102, and Brooks, *Fenollosa, op. cit.*, 294-301. As a young man, Kent spent a winter at Dublin under Thayer's tutelage. Brooks' account is based on RB's letters and what appears to be personal acquaintance with the Thayers.

23. To Alyse Gregory, 9-10-15.

24. To Elizabeth Shepley Sergeant, 8-9-15. Copy. Re RB's reference to "color diagrams and demonstration:" Thayer during the war became a foremost inventor of camouflage for the armed forces.

25. *Ibid.*, 8-17-15. Copy.

26. Untermeyer, *Autobiography, op cit.*, 104. Untermeyer continues: "Intending nothing more than a sententious generality Oppenheim said. 'Aren't we all cripples?' Amy's aggressiveness fell away from her. 'Yes,' she said, surveying her enormous girth. 'Look at me, I'm nothing but a disease.' "

27. To Elizabeth Shepley Sergeant, *op. cit.*

28. Gregory, *Randolph Bourne, op. cit.*, 108.

29. Interview with Floyd Dell, 10-15-63. A friend of RB later said, "[Randolph] could have had [Diana] back again. I wonder why he did not." Carl Zigrosser to writer, 4-12-64.

30. From M. M. Stielruthal, n.d. 31. To Alyse Gregory, 1-21-16.

32. *Ibid.*, 4 Milligan Place. Thursday. Bourne Papers.

33. To Elizabeth Shepley Sergeant, 1-4-16. 34. Zigrosser to writer, 5-29-64.

35. For material on the Zigrosser episode see, for example, To Elizabeth Shepley Sergeant, 12-23-15; From Gladys Thayer, 2-17-[16?]; From Louise de Wetter, 10-19-[16]. Also Zigrosser to writer, 4-12-64, 5-29-64.

36. From Louise de Wetter, 10-19-[16].

37. This and next quote from letters to Alyse Gregory. 11-19-16; and Cos Cob. Thursday, June [1916].

38. To Prudence Winterrowd, 3-2-13. Copy.

39. To Alyse Gregory. Cos Cob. Thursday. June [1916].

40. To Alyse Gregory, 6-4-48. Brooks or the typesetter erred when Brook's introduction to *History of a Literary Radical* said they met in "November 1914."

41. Agnes de Lima's interest in education was life-long. She already was involved in progressive education when Randolph met her. Later she was connected with the New School for Social Research. Her books include *Our Enemy the Child* (1926), *A School for the World of Tomorrow* (1939) and *The Little Red School House* (1942).

42. Material on Caldwell is from Frances Anderson Ewell to the writer, 10-28-63 and De Lima interview, *op. cit.* Mrs. Ewell now lives in Jacksonville, Fla., where she participates in the civil rights movement.

43. To the writer, 10-20-63.

44 In Box 6 there is a note scribbled on a scrap of paper apparently from one of RB's fellow Village lodgers: "Kindly give the people in this house a rest with your practicing on piano. Its a nuisance."

45. To Alyse Gregory. Milton. Sunday. [November 1916].

46. To Elizabeth Shepley Sergeant, 12-6-16. Copy.

47. To Alyse Gregory, 11-10-16.

48. To Elizabeth Shepley Sergeant, 10-10-15. Copy.

CHAPTER VII

1. "An Examination of Eminences," *Dial,* 65 (12-28-18), 603.

2. Goldman, *Rondezvous with Destiny, op. cit.,* 174.

3. Alfred Kazin, *On Native Grounds: An Interpretation of Modern American Prose Literature* (New York, 1942), 166.

4. *Patria Mia* (Chicago, 1950), 42, 74. Pound's MS was lost in 1913 by the eventual publisher, Ralph Fletcher Seymour of Chicago, but found 37 years later among financial records. Pound once challenged another poet to a duel because he was, Pound said, "stupid."

5. Quoted in Charles Norman, *Ezra Pound* (New York, 1960), 86-87.

6. From the promotion circular for *Seven Arts* quoted by Oppenheim in "The Story of the *Seven Arts,*" *American Mercury,* 20 (July 1930), 157.

7. Waldo Frank, *The New America* (London, 1922), 217.

8. Kazin, *On Native Grounds, op. cit.,* 184.

9. *Ideas Are Weapons* (New York, 1940), 534.

10. This material and that of next five paragraphs from "Our Cultural Humility," *Atlantic,* 114 (October, 1914), 503, 505-06.

11. *Ibid.,* 506. RB was not farsighted where the Armory show was concerned: it was largely responsible for liberating American artists from a long servile alliance with tradition.

12. *Ibid.,* 507.

13. This material and that of next seven paragraphs from "The Cult of the Best," *New Republic,* 5 (1-15-16).

14. See John Henry Raleigh, *Matthew Arnold and American Culture* (Berkeley, Calif., 1957), Chap. IV, *et passim.*

15. This and next three paragraphs from "Education in Taste," *New Republic,* 6 (3-4-16), 122.

16. To Carl Zigrosser, 11-3-13.

17. "Our Unplanned Cities," *New Republic,* 5 (1-1-16), 202.

18. "The Architect," *New Republic,* 5 (1-1-16), 222. Also: "A Little Thing of

Burnelleschi's," unpublished four-page MS. Bourne Papers. n.d., but address at beginning indicates 1914 or 1915.

19. "Real Estate and the City Plan," *New Republic,* 6 (2-19-15), 60-61.

20. "Town Planning and the Law," *New Republic* 1 (12-19-14), 27-28.

21. "An Experiment in Cooperative Living," *Atlantic,* 113 (June 1914), 826, *et passim.*

22. Robert E. Spiller (*et. al.*), *Literary History of the United States* (rev. New York, 1957), 1137.

23. "The History of a Literary Radical," *Yale Review,* 8 (April 1919), 468-84.

24. "Pageantry and Social Art," unpublished six-page MS. Bourne Papers, n.d.

25. From Sedgwick, 10-26-17. See also RB's essay "Paul Elmer More," *New Republic,* 6 (4-1-16), 245-47, in which he reviews and attacks More's *Aristocracy and Justice.*

26. "A Stronghold of Obscurantism," *Dial,* 62 (4-5-17), 304.

27. Susan J. Turner, *A History of The Freeman: A Literary Landmark in the Early Twenties* (New York, 1963), 63.

28. "Sociological Fiction," *New Republic,* 12 (10-27-17), 359.

29. *Ibid.* But if the craftsmanship of a sociological novel was abominable, RB denounced the work. See, for example, "The Belgian Carthage," *Dial,* 63 (10-11-17), 343-44, a review of George Eekhoud's *The New Carthage.*

30. "Desire as Hero," *New Republic,* 5 (11-20-15) Supplement, p. 5.

31. "The Art of Theodore Dreiser," *Dial,* 62 (6-14-17), 509. See also "Theodore Dreiser," *New Republic,* 2 (4-17-15), Supplement, p. 7-8. Contrast RB with H. L. Mencken's pommelling of Dreiser which first appeared in Mencken's *A Book of Prefaces* (1916).

32. "Purpose and Flippancy," *Dial,* 64 (6-6-18), 541, in which Mary S. Watt's *The Boardman Family* is reviewed.

33. "Traps for the Unwary," *Dial,* 64 (3-28-18), 277.

34. *Ibid.,* 279. See also "Mr. Bourne on Traps," *Poetry,* 12 (April 1918), 90-94, Harriet Monroe's reply to RB; then "The Reply Courteous," *Poetry,* 12 (September 1918), 341-44, a reply from RB and Brooks to Monroe; then "'Aesthetic and Social Criticism'" *Poetry,* 13 (October 1918), 37-41, a final sally by H.M.

35. "Criticism in America: I. The Origins of a Myth, *"Bookman,"* 72 (June, 1930), 245. The other two parts of the essay were "The Revival of the Anti-Humanist Myth," (July 1930), and "The End of the Anti-Humanist Myth," (October 1930). Another observer credits RB with reviving the 19th century theory of the book review as an independent inquiry in which the reviewer turns up his own information and developes his own views. This restored, Stanley Edgar Hyman says, one of the most fruitful methods possible for sociological criticism. *The Armed Vision: A Study in the Methods of Modern Literary Criticism* (New York, 1948), 181.

36. See RB's "The Suicide of Criticism," *Columbia Monthly,* 8 (March 1911), 188-92. Spingarn's position had been stated in an address at Columbia in March 1910, "The New Criticism." Then a book of the same title appeared in 1911.

37. Henry Steele Commager, *The American Mind: An Interpretation of American Thought and Character Since the 1880's* (New York, 1950), 410.

38. *The Responsibility of the Artist* (New York, 1960), 72-73, *et passim.*

39. RB never said social art was the *only* art, but he said he would approach art from a social viewpoint.

40. "A Moral Equivalent for Universal Military Service," *New Republic,* 7 (7-1-16), 217. Next two quotes, *ibid.,* 218.

41. "An Hour in Chartres," *Atlantic,* 114 (August 1914), 217.

42. "The Price of Radicalism," *New Republic,* 4 (3-11-16), 161.

43. This and next seven paragraphs from "Trans-National America," *Atlantic,* 117 (July 1916), 86-93.

44. RB in "The Jew and Trans-National America," *Menorah Journal,* 2 (December 1916), 280, said he first got his idea of trans-national America from two articles in the *Nation* by Horace M. Kallen, later the author of books on the subject. The articles were "Democracy Versus the Melting Pot, " Part I, 2-18-15, and Part II, 2-25-15. Kallen's point of departure was E. A. Ross's *The Old World and the New.*

45. "The Jew and Trans-National America," 283.

46. "Trans-National America," 96. For comments by a later writer who argues that RB's fears about American culture were realized see Dwight MacDonald, *Against the American Grain* (New York, 1962), 35-38.

47. One might expect that RB would have written music criticism. Almost all critics, he said, write—some vivaciously or learnedly—about musicians and musicial works, but rarely about music. "Music is perhaps the hardest thing in the world to write about. Words and tones do not lie kindly together. Music is so untranslateable a language that words, whether they are merged with the music, as in the song of opera, or whether they come as criticism and interpretation always seem to be subjugated to the musical will and dragged in curious denuted fashion behind it." "Studies in Tone Poetry," *New Republic,* 4 (8-7-15), 26. Again: "Somehow I was never able to write about music, never able to mix it with words; it seems so entirely apart from the world of ordinary speech and action, an essentially untranslateable language, which ordinary words quite ludicrosly fail even so much as to describe. Music is a real inner sanctuary to which one retires alone, I think: certainly I have never felt that it was very communicable, perhaps because I have been always with unmusical people, or people that I knew were not getting it in the way I was." To Prudence Winterrowd, 6-30-13.

CHAPTER VIII

1. *The World War and American Isolation,* 1914-1917 (Cambridge, Mass., 1959), 437.

2. Robert Endicott Osgood, *Ideals and Self-Interest in America's Foreign Relations: The Great Transformation of the Twentieth Century* (Chicago, 1953), 259.

3. Quoted Goldman, *Rendezvous, op. cit.,* 189.

4. *End of American Innocence, op. cit.,* 363. May excludes business from the "beleaguered defenders."

5. Osgood, *Ideals and Self-Interest, op. cit.,* 258.

6. Ralph Henry Gabriel, *The Course of American Democratic Thought* (2d ed. New York, 1956), 391.

7. Richard Hofstadter, *The Age of Reform: From Bryan to F.D.R.* (New York, 1960), Vintage paperback, 275.

8. Gabriel, *Democratic Thought, op. cit.,* 398-99.

9. Quoted, *Ibid.,* 394.

10. *Propaganda Technique in the World War* (New York, 1927), *passim.*

11. Preston William Slosson, *The Great Crusade and After,* 1914-1928 (New York, 1930), 32.

12. Quoted H. C. Peterson and Gilbert C. Fite, *Opponents of War, 1917-1918* (Madison, Wis., 1957), 11.

13. Quoted Samuel Sillen, "The Challenge of Randolph Bourne," *Masses and Mainstream,* 6 (December 1953), 29.

14. To Alyse Gregory, 1-21-16.

15. "Continental Cultures," *New Republic,* 1 (1-16-15), 14-15.

16. This and next two quotes, *ibid.,* 15.

17. "A Glance at German 'Kultur,'" *Lippincott's Magazine,* 95 (February 1915), 22. Next three paragraphs, *ibid.,* 23-24, 28.

18. This and next paragraph "American Use for German Ideals," *New Republic,* 4 (9-4-15), 117-18.

19. "Bumptious Psychology," *New Republic,* 4 (9-11-15), 27.

20. This and next two paragraphs from "Mental Unpreparedness," *New Republic,* 4 (10-30-15), 143-44.

21. "The Reality of Peace," *New Republic,* 4 (10-30-15), 322. Next quote, *ibid.,* 323.

22. Walter Lippmann took a leave from the *New Republic* soon after America entered the war. He later said (Lippmann to writer, 4-9-64) that there "undoubtedly" was a sharp difference of opinion between RB and the editors. However, if there were any open clashes, Lippmann does not remember them or they took place after he left. "For myself I have only an affectionate memory of him and the happy memory that, as an editor during the time I was with the *New Republic,* I was his constant supporter."

23. Alvin Johnson to writer, 10-13-63.

24. Frederick Hoffman (*et. al.*), *The Little Magazine: A History and a Biography* (Princeton, 1947), 89.

25. Oppenheim, "Story of the *Seven Arts,*" *op. cit.,* 157.

26. Interview with Waldo Frank, 10-31-63.

27. Oppenheim, "Story of the Seven Arts," *op. cit.,* 163. Next quotations, *ibid.*

28. Frank interview, *op. cit.*

29. Since the *Seven Arts* war essays were published in 1919 in *Untimely Papers* the latter shall be the citation.

30. *Untimely Papers* (New York, 1919), 24. Next quote *ibid.*

31. "International Dubities," *Dial,* 62 (5-3-17), 387-88, and "Doubts about Enforcing Peace," unpublished six-page MS. Bourne Papers.

32. *Untimely Papers, op. cit.,* 35.

33. *Ibid.,* 44.

CHAPTER IX

1. *Untimely Papers, op. cit.,* 62. Next quote, *ibid.,* 65.

2. See Gabriel, *Democratic Thought, op. cit.,* 395.

3. *Untimely Papers, op. cit.,* 68-69. Next quote *ibid.,* 75.

4. Albert Shaw (ed.), *The Messages and Papers of Woodrow Wilson* (New York, 1924), Vol. I, 405-08.

5. For a discussion of this transformation which Bourne considers, see Osgood, *Ideals and Self-Interest, op. cit.,* 263, Chap. 11, *et passim.* Osgood does not criticize Wilson harshly. His approach is more from the standpoint of how peace proposals were changed under the stress of war and how the change was an understandable, if not necessarily desirable, outcome of the logic, forces, and mentality of the times.

Ernest R. May's *The World War and American Isolation, op. cit.*, is on a larger scale internationally. Grey Wilson, and Bethmann-Hollweg are the stars. While diplomacy is the matter at hand, Wilson's struggle with his conscience also is graphic.

6. The idea, but not the phrase as RB expressed it in quotations, is in the June 14 oration.

7. *Untimely Papers, op. cit.*, 80-81. Next two quotes *ibid.*, 89, 99.

8. What happened, it has often been contended, was that war fervor in the United States was just reaching its peak when the Armistice was signed, and therefore was drained into the red scare. The ugliness of that episode in U.S. history comes through in Robert K. Murray's *Red Scare: A Study in National Hysteria, 1919-1920* (Minneapolis, 1955).

9. *Untimely Papers, op. cit.*, III. Next quote *ibid.*, 113.

10. Included were "The Future of Pacifism," 7-28-17 and "Conscription of Thought," 9-1-17.

11. This and next six paragraphs "Conscience and Intelligence in War," *Dial,* 63 (9-13-17), 193-95.

12. *Untimely Papers, op. cit.*, 115.

13. *Ibid.*, 117. Norman Thomas later wrote: "John Dewey used his pontifical position among young intellectuals to misinterpret and almost ridicule the objectors whose case he, the prophet of the new education, did not understand. No wonder Randolph Bourne in his loneliness was inspired to write "The Twilight of the [sic] Idols.'" Footnote reads: "Prof. Dewey later championed the cause of political prisoners." *The Conscientious Objector in America* (New York, 1923), 262-63.

14. This and next three paragraphs from *Untimely Papers, op. cit.*, 118-19, 121, 217, 130-31.

15. See, for example, the harsh judgment of Charles Madison, in his *Critics and Crusaders: A Century of American Protest* (2d ed. New York, 1959), 440. Madison modifies his judgment, however, on the next page. See also Harold Stearns, *Liberalism in America: Its Origin, Its Temporary Collapse, Its Future* (New York, 1919), Chap. 8, *et passim.* The book is an intriguing analysis, very much the product of its time. It is not a criticism of RB. It is notable because it was highly praised in some parts at the time and because Stearns' criticisms of pragmatism often coincide with RB's. Stearns very likely read RB carefully and was influenced by him.

16. For example: "For those who live, the world is not livable except through triumph over the despair of death, and over a religion which is little more than an evasion of that despair. The only consolation permitted is to feel one's self cooperating with the intelligent forces that are making for the better ordering of the world." From "Seeing It Through," *Dial,* 1 (5-19-20), 565.

17. "The Liberalism of Randolph Bourne," *Freeman,* 1 (5-19-20), 237.

18. Austin Fagothey, *Right and Reason: Ethics in Theory and Practice* (2d ed., St. Louis, 1959), 559, and Chap. 34.

19. "The Liberalism of Randolph Bourne," *op. cit.*, 337.

20. *Fenollosa, op. cit.*, 309.

21. "Story of the Seven Arts," *op. cit.*, 163.

22. [Louis Untermeyer, ed.], *The Letters of Robert Frost to Louis Untermeyer* (New York, 1963), 60.

23. To Oppenheim, 9-20-17. Oppenheim Papers. N.Y. Public Library.

24. To Amy Lowell, 9-19-17 [sic]. Oppenheim Papers. Copy. I believe Oppenheim misdated the letter, although it is possible that his letter is a reply to an earlier letter from Miss Lowell which is not in the papers.

25. *Fenollosa, op. cit.*

26. To Oppenheim, 10-22-17. Oppenheim Papers.

27. Frank interview, *op. cit.*, and in less detail Frank's *The Re-Discovery of America: An Introduction to a Philosophy of American Life* (New York, 1929), 318, where he says: "The organ's disappearance after one year is not due to the War, as is commonly supposed, but to the war between [sic] the individuals of the group—to their mutual distrusts and spiritual failures."

27a. *Fenollosa, op. cit.*

28. "Story of the Seven Arts," *op. cit.*, 162.

29. Frank also said in an interview, *op. cit.*: "Oppenheim sunk the ship, so to speak. He was very bitter about Brooks and me and we somewhat toward him, but none of it was personal. James wouldn't allow the collective editorial board. Actually, however, I was the one who got the magazine out. The point had come where James didn't have too much to say. He neglected the magazine. He was very much caught up with poetry just then." See also Louis Untermeyer, *From Another World, op. cit.*, 83ff, for account of *Seven Arts* and RB's connection with it. According to Untermeyer, Amy Lowell said she would back the magazine on the condition it avoid the war issue. Oppenheim refused.

30. "Story of the Seven Arts," *op. cit.*, 164.

31. *Untimely Papers, op. cit.*, 6.

32. *The Street I Know* (New York, 1935), 162.

33. *Liberalism in America: Its Origin, Its Temporary Collapse, Its Future* (New York, 1919), 15n.

34. See "The Idea of a University," *Dial*, 63 (11-27-17), 509-10; "Those Columbia Trustees," a letter to the N.Y. *Times*, 10-20-17; and a letter to the N.Y. *Tribune*. The latter is a clipping in Box 6, Bourne Papers, n.d.

When young Joseph Freeman, then a Columbia student, heard that Dana had been fired, he went with a friend to Dana's room where Dana was packing. Freeman and his friend ostensibly were the cause of the firing. The "proof" that he had taught disloyalty and sedition on the campus was that he had induced the two students to go to the People's Council convention in Chicago. Dana replied truthfully that he never saw the youths until the time of the convention. If he alone were cashiered, he would keep quiet, Dana promised. If not, he would make a scandal in the press.

RB was sitting in the room on a desk, swinging his legs when the students entered. "And now that you have been expelled, Harry, will you make a scandal?" Bourne asked.

"Certainly not," Dana said. "I've given my word as a gentleman."

"That's the trouble," Bourne replied with a wide grin. "You look upon all this as a gentlemen's quarrel. You lack Homeric anger." Joseph Freeman, *An American Testiment: A Narrative of Rebels and Romantics* (New York, 1936), 105-06.

35. "A Primer of Revolutionary Idealism," *Dial*, 64 (1-17-18), 69.

36. "Our Enemy Speaks," *Dial*, 64 (5-23-18), 486.

37. "That Spirit of Malcontentedness," unpublished two page MS. Bourne Papers.

38. To Brooks, 2-27-18. Aparently a copy. Also in condensed form, *Twice a Year*, Fall-Winter 1938, 50-55.

39. "The Disallusionment," 14-page unpublished MS. Bourne Papers. There is internal evidence, however, that the MS was written very early in the war, instead of much later as I judge it to have been. Next quote *ibid.*

40. To Everette Benjamin, 11-26-17.

41. To Alyse Gregory. From Hampton, Va. Tuesday [1917].

CHAPTER X

1. Published in *Untimely Papers, op. cit.* Unless otherwise cited material in this chapter is from the essay.

2. Quoted Millis, *Road to War, op. cit.*, 454.

3. "Randolph Bourne and Two Generations," *op. cit.*, 74.

4. *Fenollosa, op. cit.*, 312.

5. "The American Revolution: Revisions in Need of Revising," *William and Mary Quarterly*, 14 (January 1957), 11-12.

6. Three studies later showed how clairvoyant RB was concerning the battering civil liberties were taking and would continue to take so long as America was at war. One work, Stanley Coben's *A. Mitchell Palmer: Politician* (1963), charges Wilson with heavy responsibility for the outbursts against civil liberties. A strong accusation also is made against the people in general. Donald Johnson's *The Challenge to American Freedoms: World War I and the Rise of the American Civil Liberties Union* (1963), supercedes, but does not render obsolete Norman Thomas's *The Conscientious Objector in America* (1923), although they are not of course the same kind of book. And a work by William Preston, Jr. *Aliens and Dissenters: Federal Suppression of Radicals, 1903-1933* (1963), also makes RB appear the prophet, although RB is not mentioned in the work. Preston does *not* see the Red scare of 1910-1920 as an aberration of the war and the Russian Revolution. He convincingly traces the roots to the 1890's and and discusses (1) a long established system of drumhead deportation hearings, (2) nativism growing out of industrialization and urbanization, and (3), deep-seated worry about the nation's future, particularly by the middle class.

7. Quoted "Randolph Bourne and Two Generations," *op. cit.*, 71.

8. *Ibid.*

9. "The Liberalism of Randolph Bourne," *op. cit.*, 237. Mark Harris in "*Randolph Bourne, A Study in Immiscibility, op. cit.*, 189n, quotes the Dorothy Teal MS as saying that RB planned a book on the State and discussed it with Laski at Harvard in 1917 where the latter was visiting professor.

10. De Lima interview, *op. cit.*

11. *Randolph Bourne, op. cit.*, 126.

CHAPTER XI

1. Swain to Messitte, *op. cit.*

2. 5-31-18.

3. Dell to writer, 9-6-63.

4. To Mother, 11-4-18.

5. Dorothy Teall to Agnes de Lima, 6-2-32. The letter also says that RB allegedly then got at Dewey by writing "Twilight of Idols," but points out that it was written before the review of Alexander's work. Johnson probably was right on the essentials, however.

6. *Ibid.*

7. Lovett to Blanche Messitte, 9-18-37. Copy. Lovett also discusses the matter in his autobiography, *All Our Years* (New York, 1948), 151. Re RB's death: "I was disheartened at losing the most important contributor to the literary function of the *Dial*."

8. Rogers to writer, 12-24-63.

9. Elsie Clews Parsons to Bourne, 6-24-18.

10. To Mother, 10-12-18.

11. To Mother, 11-4-18. This letter may have been written in October, but misdated.

12. *The Street I Know, op. cit.*, 149.

13. *Fenollosa, op. cit.*, 312.

14. Watson to Charles Allen, 5-25-43, quoted Frederick J. Hoffman, Charles Allen and Carolyn F. Ulrich, *The Little Magazine, op. cit.*, 198-99. Waldo Frank told this writer that Watson was one of the angels Thayer lined up to save the *Seven Arts.* Thayer, a highstrung man, had a breakdown in 1927. In 1965 he still was living in a European sanitorium.

15. Alyse Gregory, *The Day is Gone* (New York, 1948), 135, 153.

16. *The Street I Know, op. cit.*, 138.

17. To Mother, *op. cit.*,

18. 7-27-[17]. From Provincetown. Next quote *ibid.*

19. *Fenollosa, op. cit.*, 259. Brooks in writing of this walk to Provincetown, etc., correctly dates it as 1917, but confused some of the events of the summer of '18 with those of '17. Internal evidence in an undated letter to Alyse Gregory from RB (which Brooks used) headed only "Sound Beach, Monday" shows it was written in '18.

20. Sound Beach, Monday [1918].

21. From Elsie Clews Parsons, *op. cit.* She asks whether RB's planning to spend part of the summer in Bloomfield meant he would not go west. See also RB to Alyse Gregory, Stonover Farm, Lenox Mass., Saturday [1916].

22. To Alyse Gregory, White Plains, Wednesday, [July 1917].

23. The following account is mostly from De Lima interview, 10-8-63, and from Agnes de Lima to Alyse Gregory, [1948], Bourne Papers. And for a few place names, Brooks, *Fenollosa, op. cit.*, 319-20.

24. De Lima to Gregory, *op. cit.*

25. "Story of the Seven Arts," *op. cit.*, 163.

26. Teall to De Lima, *op. cit.*, Teall was reporting a story told her by another of RB's friends, Salwyn Shapiro.

27. Gregory, *Day is Gone, op. cit.*, 154.

28. To Alyse Gregory, Sound Beach, Monday [1918]. Paul Strand was a widely known and successful photographer.

29. *Farewell to Reform, op.cit.*, 299.

30. Dorothy Teall to Agnes de Lima, 12-14-31.

31. On 12-4-18, Frederick Keppel, RB's friend and a Columbia Dean, wrote RB, in his capacity as third assistant secretary of the Navy, a one-sentence letter (Bourne Papers): "In reply to your letter of November 30 I have to tell you that we are already looking into the situation against which you protest and I expect to have a report on it at once." A check with Navy Department sources and the National Archives failed to turn up any Keppel or RB letters.

32. Frances Lundquist to writer, 2-11-64. F.L. had been introduced to RB during Columbia days by his friend Read Lewis. The friendship between F.L. and RB was renewed when he returned from Europe and they both were living in the Village. F.L. was a journalist.

33. Description from De Lima interview, *op. cit.*

34. De Lima to Gregory, *op. cit.*

35. Gregory, *Randolph Bourne, op. cit.*, 109.

36. *Ibid.*

37. Friday, Hampton Institute, n.d. Copy.

38. From Hampton, n.d. Copy.

39. 8-10-17. Copy.

40. De Lima interview, *op. cit.;* De Lima to Gregory, 4-12-[48?].
41. Branstater interview, *op. cit.* 42. Amidon to Gregory, *op. cit.* Next quote ibid.
43. "Story of the Seven Arts," *op. cit.* 44. Amidon to Gregory, *op. cit.*
45. Teall to De Lima, *op. cit.*
46. Small brown book entitled Bibliography, Box 4. Bourne Papers.
47. Natalie Fenniger to Esther Cornell, *op. cit.*
49. 10-26-17. 48. *Fenollosa, op. cit.*, 311-12.
50. To Alyse Gregory, Hampton, Va., Tuesday [1917].
51. Quoted Gregory MS, *op. cit.*, 122. 52. Johnson to writer, 11-18-63.
53. 11-21-18. 54. De Lima interview,*op. cit.* 55. Rogers to writer, *op. cit.*
56. Unless otherwise indicated, the following material is from De Lima interview, *op. cit.*
57. Possession of Mrs. Ruth Bourne Branstater.
58. Gregory, *Day is Gone, op. cit.*, 165.
59. Rosenfeld, *Port of New York, op. cit.*, 225.
60. Possession of Mrs. Ruth Bourne Branstater.
61. "Story of the Seven Arts," *op. cit.*, 164.
62. Frances Anderson Ewell to writer, *op. cit.*
63. "He was so brave that I want to be worthy of him," Sarah Bourne wrote to Agnes and Esther. "I often told him that I believe he could do anything. I can't understand how I came to have such a gifted son . . . . I like to remember that all the best that came to him came through his own efforts and determination to win out in spite of weakness. . . . He has been such a good son and my best times have come through his generosity." Quoted Gregory, *Randolph Bourne, op. cit.*, 135. n.d.
64. Thomas to writer, 10-3-63.
65. "The Image of Randolph Bourne," *New Republic*, 54 (9-24-30), 152.
66. Esther never really recovered from her bereavement, although she threw herself into work at the New School for Social Research in the 1920's. She had many proposals but did not marry. About 1930 she wrote each of her friends a letter saying she was sick of her life. She never was seen again. Bryn Mawr alumnae records show only that she was said to have died.

CHAPTER XII

1. To Mary Messer, 2-7-14.
2. *History of a Literary Radical, op. cit.*, 19.
3. *Tired Radicals and Other Papers* (New York, 1921), 9-15.
4. "What Is Opinion?" *New Republic*, 4 (9-18-15), 172.
5. "Generation d'apres-guerre: Bourne and Psichari," *Poet Lore*, 41 (Autumn 1930), 435.
6. Bourne to Brooks, *op. cit.*
7. Frank to Blanche Messitte, n.d. [circa 1937]. Copy.